BLISSFULLY RAVAGED
IN
DEMOCRACY

ADVENTURES IN POLITICS
1980 - 2020

Praise for The Author

"I just LOVE the way you write. Your wit and turns of phrase and insights are so unique and beyond compare. You must write many books!"

Carolyn Cassady
(wife of Neal and love of Jack's life)

"My God, you're the very spirit of Jack! He would've *loved* you!"

Edie Kerouac Parker
(Jack's first wife)

"This is an exceptionally fine piece of work on your part. Marvelous dissertations and mightily written rapportage!"

Henri Cru
(Remi Boncoeur in *On The Road*)

"I like your distinctive narrative voice. You are a great stylist."

Sterling Lord
(Kerouac & Kesey's literary agent)

"Hombre, let me say right off – you are a hell of a writer! This piece you wrote is just wonderful. I love it! It felt like I was there ..... what a treat."

Walter Salles
(director of *On The Road*)

"You're not an *On The Road* scholar — you're an *On The Road* character!"

Teri McLuhan
(Marshall McLuhan's author/filmmaker daughter)

"You can write your ass off!!"

David Amram
(Kerouac's principal musical collaborator)

"You erase the period after 'Jack Kerouac.'"

The Wizard of Wonder
(21st Century Merry Prankster)

More Praise for The Author

"Brian Hassett is definitely NOT a typical scholarly researcher! Instead, like all good gonzo reporters, he set out on a personal journey to immerse himself in the movement that started with the Beats, went through the hippies, and has reached into so many corners of America. His memoirs are fascinating, must-read reporting for anyone -- from students writing term papers to young seekers searching for the meaning of life."

Lee Quarnstrom
(author, journalist & original Merry Prankster)

"I am so impressed by Brian's understanding of what he wrote. Other people have knowledge, but he really 'got it.' His impressions of those I know and love were lessons for me, too. He is an astute, keep-it-simple-&-real author ... and I'm proud to also say a Friend."

Anonymous
(aka Linda Breen, original Merry Prankster, who got On The Bus in Calgary in '64)

"The stories of your adventures are always intriguing and fun. Despite what's going on in the moment — you have an outlook on the world that is just joyful. And I love your play with words."

Jerry Cimino
(founder & curator of The Beat Museum)

"You make lightning strike."

Brad Kepperley
(Aretha Franklin's horn player)

"If it's happiness you want, Brian Hassett seems to have found it."

Bill Sass
(Edmonton Journal)

"People like you are extremely helpful and inspiring."

Susan Ray
(widow of film director Nicholas Ray)

Merry Pranksters' Praise for
The Hitchhiker's Guide to Jack Kerouac

"I'm reading your book and enjoying it immensely. Surprised and enlightened. I'm still laughing from what I read last night. Laughter is the best medicine, and you gave me some big howls. The repartee is so well rendered, and your Ken Babbs descriptions are right on. And very funny. The general mayhem aspect is also spot on. Thanks for the rerun! I was there for part of it with Barlow. Congratulations on creating an awesome read. And thanks for the blast of light! You rock!"

Mountain Girl
(Carolyn Garcia)

"When you meet Brian through his words, you will know right away why we like travelling and doing things with him. It's not just what he does, but how he does it. You'll see. And it's how he describes it. He writes the way he talks, and lives the way he writes. Which reminds me of my Dad and Uncle Jack."

John Cassady
(only son of Neal & Carolyn Cassady)

"If you have read Kerouac, and are interested in his life and work, and the movement he and his friends inspired, and the effect it has had on our lives since, I suggest reading Brian's fine book. If you have not read Kerouac, I suggest you do so."

George Walker
(Hardly Visible)

"All the details were perfectly right on — which is so rare and admirable — and appreciated by people like me who are irritated by mistakes. Almost universally writers get one thing or another 'off' or backwards or off to one side. I'll put a book down if I find one or more — but I read yours non-stop right to the end as soon as I started it. It was quite the book!"

Roy Sebern
(original Merry Prankster who first painted
"Furthur" on the front of The Bus)

"This is good stuff."

Zane Kesey (son of Ken & Faye)

BLISSFULLY RAVAGED
IN
DEMOCRACY

ADVENTURES IN POLITICS
1980 – 2020

BRIAN HASSETT

GETS THINGS DONE PUBLISHING

First Edition — April 2020
Second Edition (2.5) — May 2020

Reprinted by permission:
Paul Tsongas op-ed, *Vancouver Sun*, 1992
Bill Clinton Inauguration article, *Interchange Magazine*, 1993

Front cover photo taken at Obama's first inauguration — just
hours before the book title was coined.
Cover photo stories covered on p. 451-52.

Cover design and production by the Michelangelo of books —
David S. Wills.

**The book's large font and open space is intentional.
Books should be fun and easy to read and not a chore.
You're welcome.**

For more information and to stay up to date . . .

BrianHassett.com

Facebook.com/Brian.Hassett.Canada

or email — **karmacoupon@gmail.com**

This book is dedicated to

Everyone who participates
in democracy

Table of Contents

DESSERT

It was an emotional, joyous and
cold day when Barack Obama was first
inaugurated in January 2009. When
I got back to the apartment at the end
of that historic Adventure, it had all
been so overwhelming, and my fingers
were so frozen solid, the only words my
hands could muster were . . .

Blissfully ravaged in democracy

Introduction

Founder, Curator and Director of The Beat Museum

Sometimes you meet a person who thinks like you do, who views the world through a similar lens. For me, Brian Hassett is one of those people.

We're all products of our times, and Brian, being slightly younger than me, came of age in a different decade so our experiences are somewhat different. But Brian understands history and he knows how everything in life must be viewed through an historical context. I believe an understanding of history is critical to an understanding of life. And Brian holds that same view.

Years before I ever met him in person, I had heard about Brian Hassett from our mutual friend

John Allen Cassady, son of the Beat muse Neal Cassady. John and I had first met in 1994 when he drove his mother Carolyn Cassady to a book signing at my wife Estelle's bookstore in Monterey, California. While Estelle interviewed Carolyn on stage in front of a hundred fans about the adventures she and her husband Neal had with writer Jack Kerouac as vividly described in her book *Off The Road*, her son John Allen and I walked across Alvarado Street to the Mucky Duck to grab a drink and swap stories.

I don't remember if it was on that first night that John told me about his friend Brian Hassett who lived in Manhattan and worked in the rock 'n roll world and had written for *The Rolling Stone Book of The Beats*, maybe that came later, but I do recall Brian's name coming up many times over the years when John and I would meet up at various Northern California Beat Generation events, or for leisurely hikes in Big Sur with another mutual friend Steve Edington who was then President of Lowell Celebrates Kerouac.

I clearly remember John Allen and I discussing the possibility of meeting up with Brian in Toronto for a Beat Museum on Wheels event when we were planning our first East Coast tour in 2004 driving from California in The Mighty Beatmobile. Unfortunately Canadian Customs insisted we inventory every single item we had on board in both the 35-foot RV and the 16-foot trailer that acted as a rolling bookstore. This would have delayed us for days, so Brian and I were not destined to meet for another decade.

The moment of that great occasion didn't occur until June 2015 when he came to San Francisco to host multiple panels at The Beat Shindig at Fort Mason sponsored and coordinated by The Beat Museum. This became the largest Beat Generation gathering in the world since Allen Ginsberg organized the 1994 & '95 NYU Conferences. One day leading up to the Shindig, I was rushing down the stairs from my Beat Museum office when I turned a blind corner and bumped into a guy I immediately recognized as Brian. We both stood back for a moment — realizing we were finally meeting face-to-face after having interacted from afar for so many years. A big spontaneous bear hug ensued, and it was like we had never not known each other. And that has proven true so many times since.

As I write this introduction for Brian's latest book — his long awaited collection of stories on politics as he has known it up close and personal and as only Brian can tell them — I'm sitting in my office in North Beach directly across the street from Lawrence Ferlinghetti's office at City Lights Bookstore, delayed in writing and glued to the TV because of the impeachment trial in the U.S. Senate of Donald J. Trump.

It's fitting for me to be in this situation. I've come to know Brian through our association with the Beat writers, and along the way we've discovered our mutual love of politics, and us having similar dispositions. And just as Brian knows the Beats and the Pranksters like few people I've ever met, and can spin a tale and draw connections most people would never even consider with an inimitable style that is as distinct as it is entertaining, I know he can do so in the political arena as well.

Brian is the kind of guy who is always inquisitive, always into multiple storylines and overlapping dramas, and who suddenly drops everything and takes to the road because there is a story to uncover, a secret to suss out, or an experience to be had.

Brian is the guy who "shows up." He showed up at The 25th Anniversary of Kerouac's *On The Road* in Boulder in 1982; he showed up for Bill Clinton's inauguration; for the *On The Road* auction in NYC in 2001; for Obama's 2008 election night and inauguration; and to be with Carolyn Cassady in 2012 when she needed him.

Brian Hassett knows history and politics as well as anyone I've ever known. He has a way with words, his ideas flow effortlessly, and his stories are cogent, brilliant and always on point. Brian brings connections together with gee-whiz enthusiasm and exacting detail most people have never even considered. He has uncovered Beat mysteries that lay dormant for decades and he relates those stories in unique and compelling ways. And now he's tackling politics.

As Carolyn Cassady always liked to say — "Brian gets things done."

Let The Games Begin

A lot of people got discouraged during 2016 — first the Berners supporting Sanders in the primary, then most of the nation with "the perfect storm" of the November electoral college disaster. Twice in my lifetime has this antiquated 1700s electoral college voting concept resulted in the loser of the vote becoming President. And both those times resulted in the #1 and #2 worst Presidents (by a long shot) that this country ever had the misfortune to have.

There is no other elected office in America you can win without winning the actual vote — and it just happens to be the most important one. Maybe this was a good idea back in the horse-&-buggy days, but it sure ain't democracy in the 21st century.

Citizen participation goes back to ... well, the Greeks (if you were a white native-born male 2,500 years ago), or women in America for the last hundred years, and minorities kinda mostly since 1965 (except since 2013 when the Roberts Supreme Court dishonorably rolled back the Voting Rights Act), and all of us who want who choose have been involved in the primary process since 1972. A lot of (particularly young) people seem to think the political world started in 2016 ... and for them it's been nothing but a disaster.

This is a terrible thing — and we have got to collectively work to re-engage and fix as best we can a flawed system.

In these pages I'm going to share some Adventure Tales about engagement in politics. It's a helluva fun pursuit — and the winner gets to run the country. And speaking of running, there was a great documentary in 2007 called *Run Granny Run* about the inspirational Granny D from New Hampshire who ran for the U.S. Senate in 2004 at age 94. In it she said a line I've repeated often — "Democracy isn't something we have, its something we do."

That should be carved into marble in Washington somewhere. At least I'll carve it into this paper and maybe your brain.

"Democracy isn't something we have, its something we do."

And we've all got a lot to do! 4 in 10 Americans think donald trump is doing a great job as president. (!) This makes zero sense to 6 in 10 Americans, but what this book is going to hopefully help do is get those 6 in 10 back to being passionately involved in the grand experiment that is America.

We're each here for only a small sliver of time. I have many friends who have been engaged in politics and governance for longer than I've been alive; and I've got many younger friends who are still going to be involved in it (hopefully) long after I'm gone. But we each have to be engaged proactive stewards for the small window we're here.

Perhaps this is a good time to talk about age. According to my birth certificate from Kenya, I mean Calgary, I am supposedly 58 years old as I type this in early 2020 — but obviously there's been some mistake because I feel like I'm 18. And I think the same drunk clerk was in the records office for a while because I know a bunch of people older than me that will swear on a stack of *On The Roads* that they are not the age their birth certificate says they are.

One of them is my 80-year-old stage partner, George Walker, who just put a new roof on his house by himself while simultaneously rebuilding a 1939 Furthur bus called Farthur to take *On The Road* in 2020. I also perform regularly with Jack Kerouac's principal musical collaborator, David Amram, who is a still-improvising & wailing jazz cat at age 89. And I finally tracked down and interviewed Locke McCorkle who had the house in Mill Valley where Gary Snyder and Kerouac stayed that prompted *The Dharma Bums* adventure, and he told me that even though he'd just stopped racing motorcycles at age 85, he felt like he was 35. So, everybody reading this book who's under 90 years old, there is no excuse for not having full engagement in this life.

And this also relates to the current leader of the Democratic Party, Nancy Pelosi, who turned 80 in March 2020, as well as three of the four frontrunners in the Democratic primary — Joe Biden (77), Elizabeth Warren (70), and Bernie Sanders (78) — who are all bounding and bouncing with the same kind of vibrancy as Granny D or the jazz cat or the guy up putting on the new roof. 70 is the new 30. 80 is the new 18.

The Grateful Dead's Phil Lesh also turned 80 in March 2020 and he's actively involved in Get Out The Vote (GOTV) actions — as are all the members of Dead & Company.

Phil Lesh from the Grateful Dead.
Listen to Phil.

If smart people in their 70s and 80s have not given up hope, have not become cynical, are still working hard every day to make the world a better place, that should be instructive to anyone in their teens or twenties or thereabouts that giving up is not an option. Or wise. Saying of candidates and political leaders "they're all the same" is a cop-out and abdication of the rights and powers of citizenry. Just ask Granny D.

I was born and raised in Winnipeg — Western Canada — in a world with a mocking disdain for everything American, and anything from the East. I didn't fit in in the least — left as soon as my "finish high school" requirement box was ticked, never looked back, and became an American by choice as soon as I was able. I spent nearly 30 years in Manhattan, and am now back in the land of red-&-white outside Toronto, with the minute-by-minute madness of Manhattan no longer taking up every day of every week of every year, and time and distance to reflect on that massive round-trip road trip.

Although Americans love to pride themselves in being "#1" at everything — their system is the worst for democracy. In Canada (and the U.K.) a national election is called — and the whole thing's over in six weeks — and costs 1/1000th what 2020 will cost America, not to mention the thousands of hours of print and broadcast and social media reading about the bickering between any two people.

But what America has is characters, drama and stakes. And as a friend said at the end of yet another great Grateful Dead show back in the Jerry days — "That's why I keep comin' back."

Who wins these compromised elections gets control of the biggest property on the Western World gameboard. And when I say "compromised" — what I mean is gerrymandering and voter suppression and the candidates' requirement of taking big money from big business (codified by the anti-democracy "Citizens United" Supreme Court decision of 2010) in order to buy media ads and hire staff in

50 states and coordinate more fundraising to pay for more fundraising.

America is leading the world in democracy-destroying gerrymandering — at least the 37 states that allow it — where the state government fences in all the voters of the opposing party into one or as few congressional seats as possible, then gives the whole rest of the state to themselves. This is reason 1001 why getting involved your state government is as important as engagement in a presidential election. And I may as well say it — it's actually more. And you know what's even more important than your state government? Your city government. I know it ain't sexy, and it ain't gonna be all over the TV and social media, but who your mayor is makes a bigger difference in your life than who your president is.

I know in people's heads they see the face of the president as the political person overseeing their life. But the counterintuitive truth is your quality of life, in general, is determined far more by your city council than your federal congress. Whether your water's clean, your power's on, you don't get robbed on the way to the store, you've got paved roads to drive on, whether the literal and metaphorical trains run on train, what your property taxes are (which generally takes more of your income than your income tax) — all that stuff that really is your life is more your city and state governments than it is federal — so if any of this sinks in at all let it be for you to give as much of a damn about who runs your city as Washington. Sadly, municipal elections usually have less than half the turn-out of the already low federal election participation — which was 61% of eligible voters in both 2012 and 2016. Those people whose names you probably don't even know, get elected by about 20% of your neighbors, and have more to do with your day-to-day quality of life than all the presidents of your life combined. Or thereabouts.

But of course if this book was about mayoral elections, you wouldn't be reading it. It's about "the show." Which we love. It's the big one ... with the leg-kicking Rockettes and half-time rock stars and fireworks of exploding heads every night on the TV sets of America. Not the preseason. Not the regular season. Some people watch that stuff — but everybody tunes in for the playoffs. Which, in U.S. Presidential politics, means from the summer conventions through the November elections. Or many don't really tune in until the first Presidential debate in late September (usually) — but it's the same four years as every Summer Olympics when we wave our flag and wear our team jersey and celebrate the thrill of victory or the agony of defeat.

And every election I've lived through was (rightfully called) "the most important election of our lifetime." I dunno why that is or why it's true, but it is. Well, maybe '96 wasn't when Bill Clinton was just holding serve against the Roll–Hemp ticket. I mean, Dole–Kemp. We're always at war or some damn thing. But now there's a proudly overtly racist fascist sociopath in the White House who's cultivated a cult of straight-arm saluting devotees committed to re-electing "the greatest president we ever had."

And so here we are.

25 different men and women from all demographics and backgrounds and philosophies threw their lives in the ring to be the 2020 Democratic nominee. At least this part of the grand game is a healthy democracy. Voters can

choose from longtime socialists like Bernie, or longtime businessmen like Bloomberg, or practical centrists like Joe Biden, or non-politician outsiders like Andrew Yang.

I've been On The Trail on way or another since first seeing third party candidate John Anderson in 1980, to catching every candidate in New Hampshire in 2020 — 40 years *On The Road* as another Adventurer coined it — and you're holding a good chunk of it in book form for the first time. Throughout this process of writing lots of new pieces up through March 2020, I also found old clippings of stories past, old photographs & buttons, rediscovered old memories, and followed a paper trail of typed tales back to when computers were only props on *Lost In Space*.

Now there are bots and trolls, and as the old saying goes, now more true than ever — "A lie can travel halfway around the world before the truth gets its boots on." We are all living through a redefining of what democracy and even what "truth" is.

I'm glad you've joined in this Adventure, and hopefully reading this book will inspire you to get involved and create your own stories for eternity.

How Rock Concerts Led To Politics

1980 – 1984

For most of the 1980s I lived in Phyllis & Eddie Condon's palatial apartment on Washington Square North in Greenwich Village, New York City. The NYU Program Board from where I ran the concerts was in the Loeb Student Center on Washington Square South — about a 3-minute walk away — if you didn't dawdle in the never-ending circus that was Washington Square Park. I halfway lived over there in what was my first "office" — and could do anything I wanted.

At this point I knew very little about American politics or how Washington worked, having grown up in Winnipeg, Manitoba, Canada.

The first time any of this entered my fort-building,

1

hockey-playing childhood was the Watergate hearings that preempted all four of our TV channels that summer of '73. Then there was the newsflash of seeing the giant "NIXON RESIGNS" headline in a newspaper box in as big letters as the "WAR IS OVER" or "MAN ON MOON" headlines I'd seen in books — and realized this was the first historic event of my young conscious life.

In Canadian schools, we were probably taught as much about American government as Americans were taught about Canada. I knew they had Presidents, and George Washington was the first, and 1776 was a big deal for some reason, but that was about it.

Unlike all my friends in Winterpeg, after reading *Rolling Stone* and other music magazines, I knew I wanted to live in America — a universally unpopular opinion in a small Canadian prairie town. As soon as I finished my mandatory service in high school, a couple of buddies and I loaded up the van and drove to Californey with visions of bikini beaches and waving fields of pot dancing in our heads.

The First Presidential Candidate

At one point on that crazy trip we were down in San Diego and climbed over the wall to sneak into their famous zoo. Just after we got inside, who should come walking right past us in that spring of 1980, but presidential candidate John Anderson! The white-haired bespectacled free-thinking Republican had just started running Independent as a counterpoint to Reagan's ultra-right-conservatism. But we weren't really too hip to the details. All we knew was he was throwing a monkey wrench into American politics and that was good enough for us.

My fellow Canadian runaway, I'll call him Joey, was about the only other person I knew who was really into American politics and culture, and of course we'd never seen a real-life American presidential candidate in the flesh before, and we rushed right up to him in our 18-year-old enthusiasm and shook the hand that shook the hand of P.T. Barnum and Charlie Chan. Even got me a bumper sticker from his entourage of maybe a half-dozen people — my first bona fide campaign ephemera!

World War III

A week or so after that, we found ourselves in yet another first — hanging with a real-live Vietnam War veteran — something that just didn't happen in Winnipeg.

We were at his house somewhere around L.A. on the edge of the desert when the drugs began to take hold. It was only five years since the end of that failed war, and a few more since Watergate and the Pentagon Papers, and we all knew the government lied to us and was up to no end of nefarious no good. This vet was much older and wiser than us, and had fought in the heart of one of their most heinous lies, and he was filling our impressionable young minds with fresh sinsemilla and juicy details of the latest conspiracy theories.

He kept all the lights low as though he was still hiding in the dark in the jungle. And as he was regaling his wide-eyed captives with elaborate tales of how the world really worked, the silent flickering rabbit-eared TV in the corner suddenly broke away from the regular late night broadcast with Breaking News of a secret rescue mission to free the American hostages in Iran that had gone horribly wrong. Or was it really an invasion? Helicopters crashed, soldiers were dead, and another war maneuver by the U.S. government ended in death and disaster. We sat up for hours in a pre-CNN world manually flipping the round channel knob to get any information we could. We were sure, in our vividly stoned Everything-Has-Meaning minds, that there was a grand "reason" why we were hanging with a real front-line war soldier the night World War III started.

The Reagan–Carter Debate

A few months later — October 1980 — was the presidential debate between Jimmy Carter and Ronald Rayguns. In more Le Grande Synch Dept.: It just so happened that their one-&-only debate was scheduled on one of The Grateful Dead's two nights off during their historic 8-show run at Radio City Music Hall — of which I attended 5 — and every one in the first 3 rows because I camped out on the sidewalk for tickets outside Rockefeller Center all weekend in about my second week in America. Those plush acoustic/electric 3-set beauties were my 2nd, 3rd, 4th, 5th & 6th Dead shows! No wonder I got hooked.

I knew I had to experience the debate because it seemed to be a very big deal in this new country I found myself — one month into what would become a decades-long Adventure in America. And I was determined to *understand* this place.

I went to the historic counterculture Judson Church residence hall on Washington Square South and watched it on a big tubed 1970s TV in the common room full of smart young politicos making observations so far beyond me that I realized I was an utter neophyte in a very complex but exciting world. I still remember where I was sitting in the room as I listened for the first time to this assemblage of funny, wise-cracking American  college students with politics and history surging through their veins. I'd never been immersed in that culture before — or even really knew there *was* such a culture! Politicos — in the flesh! "So *this* is what that world's like!"

I barely had a clue who the candidates were — but I knew if that crazy right-wing geezer got elected things were gonna be really bad.

And that was about it. 1980 thru '84 was a sex, drugs & rock 'n' roll frenzy in college in Greenwich Village — while still pulling off 13 A's and cranking out NYU in three-and-

a-half years insteada four so I could pay them less money
and get out into the real world sooner. During those years
I rarely spent any time thinking about politics. Reagan was
President, yuppie greed was "cool," and it was all pretty
depressing. Plus, I thought the whole science of politics was
so far beyond me — and it seemed like something we had no
control over anyway. Turns out I was wrong on both fronts.

The Moment Everything Changed

One day in early 1984 — yes, that "*1984*" that living under
Reagan really felt like — I was finishing up some stuff
in the concert production office on the main floor of the
Student Center when I heard someone talking through a
loudspeaker coming from LaGuardia Place — the little side
street off Washington Square South. But loudspeakers and
loud noise were pretty much the norm around Washington
Square Park — there was *always* crazy shit going on.

Then all of a sudden there were huge cheers for
something — bigger than normal. So I got up from my
desk and walked into the lobby — which was about 8 feet
above street level — and through the wall of floor-to-ceiling
windows I laid eyes on my first political rally.

There was a man standing on a little stage at the
end of the street with his back to Washington Square
Park, facing south down the urban canyon packed with
enthusiastic faces. I can't remember if he was on a semi
trailer bed or if they did some quick stage set-up or what
— cuz I don't recall anything being there when I walked
into the building. But now the whole block was filled with
excited, fist-pumping rock 'n' roll people. And they were

6

cheering for what some guy was *saying* — not what he was *playing*. But it sorta made sense cuz the dude looked kinda Kennedy-cool and was riffing with some cocky Mick Jagger confidence.

I'd been working in rock 'n' roll since I was 15 — toured Western Canada with Yes by the time I was 17, and worked with Bill Graham putting together The Rolling Stones tour by age 20. I knew this scene. The stage, the PA, the crowd, the cameras, the screaming fans. Done. Except I was looking at somebody who could be running the country.

This was the same crowd — the same energy — the same showmanship — as everything I'd ever done in my life. It's showbiz, man. But this was for the man who could be the leader of the free world. That's even bigger than The Rolling Stones!

Turns out the guy's name was Gary Hart. This was not the "Monkey Business" campaign — that was 4 years later. This was his first — which was actually a lot like Bernie Sanders' in 2016. He was a little-known Senator from a non-major state who galvanized the young while going up against the obvious party favorite — Walter Mondale — who'd been Vice President 4 years earlier and was the de facto nominee.

I got swept right up in it. The underdog's struggle. The new ideas. The new voice. The challenge to the system. The "volunteers of America."

Looking out that window, on that sunny unexpected spring afternoon in Greenwich Village — my life changed.

I walked down the steps into the cordoned-off street in open-mouthed awe — taking in something I "knew" but had never experienced. Like Judson Church, I remember exactly where I stood against the building next to the old

7

white-haired guard I knew who let me stand there while
he kept the sidewalk clear, as I looked left to the rock
star on the stage, and then right to the block-long crowd
listening and cheering that reminded me of the street crowd
photographs on the *Live Dead* album. This was rock 'n'
roll. *This* I understood.

These people had the same passion in their faces,
the same guttural thrill in their cheers, the same intangible
electric energy as all the best music shows I ever worked or
attended. It's a buzz that can also be felt in a large sports
crowd when the home team scores. Or in a Baptist church
on a Sunday morning. There are a few places to experience
this collective positive-minded celebratory energy. But a
political rally is definitely one of them.

And I've been actively participating in every primary
and election since.

Political Parties
1988

1988 was the first presidential primary and general election where I was all-in from the git.

I had just gotten married on New Year's Eve leading into 1988 and we were newlyweds in our 20s living invincibly in Manhattan with two incomes and lotsa friends and most everybody was in the arts and vibrantly involved in the world and you can only imagine. The force was strong with these two.

1987 leading into that election year was the first time there'd been a wide-open Democratic primary since 1976 which had resulted in "the great leap of faith" candidacy of the Nixon antithesis Jimmy Carter.

All during '87 we threw parties at 27 Washington

Square North where I'd been living for six years in
Eddie Condon's widow Phyllis's magnificent apartment
overlooking the park. In '87, Phyllis had finally gone into
the hospital and eventually passed away, so for a while it
was pretty much just me and my soon-to-be fiancé, who I
proposed to on that very Washington Square North roof
on a beautiful spring night after a deep-groovin' Grateful
Dead show out at the Brendan Byrne Arena. We came
back into Manhattan still blazing and went up on the roof
of the 7-story building, and I came prepared for whatever
may happen, and she was sitting up on this kinda chimney
protrusion with the city lights flickering like stars all around
her pretty face. We were as high as the skyscrapers and she
said this has been the most amazingly perfectly unbelievable
night of her life, and "How could anything ever be more
perfect?"

And BOOM!

I dropped to one knee, pulled out the ring box from
my pocket, and asked, "Will you marry me?"

She laughed and beamed and caught herself and
remembered to say "Yes" cuz it was all so funny and surreal
but real and we knew it.

And that was the whole backdrop world the '87
primary and '88 general were laid over.

This was the first primary that really happened full-
bore a full year before the first Iowa caucuses, and 1987 was
crazy all the way around. We went to a ton of Dead shows
— it was the summer of the Dylan-Dead merging and the
nine Dead shows at Madison Square Garden in September
climaxing with the big rainforest benefit, and at the same
time, Oliver North was pleading the Fifth in the Iran-Contra

hearings; and there was that disturbingly crazy Robert Bork / Anita Hill Supreme Court showdown. Thatcher was running England with Ray-guns in the U.S. and conservative Brian Mulroney the Prime Minister of Canada; Ronnie's Secretary of the Interior James Watt was selling off the national parks to oil prospectors; the Profiteer-in-Chief was all about "deregulating" environmental laws; his wife launched her simpleton's "Just say no" campaign, which was promptly followed by the "This is your brain on drugs" fried egg commercials all over TV; "yuppies" were a thing, and that *Wall Street* movie was big including the unfortunate line "Greed is good" — and it was really an ugly selfish time. At least as far as politics and governance goes.

But one thing that mitigated it all was that we had this great next-generation candidate who reminded everybody of John F. Kennedy — Gary Hart. He'd finished second to ol' Walter Mondale in '84 and was the runaway front-runner as '87 began and '88 loomed. This was gonna fix everything.

Until it all came crashing down.
May 7th, 1987 — "We interrupt this program . . . Gary Hart is dropping out of the race!"
What?!
This was a guy who lived in Colorado on a street named Troublesome Gulch (really) and had his picture taken with a young babe in a mini-skirt on his lap next to yacht called Monkey Business (yep) and who told E.J. Dionne in a profile in a Sunday *New York Times Magazine* published May 4th, 1987, "Follow me around, I don't care. I'm serious. If anyone wants to put a tail on me, go ahead. They'll be very bored." There was never any proof that he

and the babe actually had an affair and they both denied it, but Boom! — just the *implications* in the world of 1987 were enough to end the candidacy of a smart charismatic PAC-free next-gen leader.

If yer into it, there's a good 2018 movie about all this called *The Front Runner* with Hugh Jackman, and it's pretty accurate as far as dramatizations go.

Suddenly all the Dems were left with was a *Saturday Night Live* sketch of goofball candidates. There was the odd-talking, horn-rimmed-glasses-and-bowtie-wearing Paul Simon (not the singer) from Illinois who Al Franken satirized perfectly on the aforementioned *SNL* always referring to his "bowtie" with great comedic emphasis. And then there was the nondescript Midwestern centrist Dick Gephardt who was so blond it looked like he didn't have any eyebrows, which began a running joke of him having "eyebrow envy." And then there was Arizona's bumbling Bruce Babbitt with his bizarrely Nixonian speaking inflections and a mortician's personality. Then there was the painfully robotic Al Gore as the neighborhood bank manager dad who yelled "you kids turn that music down." Joe Biden was in there for a while and seemed like a real prospect until the Dukakis campaign leaked a tape to the press of him giving a speech where he quoted British politician Neil Kinnock without attribution, and this was such a "crime" back in those innocent days he had to drop out because of it. And yes, Michael Dukakis, the professorial explainer-in-chief who was trying to ride the Massachusetts Kennedy image after Hart had dropped out, became the nominee, at least until it all blew up when he took a ride in a tank wearing that painfully goofy helmet.

With this interchangeable lineup of uninspiring suits

with the same haircut, the one guy who stood out to me was Jesse "Keep Hope Alive!" Jackson who was the only real Reverend orator in the whole group. Yes, positions and integrity and accomplishments are important, but I want somebody with a little fire in their belly who can ignite that in others.

We all knew who all the candidates were because they had about a dozen debates (and we hosted nearly as many parties), so there was massive exposure for all of them. Although the Dems weren't exactly fielding an all-star team of visionaries, at least the parties and the networks were gamely getting them in front of voters en masse for really the first time. CNN was now in everybody's home with cable, and everybody's home *had* cable by then. *Larry King Live* was already a staple at 9PM, and shows like *Crossfire* and *Evans & Novak* were an alternative to the *The Cosby Show* and *Alf*. And C-SPAN was also on the cable air broadcasting uninterrupted political coverage 24-hours-a-day for those who didn't want a talking head telling them what they were seeing.

In yet another excellent example of how television was working, NBC did a debate where they had the six Democratic nominees ask each other questions for 20 minutes or so, then they'd flip to the six Republican candidates asking the same general questions so viewers could see both parties discussing issues among themselves back-to-back. Plus, back then it was a much less polarized time, and candidates were polite with one another. Debates were actually mature, civil conversations.

By the time of the conventions in the summer of '88, my wife and I had moved into an apartment with a backyard on the Upper East Side, right around the corner from Allen Ginsberg's legendary pad on York Avenue where Herbert Huncke stayed and John Clellon Holmes wrote about in *Go*, and this is where I began my life as the host of political parties in earnest. We were all living in Manhattan and had a thousand options every night of the week, but one of them was this crazy Canuck hosting and comically commenting on the political conventions of all things! It was a running joke with the assembled that a Canadian was teaching *them* about American politics, but to my eyes, how could you miss this show? It was like a Super Bowl or Stanley Cup party, which I also threw plenty of. People found Canadian beer in the delis to bring, we played ball hockey in our back yard, and all took road jars and bombers over to Carl Schurz Park along the East River after the show was over.

Texas Governor and all-purpose badass Ann Richards gave the keynote address that convention, and brought the house down with, "Poor George. (pause) He can't help it. (longer pause) He was born with a silver foot in his mouth."

Then Jesse Jackson, who ended up winning 13

14

states (!), showed the world what a great political speech looked like. People were still talking about Mario Cuomo's "A Tale of Two Cities" keynote address in '84, which at that point was accepted by both sides of the aisle as the greatest piece of oratory by any sitting American political figure since JFK's "Ask not what your country can do for you ..." inaugural speech back in 1961. But then enter — the Baptist preacher! He'd honed his skills under Martin Luther King Jr., and worked up his chops throughout both the '84 and '88 campaigns, and by the time the candidate with the second most delegates who darn-near won the thing hit the convention stage in Atlanta, he was gracious and powerful, confessional and poetic, passionate and convincing, and when he began repeating the "Keep hope alive!" climactic refrain he had my whole apartment screaming like a guy just scored the winning goal with one second to go!

By the time Dukakis came out a couple nights later, introduced by his Oscar-winning actress cousin Olympia Dukakis, it sure confirmed to me that my first choice (Jesse) was still my first choice. Professor Mike's a good man, but he couldn't deliver an inspiring speech to save his life. Maybe I'm a superficial guy, but I want my leaders to inspire me. Obama sure as hell did that. Reading Lincoln's speeches sure did that — appealing to "the better angels of our nature." Winston Churchill knew how to do it. John Lewis does it just every time I hear him speak. It's not unlike a coach or team captain in sports. You need someone in the locker room of life to fill us players with a sense of purpose, a call to destiny, a bigger meaning in the face of daily struggles.

Professor Mike was practical not emotional; book smart not street smart; professorial not inspirational. Off stage, he's actually a nice guy with a sense of humor and a heart of gold (relatively speaking for a politician), but Team Captain material he is not. If you ever saw that movie *What About Bob?*, he was kind of the Richard Dreyfus character. He wasn't somebody you wanted to jump in the car with and go on a four year road trip.

After nominating Walter Mondale in '84 and now Dukakis in '88, I was learning the hard lesson that we weren't the party that would pick a Gary Hart or a Jesse Jackson. This was a lesson young Bernie Sanders supporters would learn in 2016. We're not conservative like Reagan was conservative. We're conservative like our parents who are making sure the bills get paid and we don't get arrested. In other words, we're not the fun Bill Murray character in *What About Bob?* (or in just about any other Bill Murray movie), we're the party of "dad" . . . or "mom" in Hillary's case. It's no wonder young people are sometimes chagrined and don't wanna party with our party. But there's more dads & moms who go to the ballot box than there are young people — who by and large don't frickin' vote. I hope this book engages some of them to do so. Like in life, you don't always get your first choice in everything, but the blue team is sure a lot more on your side than the selfish science-denying bigots on the other side.

And speaking of appealing to the young, oh my gawd, at the Repugnant convention the next month, George Bush made the big announcement of his first appointment as a potential Commander-in-Chief, nominating a Barbie Doll as his Vice President. I mean, Dan Quayle makes Sarah Palin look smart. With cameras rolling Quayle told a kid in a classroom to spell "potato" correctly by putting an "e" on the end. At another event he started talking about the TV show

Murphy Brown like it was a documentary. Or I always loved his, "What a waste it is to lose one's mind. Or not to have a mind is being very wasteful. How true that is."

There are whole *books* on all the stupid things Dan Quayle said. And *this guy* was how Republicans thought they would appeal to young people. Still blows my mind this *Sesame Street*–level intellect was a heartbeat away from being President.

It was also at this convention where Bush tried to distance himself from the selfish Reagan extremism he'd wrapped himself in like a dirty shirt for eight years — now saying he saw "a thousand points of light" in America. But it was something else he said in his acceptance speech that he would be forever remembered for — "Read my lips, no new taxes" — which made all the soulless help-nobody "Christians" in his audience scream like an arena rock star breaking out his biggest hit.

And of course *that* was what Republicans could never forgive him for four years later. It wasn't the fact that he was so out of touch with life in America that he'd never seen a scanner at a store check-out before until he made a photo-op appearance in one, or that he never embraced the radical extremism that his predecessor and now our current Repugnant President stokes, or that he invaded Panama and killed hundreds of civilians for crass political Wag The Dog press purposes. No. The unforgivable crime of George H.W. Bush for selfish Republicans was that he actually worked with Democrats and had the gall to accept some modest tax increases to pay for a government his former boss had decimated and defunded.

But it was after the conventions that things really got ugly. The guy who took Richard Nixon's Bachelor of

Arts of "dirty tricks" and turned it into a PhD of amorality, Lee Atwater, concocted the "Willie Horton" ad that stood as the low-water benchmark until the current Racist-in-Chief started calling Mexicans "rapists" on Day One of his campaign. As despicable as Reagan was, he never led with the race card. And as much as H.W. is remembered as a decent person in comparison to many Republicans who have followed, it should never be forgotten how low he stooped to defame an honorable man who was his opponent. If you can't win on the merits of a debate of the issues, you shouldn't win.

And speaking of debates! They were also cause to throw some more great parties — which built in attendance with each one. But the most memorable was the vice presidential with Lloyd Bentsen and Dan the Ken-doll. Little known fact — this was when "deer in the headlights" was first coined.

It's true!

You picture his dimwitted sister Sarah Palin winking into the camera and playing the spotlight for all it's worth, but Quayle looked like Dick Cheney was about to shoot him in the face.

Except it was reporters.

Brit Hume and Tom Brokaw in particular. Oh gawd it was funny. First Hume asked him what would be the first thing he would do if for some reason he had to become president. And little Danny answered, "First I would say a prayer," prompting every comedian in the country to write some variation of, "So would we all!"

And then of course Danny blathered some platitudes afterwards, which sparked something I've never seen before or since. Another moderator, Tom Brokaw, asked his predecessor's question again because Quayle hadn't answered it. And again it was Deer In The Headlights time. Then, get this, Brokaw asks it *again!* Like I say, I've never seen this happen before or since. And it *should* happen. If a candidate evades a question — ask the damn question again, and keep asking it until they answer. Cuz this time it led to one of the most memorable moments in all presidential debate history. Quayle babbled out whatever nonsense he'd tried to memorize before the debate, including the unfortunate line (for him), "I have as much experience in the Congress as Jack Kennedy did when he sought the presidency." (Doh!)

Standing next to the pull-the-string Barbie Doll on stage was Kennedy's Texas pal Lloyd Bentsen. And you all know what happened next. Probably the most devastating line in the history of nationally televised debates — "Senator, I served with Jack Kennedy. I knew Jack Kennedy. Jack Kennedy was a friend of mine. Senator, you're no Jack Kennedy."

Boom!

My neighbors musta hated me that political season. We were cheerin' and laughin' and yellin' louder than a room fulla drunk Ranger fans. 'Course, in those years, we prolly had more to cheer about than they did. But it was a helluva campaign. By the next one in '92 *everybody* was into it. A pot-smoking shades-wearing sax-playing baby-boomer knocked out the last of the old World War II guys, and a kooky billionaire midget ran as a third party. Seriously. Look it up. But boy, '88 was when it all first kicked in, at least for this burgeoning politico. And I haven't missed a season since.

Becoming Tsongas's Press Secretary

1992

The political machine is huge. I know. I live in New York. There's no way you can change anything. Thugs hold the power and there's no wrenching it from them. This is 1992. It's all entrenched party hierarchy and media manipulation. There's no way you can affect a candidate or a campaign. Why are you ever reading this?

That's what I thought, too. I'm just a little idealistic Jeffersonian wandering the sidewalks like anybody else, but I thought, What the heck, why not give Tsongas's campaign a call? The guy seems like a straight shooter. Maybe I can get involved. Maybe I can go to the convention. Maybe we could become friends.

It was a long shot, but being poor, that was all I could afford to play. So I called them up. They said they were down on Greene Street. Anybody who knows New York, knows the streets are numbered. Greene Street isn't even on the map! I thought it was the name of a guy in Clue. It turns out it's in SoHo, where the couple lived and sort-of died in *Ghost* — decrepit warehouses converted into decrepit art galleries.

So I went down to the leading Democratic candidate's office. Or rather, basement. Here it was, New York headquarters for the White House, and it's a cellar with one phone, no heat, and pipes that rattle so loud you can't hear the single phone call. There's green crepe paper decorating the iron pillars, and the stationary supplies consist of boxes of his book. The leading candidate: the

largest city in the union: 1992. Go figure.

So I volunteered and they said come back for a media meeting. The next day I was offered the job of Press Secretary for New York State. I'd been a secretary before, but I hardly thought that qualified me. Nevertheless,

22

there I was riding home on the subway, pondering my new position.

This campaign is so grassroots, it's still seeds. This guy's so anti-machine, there is no machine. If there's a hidden conspiracy here, I must be part of it.

If you don't believe me, try finding your local Tsongas office. What I don't get is how he's won half the states he's run in, with no cash, no backing, and believe me, no organization. And he's running for, you know, just kind of an important position.

This campaign's so small he shouldn't even be in the race at this point. There *is* no campaign. This is Wing-and-a-Prayer Overnight Delivery.

The long and the short of it is, I didn't end up becoming Press Secretary, but I am assistant to. Call me crazy, but I was expecting to paint signs or stand in a crowd at a rally. I walked into that cellar five days ago and now I'm on the phone 10 times a day to Boston getting okays to take the initiative on whatever I want. When I met the candidate for the first time at a Lower Manhattan appearance, I was escorting Maureen Dowd from *The New York Times,* and Joe Klein from *New York* magazine to their positions. [This '92 primary was the basis for his novel, and, later, film *Primary Colors.*]

I'm not booking his schedule, but I am managing by default, and living on donuts. I keep wondering if Abraham Lincoln's campaign was run this way.

Naturally I called my folks to give them the news, but they think I'm making the whole thing up.

The Tonka Truck
versus The Ken Dolls

1992

Op-ed — Vancouver Sun, *March 5th, 1992*

As a Vancouverite who got caught in a political downpour while visiting the States, I have to report back on the primaries that are about to be decided in neighboring Washington.

After Bush, Buchanan and Clinton, most Canadians couldn't identify any of the other players in the presidential sweepstakes. Unfortunately the name recognition list leaves off the man most likely to be sitting in the White House next year, Paul Tsongas.

People seem to confuse his name with Tonka trucks. They've heard newscasters speak of "Songus," but don't know who that Tonka guy is when they see his name in headlines.

This underdog ex-Senator, it should be pointed out, has won every election he's run in, despite the media predicting he'd lose every election he's run in. Even after his win in New Hampshire, most news reports opened with Buchanan and Clinton.

Political analysts of all stripes fail to see what the voters of New England did, partly because newscasters, as part of their job requirements, specialize in appearance over substance, so it's understandable they couldn't recognize the reverse when it hit them in the face.

Tsongas looks weird, no question about it. But then FDR was no Gene Kelly. Richard Nixon was no Jack Kennedy. Come to think of it, neither was Ford or Carter. Do I have to mention Truman, Johnson, or the vomiting incumbent?

Why Tsongas is not being considered the far-and-away front runner, and people are still focused on Bill Clinton and his nice tan, reeks of the bigotry that's excluded women and minorities from the office for centuries. Not only do they have to be white European males, but now they have to be from some modeling school cookie cutter.

What distinguishes Tsongas from the rest is that he doesn't lie. This didn't do Walter Mondale a lot of good, but then honesty was very unfashionable in mid-'80s politics. Supply and demand is something Tsongas the businessman knows well.

There's a huge demand for the truth right now, and all the other rhetoric machines are failing to capitalize on it. Perhaps it's because they're deficient in the product in question.

Jerry Brown's the exception, of course, and if he wasn't such a Maynard G. Krebs, he'd probably be leading the pack right now.

So the Democratic voters of America, who for years have wanted Dems in every office but one, now have the choice between two Ken dolls, a bitter farmer, a beatnik, and a Tonka truck. No wonder the broadcasters can't get it right.

But the voters, outside of Clinton's native south in Georgia, did. Tsongas's fatherly pragmatism only comes through over time, after you stop noticing his bouncing eyebrows and his sadder-than-thou expressions. Oh, and by the way, he's funny as hell.

The Bash America Opera

1992

Unpublished op-ed for Canadian newspapers — written October 1st, 1992. It was held by the Toronto Star *and* Vancouver Sun *for a couple of weeks, but the moment & space never came together.*

As a Canadian who recently ventured south and still misses home, I have to report on a disturbing melody that's grown louder and meaner lately.

It's the "Bash America" opera, and I'm sure you've heard someone you know singing it. Unfortunately, so have the Americans. It's kind of like telling an ethnic joke within earshot of the brunt.

Visiting the States, I've come to marvel at some of the different things each of the countries does well, and it strikes me there's more reason for us to be friends with these sometimes obnoxious people than to keep badmouthing them like they're the ignorant in-laws.

Just as a kind of comical counterpoint, imagine a roomful of Americans sitting around over beers slagging Canada. Wouldn't happen. It makes me wonder if we shouldn't be just the slightest bit nice, having lived beside a giant who's been covering our behind since before anyone can remember. We've been holding hands with the biggest kid in the schoolyard for years, allowing us to pursue our dreams any way we wanted without ever having to look over our shoulder. In fact, we felt so safe we never even saw the need to put a confederation together until 1867. What kind of shape would we be in right now if we'd lived next door to Russia, or India, or Mexico?

I'm finding down here that Americans actually *like* us. I'm not kidding. They think we're more honest, polite, and trustworthy than they are. They think our cities are so clean they film all their movies in Canada so they can imagine they live here. They're going to be basing their new health system on aspects of ours, despite the yappings of their campaigning candidates. And as Canadians, we haven't exactly rejected their TV, music, fashion, soda, Bill of Rights, or national pastime either. These are the qualities of friendship.

It's nice to remember Saint Jerome in times like this: "A friend is long sought, hardly found, and with difficulty kept."

I don't know, is it crazy, or should we try to be nicer to each other for a week or two until we can both get back on our feet again?

With the coalition of Europe, and Japan's

Commonwealth of Independent Islands, maybe it's
time to remember who our closest teammates are, and
stop bickering about the gaudy trophies in our brother's
bedroom. He's overhearing us, and it doesn't sound so nice.
Can I just say right here that our laundry might stink too, if
we had ten times as many socks.

Americans are really trying their darnedest.
Honestly. They don't know everything, but they're trying.
They're going to be dumping their so-called "environmental
president" in November. Sierra Club membership is
soaring, and people are turning in their guns at police buy-
backs all over the country. Ronald McDonald Reagan is
back on the late-night B movie circuit where he belongs,
and they're finally admitting we were right all along about
healthcare.

But hark o' noble countrymen: the Yanks are down
and being kicked from all sides right now. Are we really like
an L.A. cop on videotape? Are we not a better people than
that?

This is global crunch time, my homies, and the
league is realigning. Perhaps it's time for just a tad of
continental solidarity.

Bill Clinton's first Inauguration

January 20th, 1993

Originally published in Interchange Magazine, *and* TransForum Magazine, *Jan. and Feb. 1993*

"We march to the music of our time."
                          Bill Clinton at his Inauguration

Little Dorothy Washington slowly snuck up to the Iron Curtain of Oz, and peaked behind the screen. Her eyes popped when she discovered only a hungry old woman hunched over on a stool, pulling what levers were left of The Evil Empire. It was kind of embarrassing. You spend half a century and all your money preparing for battle, only to find your enemy's a broken down old matron. And Dorothy was pissed. Four-Star Ike,

Dick the Magic Dragon, John Wayne Raygun, and Stormin' Norman George suddenly looked worse than silly. There was no "there" there, and the paying customers were talkin' refund. There were riots, poverty, and incurable diseases at home, while they'd sat spellbound at the feet of the their elected monarchs listening to tales of tigers in the jungle.

You should have seen the look on their tiny faces when the curtain peeled back and they discovered they'd been sitting out in the cold (war) for decades while last year's losers were all in school attending class.

"Those damn foreigners were sitting around getting smart again while I was listening to Bonzo's bedtime stories. Am I ever stupid!" Dorothy whined, hitting herself upside the head with a ballot box, and running all the way to the schoolhouse.

The Grand Pendulum reached its apex during the hundred hour ground war in Kuwait, and the recess bell clanged for change. Dorothy was picking at a daisy, wondering, "Ummm, if Iraq has the third biggest army in the world and can't even last longer than a long weekend, what are we doing this for?"

Enter: the swing era, the sea-change, electricity, spring in the step, new life, blinding fireworks, cascading karma, oh my god — Elvis is in the White House!

"What a weird dream!" Dorothy says, waking up.

Those crazy Americans have done it again. They couldn't
be content with a Paul Tsongas or a Bob Kerry or some
other nice guy in a suit. No. They had to pick a pot smoking
sax player from some state that made in-breeding just
another lifestyle choice.

As an expatriated Winnipeger who's been caught in
the gears of America for more than a decade, I decided to
rent a van, convert it into a jack-proof mobile fort, and drive
to Washington to witness the passing of the spliff.

The nugget of the whole week was the concert at the
Lincoln Memorial on the Sunday before the swearing-in.
It was televised on HBO, so check local listings. (It cost
them a bundle — they'll repeat it a lot.) It had the first all-
star performance of "We Are The World" since Live Aid,
including Michael Jackson, Stevie Wonder, Diana Ross,
Kenny Rogers, and a cast of many who I think just sort of
wandered out there.

But it was the spirit of this very black and white
audience that transcended. Kids, grand-couples, middle
class families on blankets — and everybody in a really good
mood. And no idiots. When was the last time you were in a
crowd of half-a-million people and there were no idiots?

So there you are, and there's these giant TV screens,
and there's James Earl Jones reading Lincoln's Gettysburg
Address to the point where, when he reaches the climactic
line, singing "America" in his rich baritone, and stressing
the words "the people," half the crowd is just bawling their
eyes out:

"That this nation under God shall have a new birth of freedom — and that government of *the people*, by *the people*, and for *the people*, shall not perish from this earth."

Then Jack Nicholson strolls out and the crowd starts howling and laughing and falling over. His hair is blowing straight up off his head like his toe's stuck in a socket, and he's reading Lincoln all serious-like but the whole field is just roaring and laughing along with His Freakness.

Then Aretha Franklin comes out, the queen of living soul, and *man*, can she still hit it. She sings *"Someday We'll All Be Free,"* and the whole time you're going, "Yeah, this is cool, but I wish she'd sing '*Respect.*' Not quite the place though." Then Boom! She does it! Aretha's honking on *"Respect,"* and the whole crowd of America starts shaking its collective black ass under a clear winter sky. It was so funky you forgot you were at an historic event.

Then, whoops, Dylan appears out of nowhere, and seems to surprise even Clinton. He wasn't even rumored. You can see Bill on the giant screen just bouncing in his seat like a little kid, and he's hitting Al Gore, going, "Hey Al, right on! It's Bob! I love it, haw haw. Did you set this up?! Pi-i-i-ig whiskers!" he squeals, slapping both knees with his hands. And Dylan's up there massacring *"Chimes Of Freedom."* Brilliant song choice, Bob. Too bad no one could understand a freaking word you mumbled!

Jack. Aretha. Dylan. These are the artists that the President of the United States identifies with!? Jack "Here's Johnny" Nicholson? Aretha, the touring soul goddess of love? Dylan? The poet laureate of the music of revolution?

36

The guy didn't even show up at Woodstock, and he's
here inaugurating a president? You think the times have
changed? I mean, is this possible? I don't think so.

What Were Once Motifs Are Now Symbols, to update
the Doobies. Saxophones — and shades. Okay, who wears
sunglasses? Hip people, right? "Symbol of," anyway. And
where did that come from? The '50s Beats — used to cover
up stoned red eyes. "Originally employed as a drug aid —
now handy as a presidential metaphor."

And the saxophone. Not the clarinet. Not the bass.
Not the grand piano. The guy has to wail on the saxophone
— Charlie Parker's heroin engine. The rock horn. The horn
that was too cool for big band jazz. The human soul pipe.

Let's review: The sax. Shades. Jack. Aretha. Dylan.

Open discussion question: What type of person has
these five things on the back of their baseball card?

Then out on The Mall, there's two days of open tent
free concerts featuring Bob Weir of The Grateful Dead and
thousands of twirling Deadheads at the foot of the Capital
building. Then, Los Lobos. Little Feat. Michelle Shocked.
All officially invited mind you — playing on the Great Field
of America, surrounded by Smithsonian museums, and
literally in the shadow of the Washington Monument.
Wynton Marsalis. Robert Cray. McCoy Tyner. Four ongoing sound stages. For two days, besides the Lincoln
Memorial concert. Taj Mahal. Linda Ronstadt. Blues
Traveler. Food stands from 50 states. It was Folklorama,
Yankee style. And these are the official functions.

Back in the alleys of D.C. lay copious dens of
iniquity and schmoozing that were churning in overdrive.
Refurbished warehouses, old banks turned into decadent

lounges, TV screens everywhere, CNN, C-SPAN, open bars, here a schmooze, there a schmooze, everywhere the camera's snap.

It's out of control, of course, but there's 12 years of pent-up frustration just bursting to get out. Or maybe it's 30 years, or longer. The children of the Ozzie and Eisenhower Conformity Generation, who briefly blossomed during Kennedy's spring of freedom, have finally grasped the reigns of power they had only dreamt of in the adolescence of the sixties.

The psychological spirit of America was born in 1945. That second world war victory established them as a true empire, greater than the old ones of Europe who were unable to curtail their own cancer when it rose.

It was Christened with a splash of Jackson Pollock's Abstract Expressionist painting, trumpeted by Charlie Parker's be-bop musical revolution, and its journey narrated by Jack Kerouac singing Whitman's song in the modern age. The young nation flowered, dreaming in the immensity of it. It was the Age of Aquarius. The Summer of Love. The Woodstock Nation.

But as a few of its heroes dropped, the optimism of youth disintegrated into the cocaine disco toilet stalls of the '70s. The country got sucked into the great temptation pit, like Adam, Achilles, Macbeth and Milken. "Make me Big. Bigger." Schwarzenegger. Schwarzkopf. "Bigger, Bigger. Kill. Kill." Transfixed by its own muscles and glued to the mirror, it belched, "I love myself."

Thank God that beast is dead.

America has rounded the corner of middle age, and put away its childish things. The hopeful intentions of the songs sung from the stage of Woodstock in 1969 were echoed from the stage of the Lincoln Memorial in 1993. America came home from the wars last year, and found that her family had split up while she was off becoming champion of the world.

A country rooted in Jefferson, Lincoln, Whitman and Thoreau, had somehow degenerated into Nixon, Quayle, Trump and Tyson. Not even America liked what it saw. So it changed. No matter how dramatic and funky and symbolic this Aquarian Coronation was, it's only a reflection of a much bigger change that's taken place in the mind and body of America.

Citizen to Sitting Zen

1996

1996 started off with a bang. I became an American citizen.

It all started with a little four-inch clipping from a newspaper my mother sent me from Toronto from one of those Q&A sections they used to run in newspapers when there used to be newspapers. Somebody wrote in asking about a Canadian becoming an American citizen, and it said you did not have to renounce your Canadian citizenship to do it. That had always been a deal breaker for me. I love both countries and made New York City my home for the last 15 years, but I wasn't about to renounce the country that formed me.

This little clipping prompted me to call the Canadian Consulate in New York, and thus began a year-long process of filling out forms and gathering documents. I never hired an immigration lawyer — did it all myself. I worked as a legal secretary at some of the biggest law firms in the world, so I knew my way around a legal document and wasn't scared by the language or gravity of the questions or answers. Also, I'd been a Permanent Resident (gotten my "green card" which was actually blue) after I got married in 1987, and you have to hold that status for five years before you can apply for citizenship. Another factor was — this was now the Giuliani era in New York and people were getting arrested for anything and everything. There was a real turn in the energy and openness and freedom that was New York City when that little lisping dictator took over, and if I happened to get caught up in one of his law-&-order sweeps and got a criminal record, that would probably prevent me from becoming a full-on citizen and could jeopardize my status in the country in general. But if I became a *citizen*, I'd have the same status as the president or anybody else and they couldn't kick me out even if they wanted to.

So I went down that form-completing path quite happily. At some point you have to go into the INS at 26 Federal Plaza and be interviewed to see if you know what "America" means. And if you've read this far, you already know I was teaching my fellow New Yorkers about their country and really quite embraced the whole thing. In the interview they ask you all these questions like how many justices are on the Supreme Court, and name three freedoms in the Bill of Rights, and why do we celebrate Independence Day, and what country did we gain independence from, and stuff like that that I could talk about all day. I was breezing through them all and kinda won the guy over in the process, and when we got to the question: What are the three branches of government? I answered, the White House, the Senate and the House.

And the guy went, "oooooo," like I just broke his heart. He never said and I never asked, but I think they probably gave anybody who got 20-out-of-20 right some sorta prize. I was one "judiciary" away from whatever it was.

Then after you dot all the i's and cross all the t's and wait patiently for the paperwork to shuffle through the system, I got approved and was told to go to the Javits Center for my official swearing-in ceremony. [see, also; the 2016 election night chapter, also set at the Javits Center] They're all real sticklers about rules and everything, and only actual pending citizens are allowed in to the giant convention hall, but I said "forget that!" (except I used a different word), and brought my game-for-anything Prankster girlfriend who snuck in with me (my wife and I had separated by this time). Like everything I do, I made an Adventure of the whole thing. They send you a copy of the Pledge of Allegiance with the letter so you can know what you're signing up for, and when it got to the last line, "... so help me God." I said out loud, "So help me Jerry."

They still let me in.

'96 was probably the easiest presidential election of

Becoming an American citizen.
April 17th, 1996

my lifetime. Democrats would usually lose, or like Clinton in '92 it was a real unknown going into election night. This was the biggest electoral college win for a Democrat since LBJ in '64. But it was still a presidential election, and I'll be damned if I was not going to be involved in it up to my eyebrows!

One of my big targeted objectives was registering people to vote. In Manhattan you could be pretty sure everyone you got to register would vote Democratic, and I carried those yellow registration forms with me everywhere, including into all the various offices where I worked as a temp, leaving small piles in waiting areas and such.

I became a bit of a regular at the Clinton-Gore New York campaign headquarters in Midtown. They had a whole floor of some old kinda crummy nondescript office building, but it was so exciting to go there. All of the campaign headquarters I've seen depicted in movies from *Taxi Driver* to *Primary Colors* are quite accurate to my experience. They're noisy, buzzing with scads of people all doing different jobs, multiple phones ringing constantly, bulletin boards with the latest press clippings, chalkboards with schedules and ever-changing poll numbers, and various yard signs and campaign posters on the walls, often with stacks of them on the floor below that you could take. This particular New York office headquarters was a labyrinth of small and large offices with different functions — press, accounting, get out the vote (GOTV), field operations, the advance team for appearances, volunteer coordinators, state coordinators, city field operations, minority outreach, fundraising, and I think there was one whole department just for collecting endorsements. It was all a buzzing madhouse. And it was such a contrast to poor ol' Paul Tsongas's New York headquarters in that crummy SoHo basement in '92. This was the big leagues.

I went to some planning meetings, but mostly I'd just go in to grab more voter registration forms and buttons and such to pass out, and to see if there were any rallies planned — which there really weren't too many of since we were gonna win New York by a bunch. But for once it was nice to play a season on a winning team.

Also of bizarre note, even though Al Gore invented the internet whenever he figures he did that, this was the first presidential campaign to ever have actual websites! Both were painfully rudimentary, but most of us didn't use them because we got online in those days by noisy slow dial-up connections to AOL accounts, and maybe read some message boards. The Dole site was created and maintained by two Arizona State University students who ran it out of their dorm room and a suburban bedroom. They remember their entire marching orders as being, "We need to have a website, and it needs to be better than Bill Clinton's." The Dole campaign staff themselves could barely use email, and as one of the site developers remembers, "The campaign guys would print the pages out [each new version of the site], annotate them and fax the changes back to me. I had 17 feet of faxes all over my dorm. It was so ridiculous."

Also during this time, I was temping up a storm in Manhattan. When word processing first came along in the mid '80s, there was a ton of work to be had. Not all that many people had made the leap to computers, and the bazillion offices in New York City needed people who knew MultiMate or WordStar or WordPerfect. But as more people learned the programs, there began a dropping-off in the high-paying gigs, and so I wisely morphed my way into becoming a legal secretary, cuz that's where the rates weren't dropping, and if you were really good, you could get all the work you wanted. Plus, law firms were the kinda place where they'd all be in a conference room talking for hours, while I'd be sitting at some high-end computer writing my own books and articles on floppy disks. In fact, this was when I wrote my first published book, *The Temp Survival Guide* (Citadel Press, 1997).

Temping was huge back then. There was even a short-lived sitcom based around a New York temp agency called *Temporarily Yours* on CBS with Debi *"Goodfellas"* Mazar, Seth *"Family Guy"* Green and Joanna *"West Wing"* Gleason. Once I got the book contract, I knew I wanted to write it fast & straight-through so that it would read fast.

I thought it would be cool if I could write it in a week —
and finished it in six days. There was lots of adding and
subtracting later, but the whole basic arc of the book was
written in one flowing flash.

In fact I became something of a Golden Boy
(Winnipeg reference) in the temping world, such that when
one of my agencies got a single request for somebody to go
to MTV for the first time, they called me. I was sorta the
rock star cool guy in a profession of nerdy misfits, and the
agency wanted to land MTV as a regular client, so they sent
me as their representative. Talking to other temps over the
years, we'd ask each other where the good and bad places
were to work, and I'd long heard that MTV was fun, as I
could imagine it might be.

The gig was being an assistant to one of the lawyers.
Generally speaking, legal departments aren't Party Centrals.
The whole field is not far off from accounting. But I was
an exception — cool and fun and funny — while also 100%
accurate in my work. But here was the crazy thing — they
used some word processing program I had never used in my
life. I didn't tell even the agency let alone MTV that I didn't
know it cuz I just wanted to get my ass in there, even if it
was just for one day. So as soon as I arrived I had to start
learning the program as fast as I could cuz at any minute
the lawyer was gonna drop some marked-up contract on
my desk. Well, somehow I pulled it off. By the end of the
day, the lawyer, Yvette Alberdingk, sent around an email
saying — "If you ever need a good temp, ask for this guy by
name." Couldn't believe it. It changed my life. I ended up
working there at their Times Square headquarters for the
next six great years including for the CEO Tom Freston and
the network presidents like Judy McGrath, until my parents

got sick. Since I'd left home at age 18 and was an only child, I knew I could never get this time back if I didn't spend it with them before they were gone.

Also, the mid-'90s was when there was a real resurgence in all things Kerouac and the Beats. NYU put on these two giant conferences in '94 and '95, and there was a mammoth show at the Whitney Museum of Art in '95 called "Beat Culture and the New America." Also, the Kerouac estate had changed hands from Jack's wife Stella, who didn't let anything get published, to a new guard who began releasing all these unpublished masterpieces he'd left behind in Jack's immaculately maintained filing cabinets.

It was kind of a crazy fluke — or karma — how I ended up getting back involved in this world again.

I'd heard about the conference but didn't plan to go because I had been at the *real* conference — the big one — the biggest gathering of the Beats that ever took place — Boulder '82. As John Clellon Holmes said of it — "We had come from all over the country, from all periods of Kerouac's life, and more of us were together than had ever been in one place at one time before." I ended up writing a whole book about that bad-boy — *The Hitchhiker's Guide to Jack Kerouac* — so when the first NYU summit happened in 1994 I thought arrogantly and mistakenly that I was above some middlin' poor cousin to Boulder '82.

The crazy thing is, and to be completely confessional, I think the reason I went down to the Village after work that random Wednesday in May was to go to my pot dealer's apartment. Afterwards, I went walking around my old stomping grounds of Washington Square Park. I went to the Loeb Student Center where I used to produce the concerts [see the 1980–1984 chapter] — had to kinda sneak

48

into the building cuz of course I wasn't a student anymore —
but if you just walked in fast like you knew where you were
going you could get past the guards checking for IDs if you
were smooth and invisible.

I went up to the concert hall on the second floor and
allowed the memory echoes to wash through me, including
of the big Acid Test I threw there with Country Joe
McDonald, Rick Danko, Paul Butterfield, the Joshua Light
Show and such, then I went out on the terrace overlooking
the still-swirling circus of Washington Square Park. As
I was leaning on the railing, below me, right where the
Gary Hart stage had been set up, a white Jeep with a big
"Farm Aid" sign on the side was at the front door and some
guy was unloading conga drums. Turns out it was David
Amram and tonight was the big opening show of the Beat
conference. Like I say, I had no intention of attending this
thing. It was something from my past that I wasn't much
involved with anymore, but "Geez, it looks like something's
happening." So I stuck around. And it was another one of
those life-changing moments.

Everybody was there for the big opening show,
almost all of whom I hadn't seen since '82. Carolyn
Cassady, Jan Kerouac, Anne Waldman, Ann Charters, Al
Aronowitz, Michael McClure, Joyce Johnson — and some
who weren't there in Boulder like Terry Southern and Cecil
Taylor. And by fluke, sitting right in front of me was my old
friend Teri McLuhan (daughter of Marshall) who was with
the photographer musician John Cohen.

I ended up connecting with the organizers — Helen
Kelly & Ed Adler — and finagled myself an all-access pass
to the whole conference. One thing led to another, and
suddenly I was completely immersed in the Beat world

again. And in a way, the arc that began that night hasn't stopped soaring since. Shortly after this, I began organizing shows at the downtown clubs and was once again living in Beatlandia — while simultaneously working at this giant media corporation in a shiny skyscraper in Times Square.

This was the backdrop setting for that entire '96 campaign.

1996 wasn't an election the Republicans look back on fondly, I don't imagine. First, there was the hugely unpopular and polarizing firebrand Newt Gingrich as Speaker of the House who started the whole "shut down the government" routine which didn't go over any better back then than it did when the current Best-Negotiator-in-Chief tried it a couple times. There had been a couple shutdowns before Gingrich, but they only lasted a day or two, whereas his would go on for a week or three.

And then there was the Republican primary that had two certified wackos who actually gained a little traction — Pat Buchanan, who tapped into the anti-immigration, anti-women, anti-choice, anti-arts, nationalistic faction of the Repugnant base that the Orange One would whip up twenty years later; and businessman Steve "Flat Tax" Forbes, yet another precursor of Republicans' desire to imagine themselves as titans of industry. He was primarily running, as far as I could tell, to lower his own income taxes — proposing this scheme that he and a McDonalds worker should pay the same tax rate. The other freaky thing about the bug-eyed Forbes was — he never blinked. I mean, physically. His eyes stared in a pop-eyed Deer In The Headlights way that ol' Barbie Quayle had made famous in 1988 — but with Forbes it was freakishly perpetual.

The Republican Party is not exactly the party of youth and vitality, and with Bob Dole they managed to pick the oldest major party nominee in history to run against the first baby-boomer President. He literally tottered off the front of a stage at one point, reminiscent of Gerald Ford falling down a flight of stairs, both caught on camera and replayed endlessly. He referred to "the Brooklyn Dodgers" as though they were still a team, and his age became a running joke in the late-night monologues. David Letterman — "Bob Dole is calling himself an optimist. I understand this because a lot of people would look at a glass as half empty. Bob Dole looks at the glass and says, 'What a great place to put my teeth.'"

But the comedic portrayal of Bob Dole that defined him best in popular culture was Norm Macdonald's brilliant impression on *Saturday Night Live,* including, for me, the single lasting image of the whole campaign which came (I think) in the *Weekend Update* following the election when they had Dole/Macdonald all alone forlornly dragging his luggage along the sidewalk to REM's *Everybody Hurts.*

To combat his "old" perception he picked as his Vice President a young 61-year-old whippersnapper named Jack Kemp who used to be a pro football player and whose main qualification was he still had a full head of hair.

This helped with young voters about as much as Dan Quayle did for H.W. Bush, and promptly prompted the Dole/Kemp parody buttons & stickers — Role/Hemp.

The whole thing was doomed from the start. Oh yeah, and the crazy munchkin Ross Perot ran again, even though he tried to get somebody else to front his Reform Party. But no one would, so he had to do it himself, and all the pie-charts and paid "volunteers" could only muster about 8% of the vote.

And speaking of the vote — it was the first time I ever got to cast one in America!

I wish it had been a more historic year — maybe baby-boomer Clinton's first, or Obama's first, or the first woman — but vote I did, in those huge, ancient, New York State gear-filled voting booths with the giant handles you had to pull from one side to the other to register your vote and seemed like they were old props outta Charlie Chaplin's *Modern Times*.

Casting my first vote in America.
Tuesday, Nov. 5th, 1996, Manhattan

The election night party in New York was a classic. I had worked my way into the campaign enough that I got a ticket to the big Victory Party at the Sheraton Hotel in Midtown. Knowing a thing or two about big events and campaigns, I knew they had given out way more tickets than there was room in the biggest ballroom in the hotel. Little tip: Victory Parties do not officially start until after the polls close in whatever city you're in. Theoretically, everybody's supposed to be still working on the campaign up until the last minute. In New York, being a late night town and all, polls didn't close until 9PM, so I went to the Sheraton by 8:00 and there was already a line about six people wide stretching from Seventh Avenue all the way down 52nd Street. So, natch Satch, I just went straight inside to the ballroom floor and walked in like I was doing production.

BOOM!

Spread all around the perimeter of the giant nearly empty room they had big TVs on stands like what the AV department at a high school might roll into a classroom in the '70s. And they were all set to different stations — which in those days were the Big Three networks, plus PBS, CNN and C-SPAN. I went to one of them and blended in with the small crowd of other early arrivals, everybody in a good mood. Of all the 8PM (Eastern) poll closing states, only Texas was on the board in red. Everything was looking as good on election night as it had been for the months leading up to it.

Not long after I got in there, there was a loud commotion behind me and I turned around to see a flood of people streaming through the doors. "That's weird," I thought. "They're letting them in early." I couldn't figure out why, then decided, "They prolly got told by the cops to clear the sidewalk."

And then the fun began. First of all, there were now a couple thousand revelers flooding like water into every open space in the room. And all the TV screen maps were deep blue. A lot of people would rush to the screen on the AV cart I was in front of, check the "score," then quickly leave for the network on the next TV. It was a full-body physicalization of clicking through the channels on your remote — except you had to move about 50 feet instead of move your thumb a fifth of an inch.

It seems to me there was an open bar, but don't quote me on that. For sure everyone was well buzzed and New Year's Eve joyous. And for us, it turned out 9:00 was the new midnight. That's when the next batch of states closed — New York, Wisconsin, Minnesota, New Mexico, Rhode Island — and BOOM! At 9:01 with all these new states projected to go Dem, all the networks in the land were able to say "William Jefferson Clinton will be re-elected as President of the United States!" And 2,000 of my new best friends threw their arms in the air and started screaming

54

like I hadn't heard in this town since the Rangers won the Stanley Cup two years earlier.

And then — ah-ha! *"That's* why they let everybody in early. They knew it was gonna get called as soon as the 9:00 polls closed."

This was probably the best party in America that night other than whatever Bill Clinton was throwing in Little Rock. And come to think of it, it was probably better than that. No offense to Arkansas, but we New Yorkers know how to party! And thus began an insanely joyous night.

This was the earliest a presidential election would be called in my lifetime. Well, I guess '84 was probably called early, but I wasn't involved in that one, and the wrong team won.

New York City is a very liberal and Democratic town. And it's where the money & media & power are. So every major Dem was there at the party, and most of them spoke from the stage. The esteemed and now mightily missed Senator Daniel Patrick Moynihan; our '84 Vice Presidential nominee Geraldine Ferraro; former Governor Mario Cuomo; our senior House Representative Chuck Schumer who would go on to end the nightmare that was Alphonse D'Amato and become a Senator in the next Midterms in '98; longtime Harlem Representative Charlie Rangel; Brooklyn Representative and "the Librarian of Congress" Major Owens; a young Jerry Nadler long before he'd chair the eventual impeachment hearings of another New Yorker who shall remain nameless; Representative Carolyn Maloney representing my district in Manhattan; former Mayors David Dinkins and Ed Koch; and a couple thousand or so of us various levels of operatives.

We may not have won back the House or the Senate that night, but it was still a helluva party. They had a huge balcony off the ballroom looking down from the second floor over Seventh Avenue right near Times Square which was an ideal place to smoke a celebratory joint or three beyond the noses of the new Giuliani police. There were all sorts of New York characters who had managed to find their way into the party. I remember this limo driver who carried in his wallet a picture of every cool person he'd ever driven, and had concocted elaborate stories about how they'd become best friends. And there was this comedian who was doing a one-woman show in the East Village and seemed to be making up new political material on the spot. But the most memorable was a magician in full top-hat-dapper-suit regalia who was spitting playing cards out of his mouth in the middle of conversations.

Since I was in this nice hotel where I didn't usually find myself, I did what I did in every building I ever temped in — I went up to check out the roof. Back in the pre-9/11 daze, almost every roof in the city was accessible. I went out to the deli and grabbed some beers, and came back in the hotel as a guest of the party, but pushed the top floor on the elevator. I was always tempted back then to write a book about how to get onto every roof in the city but I knew that would blow the secrets of all the sacred lookouts I'd found.

Outside every elevator door there is a floor-plan with the stairwells marked In Case of Fire. All you had to do was go to the one that had a stairway going up to a door with a sign that said "NO ROOFTOP ACCESS" and then push that door open — and Whoosh! you'd feel that big gust of 40-story-high wind and know you were home!

The thing about New York is — it's crowded. It's the greatest city in North America at least, and everybody wants to be there. But one place you could have the city to yourself was on the roof of a skyscraper. The madness was going on all around you, but you had a space the size of a building all to yourself, with 360 degree views, open air, and the adrenaline jazz of being someplace you weren't supposed to be — but were!

What was cool about this roof was the massive "Sheraton" sign. And something I first experienced on the Essex House roof on Central Park South was that you could climb up the ladder onto the iron scaffolding that the sign was attached to and boy, that is a freaky wild experience! It's one thing to be standing on a rooftop with the wind blowing around you and being able to look out into the crowns of the other architectural masterpieces that every damn building in that city is — but, boy, when you're up in the scaffolding with the wind blowing up from below, suspended on a narrow little fire escape type walkway in the middle of the air above the city, it feels like you're flying. It's the closest thing I've experienced to what a bird must feel like. And that's what I spotted on top of the "Sheraton"!

BOOM!

Find the ladder — and get higher still! Up I went until I was right there at the crown of the giant two-story-high "S" of the sign! The wind was blowing up a storm — in fact there were wonderful storm-like conditions that night, with a very low cloud cover, and in a lit-up city like New York, the illuminated flowing clouds create this undulating 3-D painting right above your head. And of course I had saved one last joint — which are always a bit of a challenge to light in these conditions — but I didn't have four stars on my tie-dyed Prankster collar fer nuthin.

I sat down on the iron slats and let my legs dangle in eternity while I pondered all we had done and all that was ahead. The Mission of the Year accomplished. The first baby-boomer President was re-elected over a turn-the-clock-back regressive geezer. The good guys won! I thought of the button I was wearing that night — "It's the Supreme Court, stupid" — playing on the '92 campaign's "It's the economy, stupid." Bill had appointed Ruth Bader Ginsburg and Stephen Breyer in his first term, and we had big hopes for the term ahead. Nobody ended up retiring in his next four years, but we didn't know that on election night.

I knew Bill wasn't Jerry Brown or Ralph Nader or anything, but he had assessed and worked the electorate. There'd been Republican presidents pretty much my entire adult life, and America was not Greenwich Village, as much as I wished it were. You couldn't be as far over on the left as my friends & I and win Ohio and Florida and all the places you had to to become President. But Clinton had tilled the middle ground. And because of that, women's rights were safe. Voting rights were safe. The environment was safe. Education was safe. Judgeships were safe. PBS was safe. Newt Gingrich and his right-wing selfish pals were up to some serious no good. And there was only one office-holder in their way. And we just held that office. And it was time to celebrate. On a rooftop in New York. Under the billowing clouds of history.

Hanging Chads
& Lost Innocence

2000

"You may say I'm a dreamer, but I'm not the only one," as John Lennon sang to the rippling waves of eternity.

Until the last two months of 2000 I believed in justice and democracy in America. I'm an optimist. I don't just see the glass as half full — I'm pouring more in while you're asking the question.

How the 2000 campaign played out — from Al Gore disowning the partner who brought him to the dance, and picking Joe "Sanctimonious Snake-Oil" Lieberman as his V.P., to the first electoral college robbery of my lifetime, followed by the anti-democratic non-justice that the Supreme Court meted out — it all popped the bubble of America for this new immigrant and citizen.

The Florida Supreme Court ruled that the votes should be recounted. Then the federal Supreme Court of a country that goes around the world killing people with a paper medal on its chest claiming it stands for democracy and justice, ruled that counting the votes should be stopped.

It was all preceded by and set to the backdrop of the Lewinsky affair and ken starr's vast right-wing conspiracy witch-hunt, brought on by the two most heinous female creatures ever to stalk the American countryside — Lucianne Goldberg and Linda Tripp. Right-wing attack dog and former Nixon dirty tricks spy Goldberg had lied to Tripp that it was legal to tape phone calls, and then coaxed her amoral flunky Trippster to con the infatuated intern that she was a friend — as she worked to destroy that young girl's life for perverted political gain over consensual adult sex — which apparently neither of the two old witches were having.

Of course, we've since learned in painful detail how this so-called "family values" sliver of American political profiteers have nothing to do with "family" or "values." Separating families at the border and attempting to deny gay Americans the right to marry and have a wedding cake has more recently exposed their rancidity. But back then, serial-cheating family-abandoning Newt "Salamander" Gingrich and later the pedophile gay sexual abuser Dennis Hastert were who the Repugnant Party put forth as their Speakers of the House of Representatives. And these two women and these two men are perfectly emblematic of the duplicity driving the Repugnant train. And nuttin's changed since the Pussy-Grabber Express rolled out of the station.

And Al Gore — who, as much as I applaud his Herculean uphill efforts to bring An Inconvenient Truth to the world's attention — allowed the ken starr narrative to dictate his campaign in an historically tragic error of judgment.

The government was operating at a surplus, the economy was booming, Bill Clinton had the highest approval rating (65%) of any departing president since Harry Truman, and Gore listened to whatever bad advice he got and ran away from the president he was connected to — and *then* named as his V.P. the most despicable Republican-wannabe pseudo-moralist psycho-prick he could find.

I'm a lifelong Democrat and I didn't even vote for this ticket, going Green instead in New York State cuz I knew the Dems would win by 15 points and wanted the Green Party to reach the automatic ballot threshold to be included in future elections.

2000 was a perfect storm — just like the freak factors of 2016 were — both disastrous outcomes that wouldn't have happened if not for a whole series of improbable events.

I don't buy into any religion, but I've learned from experience there's sumpthin goin' on beyond the surface. But all the human suffering that has happened because of both these hundred-to-one electoral calamities makes me think the anti-godster atheists might be right. I don't wanna concede the existence of a Great Spirit under any circumstances, but seeing all the atrocities both natural and otherwise that have befallen our species (and all the others), some of these bizarre occurrences have sure made me question my faith. Without even getting into everything else in human history, how could Florida have fallen .009% on the wrong side? And the less than 1% in Wisconsin,

Michigan & Pennsylvania in 2016 that put the psychopathic death-&-suffering-causing Trumpenstein monster in the White House wouldn't have happened if there was a god.

And just like the 2016 campaign, in 2000 the Repugnants created and paid to air pro Green Party ads (before they simply had to create social media memes) in several toss-up liberal-leaning swing states trying to split the left's vote. And just like 2016 with their Bernie and Jill Stein subterfuge promotions, it seems to have worked. Green Party candidate Ralph Nader got 97,488 votes in Florida . . . which Gore lost by just 537.

Extensive exit polling showed that 6% of voters who identified as "liberal" voted third party — whereas only 1% of self-identified "conservatives" did. It's a way of dividing the left (that some on the left fall for) and the right knows how to milk it.

Jon Stewart had taken over *The Daily Show* in January 1999, and in these first formative years he assembled an all-star team for the soon to be destination viewing 11PM slot on Comedy Central's basic cable channel. With core "correspondents" Stephen Colbert and Steve Carell, and occasionally Lewis Black, Mo Rocca, David Cross, Dave Attell and many all-star others, Stewart created an entirely new late-night medium for both comics and viewers. Stewart himself credited the 2000 campaign as the moment his show gelled into what millions of American would tune into for the next 20 years and counting.

Also still thriving during this cycle was *Saturday Night Live*, with Darrell Hammond doing his classic stiff Al Gore, which his campaign actually forced the candidate to watch so he could see how badly he was coming across.

Life imitating art. Hammond's prolonged, exaggerated, very Southern *"In my view* ... (pause)" start to nearly every sentence in the debate, and his repeated use of "lockbox" that Gore had come up with to protect Medicare, became national catchphrases. And to complete one of the great political comic duos of all time, Will Ferrell's bumbling, malaprop-rich, mangled-syntax George W. Bush also entered the public consciousness, including one of the words that continues to define Dubya to this day — "strategery."

And in the Cool Tidbit Department:

2000 was the election that cemented the red & blue colors for the two parties. It had jumped back and forth on different news outlets every election since color TV coverage started in earnest in 1976. In fact, that year, ABC used *yellow* for Republicans!

I remember watching the returns in 1980, and when Reagan was winning the whole Midwest, David Brinkley famously said on air that the middle of the country looked like "a suburban swimming pool," because Republicans were blue then.

Younger people and non political junkies probably don't know, but before 2000 you could have one TV network with the Dems in blue and Repugs in red, then change channels, and the colors were reversed on that network's map! It was kinda funny, kind of jarring, and kind of confusing.

Because the 2000 election dragged on into mid-December, with maps of Florida appearing regularly on TV and in newspapers, some of which like *USA Today* and the *New York Times* had gone to color printing, the colors that were used for that elongated election were burned into both the public psyche and newsroom protocol and never changed again. The senior graphics editor at the *New York Times*, Archie Tse, explained his decision as simply as, "I just decided *red* begins with 'r,' *Republican* begins with 'r.' It was a more natural association."

Florida Florida Florida

Election night — no wait, election *month* — was a frickin' nightmare.

Although it started out pretty positive.

My mother had gone 100% deaf earlier that year, and we were talking on the phone on election night using a service where somebody's on the line typing what I say so my mom could she read it on the other end. While we were on the phone sometime shortly after 8PM, my TV was on in the background, and I said, "Oh my God — they just called Florida for Gore!" And the typist — who's not supposed to say anything — reactively blurted out an obviously happy, "Oh, Wow!"

Another funny family moment — my Dad was in his 80s at the time and was kinda crabby even in his best of years, and didn't understand anything about an "electoral college" (just like most Canadians and even most Americans) but he religiously watched the CBC News every night, and every time I'd call during that two-month drag-out I'd get an earful about "that *god-damned* Florida! Why *the hell* are they still talking about that place. Isn't there any other news happening in the whole bloody country?"

Election night was the night the late great Tim Russert [see his tribute in the Dessert section] wrote on his whiteboard "FLORIDA FLORIDA FLORIDA" when everybody was trying to figure out how the election would be decided and who the next President would be — a scene *TV Guide* called one of the 100 Greatest Moments in Television History, and the whiteboard he wrote it on is now in the Smithsonian!

At about 2:30 in the morning, the news networks called the election for Bush — (even though Al Gore got more votes!) It was all that 1700s "electoral collage" bull. With Gore not embracing his popular incumbent boss, Ralph Nader and the Green Party got *four times* as many votes in 2000 than they did in the preceding '96 election, and that defection from the green-leaning left cost Gore a bunch of states. For one, he lost New Hampshire — which would have won him the Presidency — by 7,200 votes — and 22,000 voted for Nader.

I turned off the TV and was up writing an email dispatch to my political friends when the phone rang about 4:30 in the morning. "Something's happening," my *Toronto Star* reporter friend and fellow nighthawk Mitch Potter told me without so much as a "Hello." Gore was in the car on his way to give his concession speech when word reached him that Florida was in fact "too close to call."

BOOM!

You all know what happened after that. Hanging chads, butterfly ballots and Jeb Bush running the state that would make his brother president. Sure — that seems legit.

Doh!

With the f'ed up quasi "recount," Dubya ended up "winning" the state by the aforementioned 537 votes out of nearly 6 million cast!

When people say their one vote doesn't matter I wanna go full Tarantino on their ass. The Cheney Administration and its spokesman George W. Bush won 271 electoral college votes, just squeaking over the 270 goal line. To riff on Tim Russert —

NEW HAMPSHIRE

NEW HAMPSHIRE

NEW HAMPSHIRE

A similar electoral college fuck up would put an insane pathologically lying racist in the White House 16 years later. Thanks a lot, Founding Fathers. And third party voters.

May we all take these catastrophic results to heart and make goddamn sure it never happens again.

The Franken Fracas

Democracy in Action –
Sunday! Sunday! Sunday!

2004

Howard Dean town hall at the Palace Theater —
High Noon, Sunday Jan. 25th, just before the New
Hampshire primary voting on Tuesday,
Hundred year old theater, core heart downtown
Manchester,
a city & state completely consumed by the primary;
every corner and window painting a candidate's name in
red, white & blue.

Beatlemania outside the theater.
Obviously the hot show of the hour.
Paul Begala, David Brooks, Al Hunt, Frank Luntz, Jonathan
Alter . . .

Every seat filled,
Back of floor and side aisles packed with cameras and media
and people all ages in parkas.

After Dean's stump speech, the Q & A starts.
By the second question a twenty-something guy approaches
the hostess with the mic next to me in the aisle.
Weird vibes from question man.
Hostess begs off with promise he'd be next.

I'm crouching down in the aisle right beside him, also
waiting to ask a question,
Then Howard asks to take one from the balcony.
Hostess uses opp to move up to front row.
Suddenly Question Man starts to yell out about Dean
not being a real Democrat, and that he's a phony, and
why doesn't he go after Dick Cheney, and what about the
drug war, and all these non-sequiturs, and everybody's
kinda "huh?" until he mentions Lyndon LaRouche and
everybody's "ohhhh."

Some guys in dark suits try to talk him down, but he doesn't
stop.
More big guys in suits show up,
Huddle around him, then inch the huddle up the aisle to the
back of the house –
        to the darkest opposite back corner from lobby doors.
Dean keeps talking to the next audience questioner . . .
        the show goes on.

As soon as the huddle gets past the final row,
Another guy stands up in his seat —

Bigger, louder, five rows behind me, picks up the rant.
It's choreographed!
Professional protesters!
How many are here?
Coordinated political terrorists emerging from among us . . .

"You're not a real Democrat! What about the drug war?
You're part of the establishment!"
Other dark suits try to reason with the guy.
They coax him out of the seat to the aisle where
There's only me and some other girl crouched down waiting
to ask a question.

The suited ushers are thinking he's a reasonable New
Hampshire theater-goer –
         their hands held politely to guide him to the rear.
I see his eyes, his face, the anger, the punching finger-
pointing.
         "No way he's going back."
Most staffers and "security" have left with the first protester.
No one's in charge.

Sure enough, as soon as he steps out of the row of seats, he
starts down the aisle for the stage.
Big guy, six-footer, big belly, storming right towards me,
Nobody but me and the girl between him and the stage,
I leap up from the crouch —
Throw a shoulder & back block into his middle —
         solar-plexus bull's-eye Thump!
Whale stops
Bounce, blubber blubber.
My feet regain grip on downward slopping carpeted aisle,

and he charges ahead again,

BOOM!

Stay low, bounce back, "solid force," one foot way back as deep anchor.

I'm turned sideways, he tries to go around behind,

No one's stopping him.

"Stay with him. Be a wall," I'm thinking, pushing back.

He tries to go around in front of me, we crash into the row of seats,

Eyes closed, using The Force, responding to how his body moved.

This is my home turf — a theater concert aisle :-)

He keeps pushing, no one comes to the rescue;

Stay low, shoulder to his mid-section, following his center, pushing back,

Head-tucked, hunched over, holding him, huge, fat, pushing forward, "stay low."

Finally he seems to get pulled back,

Stand up,

Everybody's yelling, finger pointing, Dean supporters trying to shut him down, suits got their huddle back.

I'm like, "Holy shit!"

As soon as he's to the back, a girl stands up right in front of me and starts yelling at Dean.

I say, "Hey you guys already had lots of time, you said more than anybody else already," and I engage her in a conversation just as she started her speech and kept her attention and she stops yelling.

And while I'm talking to her, the big angry immovable whale of a guy is being ushered out in the back of the theater where it's impassable with cameras and press and campaign

staff and
The passive campaign 'security' is about as tough as a
church, so
Suddenly the guy appears over the back wall in the one open
spot where some camera had vacated.
And he starts all over again – Dean 'n' Cheney, loud 'n'
angry . . .
I feel like – "I'm dealing with the girl" who was next in their
choreography,
and had just shown you can be proactive & stop jumbo-guy,
but
Nobody's stopping him,
And I'm holding the girl with words but
He keeps on yelling, and meanwhile
Dean and the audience questioner are trying to keep talking
over it.

Finally I go, "This is nuts," and I leave the girl to go stop
yelling blubber bluster.
As I get there, there's all sorts of people sorta tapping him
on the shoulder,
And one guy in a parka (turns out to be Al Franken) tries to
pull him back from the partition.
The guy lashes out, throws a punch —
Action – people – arms – dark – flurry,
Parka-guy gets knocked to the ground;
Just as he does that — the violence has escalated and
camera gear is at risk —
The Road Warriors' babies are threatened,
And they mobilize like Special Forces, but
Too many move for the guy at once, and
He falls back into a tripod, and a camera goes over, but

There's so many people, it doesn't have room to hit the
ground.

The fire exit door's kicked open with a bang —
The area fills with sunlight —
A body flies out, coat flapping like a cape.
The door slams shut.

Emergency Room doctors rush to check cameras' vital signs,
Big parka body's still on his back on the floor,
I look down — it's Al!
"Al, no way!"
He's holding half a pair of glasses, broken at the nose,
One hand blindly fumbling among a million dark feet for
the other half.
Finds it. Holds them together. "Oh shit."

He stays on the floor in shock. Been there.
"I'll just stay here. Safe. Legs shaky. Don't stand."
A few more seconds, it's getting dangerous being down
there, too many feet.

Me and some other guy each reach a hand down and pull
him up.
He's kinda stunned, looking at us funny,
Faces a foot apart.
We've talked a few times, there's recognition,
He locks right into my eyes, scared, stunned, looking for an
answer.
"Good job, man. Way to go!" I reassure him. "You did the
right thing."

He's staring at me, nodding like he's coming back.

"He broke my glasses," is all he can say.

Dean's voice fades back in from the distance.
Finally some friend nods, "Let's go this way,"
And leads Al off to fix his specs, and
He gets taped up and is back in the game in minutes.

The Rock Party and
The Fall of New York

Election Night 2004

It was a really magic night! Until the nightmare.

Couldn't sleep the night before — up at 6 AM watching a camera follow Don Imus into his polling station with a long line of people out the door waiting to vote, and him saying, "I've *Never* seen it like *this*!"

There's reports of record-breaking turn-out in every county in the land. I dash over to the school at some low point in the news hour cycle and vote for the Green Party by pulling the giant rickety handle on NYS's ancient voting machines. I'm a strategic voter and know John Kerry was kerrying New York State by double-digits, so I try to get the Green's numbers up.

By noon, Kerry's headquarters is giddy and almost dancing, and Bush's is heads-down and dour. All the pundits are pundificating about what went wrong for Bush. The wee Shrub himself stumbles out of his voting booth looking as shell-shocked as his mother watching King George the First collapse in that great debate in '92. And the Little One's babbling even more incoherently than usual — he *knows* it isn't going his way.

This was obviously *Our* day! And the world was changing for the better!

The phone's ringin' off the hook, people stopping by. The "liberal" TV media are curling tiny smiles and radiating subtle shades of giddiness. Networks were monitoring exit polls, and they weren't reporting them over the air, but the results were in their faces.

And there were parties everywhere. NBC was outside Rockefeller Center. CNN at Times Square. Senator Chuck Schumer at the Grand Hyatt. A thousand email invites to places like The Bowery Poetry Club and Crobar hosting serious election-party all-nighters.

Got to Rock Center by 6 and it felt like warm-ups on New Year's Eve — everybody out with a smile, some rushing towards home with a big beam on, others waiting for the other ball to drop. As you entered the processional mall of the Rockefeller Cloister there was an almost beatific calm of joyous confidence. NBC, God bless 'em, had built this "Democracy Plaza," a giant Disneyland playground for fans of democracy — towers with giant TV screens and concert speakers blaring NBC and MSNBC from three different broadcast studios behind walls of glass — reflecting the transparency of their coverage — citizens and freedom-of-the-press merging in an open orgy — with Oval Office Fantasyland displays you could walk through, and a giant map of the nation on the skating rink below to be colored in as the states are won.

As I arrive, I see Tom Brokaw through the window sitting down in his chair for his final election night coverage, the only guy on the air in Nebraska when Kennedy was shot, and now signing-off his career with JFK II. I see my favorite player in the pundits league, Tim Russert, coming right towards me thru the crowd! He's got his frowning don't-mess-with-me scowl on, like he's trying to scare off any space intruders, but I go, "No way!" and give him a big smile, as in, "Stop it, Mr. Serious," and say to him "Have a great night!" and he drops his scowl and smiles for just a second, winks, and says "Thanks!"

The whole place is wild! Like being at any euphoric mass gathering of like-minded people — a Woodstock for voters, Mass with the Pope, the *real* American Super Bowl— two teams, no tomorrow, a lotta hype, dancing bears, and Las Vegas layin' odds! Except the winner of this gamble gets to turn its citizens into armed killers and our nation into a goose-stepping army of chest-pounding thugs. Or not — as the case will obviously be!

We were finally putting an end to this King George madness and everybody knew it! You could see it in the faces. Watching MSNBC prepare to go on the air, Ron Reagan Jr. was just bouncing and couldn't stop smiling. Across the table, Republican Joe Scarborough was ashen in shock and lost in thought. All around there were nothing but Kerry signs and buttons and women and Democrats and young people in a blazing rainbow of new-day joy.

Every time Kerry or a Democrat's name was mentioned on the giant screens, the whole crowd cheered. When Bush's name was mentioned, one guy clapped.

"Who's *THAT* guy?" and everyone laughs.

CNN's been hyping their Times Square broadcast for about a month, so I scooch over there before the results start coming in at 7. If the Peacock has *this* goin' on at *a skating rink*, the all-news network *in the middle of Times Square* is gonna be the center of the universe!

As I salivate thru the tourists for the feast ahead, there's the first subtle hint of, "This isn't right. What's going on?" CNN's Campaign Express bus is parked in the middle of Times Square . . . but nobody's around it. And there's the giant NASDAQ screen, but it's *not* showing CNN. There's a street-level broadcast booth, but there's only about 20 people around it. There's Larry King and Jeff Greenfield, but there's no audio on the outside of the studio. There's kids smooshing their faces against the glass, and tourists from Kansas who just want to wave home on TV. What happened to the election? This is just a glass bowl of Larryfish. And they're barely moving! Across the square, MTV's plastered for 3 stories with their Choose or Lose campaign. NBC turned Rock Center into a Democracy Disneyland. Flags are flying all over the city – and here's CNN with the sizzle of a stock ticker. Watching Larry in an isolation booth adjust his suspenders was about as awesome as watching the *Times'* print dry. So I zipped back over to the November New Year's Eve party at Rock Center.

Weaving through the Midtown canyons, some guy was up ahead washing windows with a squeegee, with some security guard standing over him, and I'm thinking, "Ope! There's some guy with 'community service'!" But as I get closer, I look through the windows he's cleaning — and it's the freakin' Fox News broadcast booth! And not a single person is standing outside! Britt Doom, Bill Kristolmeth, and that Beetle Barnes are all sittin' right there — and

there's not one fan at the window! It was almost sad — but
... not. And so reconfirming of how the night was going!
These guys were solo at a funeral that no one was attending.
Meanwhile, the Democrats were dancing in the street to
Johnny B. Goode outside Radio City Music Hall!

Back at the Rock party, the first results came in —
they only give piddly Vermont to Kerry, but a big cheer went
up anyway. There's a funny little murmur of boos whenever
they call a red state for Bush, and everybody laughs that
we're doing it. It's like the silly unflappable mood when
you're at the big home game and know your team's gonna
win tonight. People are beaming, back-slapping, and beer
drinking out of deli coffee cups — the new-age Giuliani-
Buster. "Strangers stopping strangers just to shake their
hand," I heard some Deadhead singin' on the back of a
Cadillac. We were all together and happy. This horrific
global nightmare was finally over! And we were all sharing
the moment as one!

With each passing half-hour, more and more people
were pouring into the Rock Center town square as word
was Kerrying across the land. Everyone wanted to be here.
They were calling Connecticut, Delaware, Maine, Mass and
all sorts of others for Kerry, even recent toss-up New Jersey.

On the wall of the giant phallic Rockefeller Tower
they'd rigged up (literally) two window washing rigs, draped
one in red and the other in blue, and were pulleying them
up the side of the building as each state's electoral votes
were determined, with this carny bell-ringing level marked
at about the 27th floor reading game-over 270, and these
long primary drapes streamed down to the ground forming
a giant bar graph of votes like a flowing Ross Perot chart,
New York skyscraper size.

The whole scene and vibe kept accelerating, faster and faster, the frenzy escalating with each state's poll closings. I bump into Howard Dean as he's leaving the MSNBC booth. He's covered in pancake make-up that looks so good on TV and so six-feet-under in person. He was gonna walk by, but I say, "Hey man, I was with you in New Hampshire!" and he stops and turns and says, "Hey! Thanks! That's great, thank you very much," and shakes my hand and looks me in the eye. But he seems all worried like he's going to lose again or something. I wanna pump-up the TV QB, so I slap his shoulder making a poof of makeup dust cloud his head. "This is gonna be a great night!" I say, and he's like, "Well, . . . I sure hope so (hak hak)."

I'm thinkin, "This guy's a worrywart!" But I say, "This is what we were doin' it all for!" And he says, "Yeah, I know," shakin his head in an agreeing yet discouraging way that said, "Boy, you're right. But, boy you're wrong." Like he knew somethin' I didn't yet. Then he says, "Let's keep our fingers crossed," as a handler grabs him by the arm and whisks him off to his next camera.

I start saying to people, "Say goodbye to Senator Kerry," and a long pause as they look at me strangely. "And Hello to *President-Elect* John Kerry!" and they burst into a smile and we all high-five and spill beer! It was *So* great! There was no place else in the world I wanted to be. The cell phone's ringing nonstop with calls from all over North America — some people biting their nails, others in vans biting the dust in swing-states and calling for the latest update. Then Walter calls, inviting me down to the *Daily Show* party at that sprawling Park Cafe party club. Well, okay, that's one other place I'd like to be.

Jump in a cab headin' downtown. Through Times

Square, past CNN, a hundred people now swarming around
the curving Larryfish bowl, but it's nothing like Rock Center.
The cab radio is calling Chuck Schumer the winner in
the New York Senate race the minute after the polls close
(9PM), and the Dem Ken Salazar in Colorado is beating
Adolph Coors for the open Senate seat! This is a *landslide*!
All is good in the universe!

Until I step into the other world of the *Daily Show* party.
　　　Suddenly, as Dylan says — things have changed.
　　　Giant wide-screen TVs hanging everywhere from the
ceiling like bats;
　　　　　— except loud music is blaring instead of the news,
　　　　　and no one was paying any attention
　　　　　to　*The　Election*!
　　　　　Hello?
　　　　　Grabbed a plateful of refueling salmon and stood
under the lowest-hanging bat, squinting at the numbers, but
it wasn't coming into focus, and it wasn't computing. I'd just
been dancing in throngs of victorious new world Democrats
cheering every state . . .
　　　　　but suddenly it was the state of dismay,
　　　　　— that America's greatest political show's party . . .
　　　　　didn't even have the election coverage sound up!
　　　　　as though this was just some old debate from the
C-SPAN library playing in the background and not the real-
time numbers flowing in live after years of work and only
our freakin' species in the balance!
　　　　　Bush up by 20,000 in Florida — "It must be just the
Republican districts they're counting so far."
　　　　　Then I look again, and he's up by 100,000!
　　　　　Something's wrong,

Something's wrong.

I think back to my many years of studying elections .
. . and immediately start drinking tequila.

Then Virginia, and North & South Carolina all fall
like saplings in a sudden storm . . . *and they're gone.*

We're not even close in Arkansas,

Not even close in Louisiana,

Just a hairsbreadth ahead in Wisconsin and PA.

This isn't right.

Something's wrong.

I quickly move to double tequilas.

I'd been telling people for days, "We'll know the
trend and what's going to happen by 9:30."

I look at my watch.

It's 9:30.

I'm standing under the batscreens,

screaming

inside

that something's not right . . . in A BIG Way.

Can't admit the numbers are real,

something's gotta be off,

go to another screen, another network, another
number, but it's not adding up.

Can't move,

or see anything but exploding numbers blinding
from above,

immobilized

like a bleeding soldier in the field,

I need morphine . . .

I need to be shot in the head.

82

I slump down in one of the giant curving Copacabana booths,

And once I'm off the TV screen hell I notice all these famous faces in the crowd around me, all these young actors and actresses I recognize from movies or my dreams or other parties.

Pale and goateed Ethan Hawke drops down beside me,

both of us stunned and staring up in open-mouthed shock at the numbers . . .

two wounded soldiers on the field of Gettysburg,

looking above for salvation, but dying inside as none comes,

limbs numb,

stomach-punched,

stripped of hope;

a blood-red tide rising,

drowning,

gasping,

nothing we can do . . .

I've gotta drink this through:

Who's got a light?

I know! It's . . . the *Daily Show*'s fault!

Yeah, that's it!

I picture the million dancing Democrats at Rock Center and jump back in a cab uptown with visions of ferris wheels and carousals, calliopes and clowns, and everybody was dancin', dancin' in the street!

But as the cab rounds the corner onto 50th,

a newspaper blows across the empty street in front of us.

We coulda driven on the sidewalk.

When I left here a few seconds ago (it seems) it was New Year's Eve — and now it's suddenly the hungover morning after — and it's not even midnight.

I stagger like a wounded cowpoke through the ghost-town tumbleweeds. Disembodied voices echo through empty canyons like taunting demons. The balloons had all dropped and popped, and multi-colored litter is all that's left of the dream. A dancing mosh-pit of war-ending democracy was now a ghoulish accident scene in the middle of the night — flashing lights, the absence of life and the sense of death, clusters of silent cops by yellow police tape and beaten blue barricades — and a bloody red splatter all over the white skating rink below.

The happy circus had turned into some upside-down Bizarro-world, a Twilight Zone where all the people have disappeared. And echoing through a canyon, when some state is called for Bush . . . a *cheer* goes up from some hidden pocket of insurgents! *A cheer* for godsakes! Here! In My city! The Artist's Village! . . . of liberals, democracy, our nation's first capital, Washington's oath, the birth of it all, the revolutionaries, the Beats, the spirit guides, the mystics, painters and poets, Greenwich Village and the morning *New York Times*, immigrants, minorities, and open-mindedness — the cradle that berthed be-bop and folk, that drew Lennon and Dylan and me and you — Clinton's victory convention and his First Lady becoming Senator — FDR and Eleanor's home fer god's sake! and Moynihan and Jackie O., Walt Whitman and Mr. Poe . . .

Oh no!

Another state's called for Bush,

and another faint cheer washes in where angels fear
to tread,

and the building-size red stripe is pulled higher up
the wall, closer and closer to the 270 buzzer,

but the blood-red dye's already cast in the ice,

and Bush's smirking face is on the giant screens
everywhere looking down on us like Saddam Hussein's
glower all over Baghdad,

and hidden somewhere in the haunted streets lay a
pocket of his Republican Guard

cheering

right

in the middle of Manhattan!

Someone shoot me in the head!

I'm no longer grateful — I just wanna be dead!

I wanna jump in front of a cab, but jump inside one
instead.

I can put this nightmare to rest — if I can just go to
bed;

And dream in blue rhymes, and never see red;

I promise, oh lord, if you'll just end this dread,

I'll be a good person, from this day ahead!

And I know there's a meaning, or so I've read;

That I can still carve my future and will not be led.

~ = ~ = ~ = ~ = ~ * ~ = ~ = ~ = ~ = ~

The Afternoon After:

One time I asked Beat poet Michael McClure about the unified and driving force of his "generation," and how that was missing today. And he answered, like a poet, almost in a haiku:

"Go to Texas," is all he said.
Then a long pause.
"Find opposition."

When it looked like Bush was going to win a few months ago, I thought, "Well, this is sure gonna be great for music!"

From '68 to '74, when America had its former Worst President, it was one of the highpoints in creative life for most of the American arts.

We've had a good start, but we've only got a few more years to take advantage of this war-mongering born-again chicken-hawk liar,
to channel our fire
into our art
and our lives
and be better people
and lead by example if our White House doesn't.

This kind of oppositional inspiration only comes around about once a generation!

And it's going to be a joy to collectively make the art and life-choices that matter, and stoke the fires in the smithy of our souls.

Groove forth, and thrive in the underground — just as our roots always have.

2008

The Turning Point in the Democratic Primary

The following 13 short chapters were written contemporaneously as the 2008 Democratic primary and general election played out.

The moment:

It was between 10 and 11PM on Saturday night (January 19th), the night of the South Carolina primary.

The race was a projected victory for Obama at 7:00:01, as soon as the polls closed. Obama announced he would make a speech at 9PM, giving Edwards and Clinton two hours to make their concession speeches. Edwards made his. Bill was picked up live from a rally somewhere congratulating Obama on the win (for about a sentence) and then right back into his Hillary sales pitch. Hillary is seen leaving the hotel for a car to the airport. No speech? Shortly after 9:00, Obama lays down one of his master oratories and everyone's blown away. "Is it me, or is this guy getting better every speech?"

And I keep thinking Hillary's just going to nail it, too, wherever it is she's heading to – must be something big! But it turns out it's just some regularly scheduled campaign rally — and she goes right into her stump speech like South Carolina never happened! She never thanks her staff or supporters or volunteers or anyone in South Carolina.

And then the next day she says she's going to Florida to accept "victory" there after all the candidates agreed in advance that the state jumping the primary queue disqualified it.

Here is my dispatch from the morning after . . .

I just thought I'd high-five my Obama friends — tremendous victory last night. He proved you can play clean and win big.

I'll tell you this — some things that I demand of my party's leader are civility, statesmanship, being a team player, playing by the rules, and being the steady guiding father (or mother) of the party.

Not only did the Clintons run a, shall we say, indelicate or undignified South Carolina campaign, they were blown out on the scoreboard (55% to 26%; 25 delegates to 12), and were not remotely gracious in defeat. How was she so busy after 7:00 that she couldn't stop at the podium at her headquarters for five frickin' minutes? "Congratulations to a great campaign by Barack, thanks to everybody in South Carolina, and now it's on to Super Tuesday." Not only was it ungracious of her, it's bad politics — and not becoming of someone who wants to be the leader of the party or the country. Win or lose, I demand that my standard-bearer be gracious in both victory (when it's easy) and defeat (when it reveals the quality of your character).

I first heard yesterday, then read the stories on it today, that Hillary is planning to challenge for both the Florida and Michigan delegates to be seated at the convention, despite having signed on earlier to stand with the party that no candidate will campaign in nor accept the delegates from those two states. Everybody pulled their names off the ballots in Michigan — except Hillary. And now she's planning to go to a "victory" rally on Tuesday night in Miami. Not with my vote she's not.

Rough 'n' tumble politics are part of the game. But to play any game you have to first play by the rules. To me, sportsmanship is paramount, whether in hockey or politics. For quite a while I've been rationalizing different things the Clintons have been doing. I have no problem with them getting blown out in S.C. — that happens in some states in every primary — but for her to not step up and be gracious and "Presidential" in her defeat, for her to just "issue a statement" and run out of town after the loss like a pampered brat who can't stand not getting everything her way is immature in the extreme. And then to have that W.C. Fields of a husband stumble out this morning and play another race card, dismissing Barack's classy and compelling victory as just another Jesse Jackson, and then to have this followed by her wanting to suddenly count Florida and call it a victory — well, I'm sorry, but that is not how the leader of my party behaves.

You can now count me as a *former* Clinton supporter. I've gotten on the Obama bandwagon, I've got six cold ones in my bag, and I'm saving the seat next to me for Teddy Kennedy who gets on tomorrow. And we're going to Party the right way!

Brian's Obama Endorsement
February 9th, 2008

I know you're smart enough to make your own choice. For me, I was a Clinton supporter, as I have been since 1992, but will be casting my Democrats Abroad vote for Barack Obama. I think Obama can win the presidency, bringing independents, Republicans, and new voters into the party. Most *Democrats* I know don't even want to vote for Hillary in the general. She will unite and invigorate the other side and drive up their vote against the Democrats in more races than just the presidency. Further, I don't trust her ethics or judgment or morals – based on how she's run her campaign. She played her now-signature election-eve fake tears routine again yesterday, and is on the morning news shows today claiming she won 4 states so far, still taking credit for states that don't count and didn't even have any other candidates on the ballot. If she can't be honest or play by the rules of her own party in our primary, why on earth should I believe she'd be ethical in the White House with the doors closed and the shades drawn?

One of her perceived strengths was that she'd been vetted and was still standing. But the problem is what her husband has been up to the last seven years — with him being unsupervised, I have no doubt he's been up to some shady shenanigans. I think the numerous recent news stories revealing some of them are just scratching the surface. And we can't afford to have the White House consumed for the next four years with fighting off more Clinton scandals.

I hope and assume you watched the "Yes, We Can" Obama video (dipdive.com) that's now found it's way onto the Obama website and mainstream news shows. To me, the Barack-star appeals to the better angels of our nature. If you read his books, you know he is a thoughtful, passionate, worldly man. He's fair minded, and he's honest. And he's older than Bill Clinton, JFK or Teddy Roosevelt were when they became President, so it's not like he's too young for the job. In fact, he has more experience than Bill Clinton did when he ran for the same job, so for the Clintons to be claiming Obama's not experienced enough reveals more about them and their never-ending hypocrisy than it does about Barack.

If he runs his White House like he ran his campaign, it will be both ethical and inspiring – almost the polar-opposite of his opponent. He has an unlimited ceiling of potential, both in the numbers of votes he receives as well as being a positive inspiration to the nation and the world. His appeal is so broad, the phrase "Obama Republicans" has already entered the political vernacular. Although, I sort of like "Obamicans."

This is a vote that I'm very happy to be casting. It makes me feel proud to be an American again, and be very hopeful for the future. This is not a hold-your-nose vote for the lesser of two evils, but rather for someone who inspires, who plays by the rules, shows excellent judgment on a daily basis, and will be a tremendous voice for our nation, both at home and abroad.

The Clintons are going to pull every dirty trick in the book to steal this nomination. The only way we can stop them is with our votes today.

So, vote like you mean it! The revolution will be televised.

60 Minutes —

How Obama's Up crossed over Hillary's Down

2008

The two lines have intersected.

We're watching a turning point in the nomination.

The lines had just reached parity on Super Tuesday, but Obama still actually won it (narrowly) in both states and delegates.

And he hasn't lost a contest since Super Tuesday — 5-and-oh. Or, oh-oh, if you're a Clintonian. Washington and Nebraska by 30+ points, Louisiana by 20, Maine by 15, and the Virgin Islands by 80%!!!

If you don't know, they both did interviews for *60 Minutes* tonight (Feb. 10th), and the newsmasters caught it. It was like an interview with the winner, and the loser, of the race. You could see it in Hillary's face, and hear it in her words.

Her line about, "I've accepted and am at peace with whatever happens — it will be what's supposed to be." (or however she said it), and "I love being a Senator from New York." etc. She knows. And Katie Couric, to her credit, one of the best in the business, got it out of her.

What did YOU do on Valentine's Day?

2008

Those lovable nuts, Hillary & Billary, spent the day (apart of course) cruising around the countryside, choosing the day for love to unleash their harshest-ever smear campaign against Barack Obama.

Barack, by contrast, took the entire day off from campaigning and spent it with his wife (and kids).

Tells me everything I need to know.

So, . . . Miss Inevitable & Sick Billy have gone double-dirty negative instead of being "experienced" statesmen. And did you catch how their Pennsylvania surrogate, Governor Ed Rendell dropped the race card yesterday? Loosely, "There's a percentage of people in my state who won't vote for a black man" — giving the racist bigots of PA cover to keep the crosses up on their lawns. I kinda can't believe it. And this is just gonna be the start of it.

This negative crap is going to wipe out Hillary's female empathy vote, and tip so many Dems who are teetering on the fence in Obama's favor. These are things you just don't do, especially in the Democratic family. We know where the other side stands, and we expect it. But playing the race card goes against everything Democrats stand for.

Hillary's Negatives 2008

Back when I was so much younger then, a Hillary supporter, I knew there was a lot of, well, anti-Hillary people out there. She wasn't like any other Democrat. Nobody said or wrote really negative things about Edwards or Biden or Obama or Richardson, . . . but Hillary! It was weird, I didn't get it, so I began asking people what it was they didn't like about her.

I started writing this with the objective, "These are the obstacles ('negatives') we have to erase in order for her to win the nomination." Well, . . . *that* didn't work out so well.

Based on discussions with about a hundred people in numerous online and physical locations, I came up with the following list of problems and perceptions:

She's . . .
— calculating, with an air of dishonesty; phony, inauthentic, don't trust her;
— conniving, manipulative, "political" in the worst sense;
— she exudes an air of entitlement, being "anointed"

the Dem front-runner, she acts privileged and thinks she deserves to be crowned;

— that if she's elected she'll not only keep the negative polarization of Washington raging, she'll probably just make the atmosphere worse;

— that she doesn't play by the rules, and/or plays dirty;

— don't like the idea of the Clinton-Bush stranglehold on the presidency for 28 years;

— that she "rolled over for Bush & his cronies" – that she wasn't really a Democrat – she gave in to the Right too much;

— her shrill voice and cackling laugh – it's *amazing* how many different people have said this to me – probably a third or more of all respondents mentioned it;

— she's in the pocket of big business;

— takes tons of medical industry lobbyists' money while claiming to be fighting against them;

— she only has stature or fame because of being married to Bill – doesn't deserve where she is;

— "the boys are picking on me" line after the debates;

— the resonating "Crybaby for President" t-shirts;

— not leaving Bill after Monica (compromised ethics & power-hungry to stay with him);

— simply by being a "Clinton" which is a dirty & motivating word to many Republicans (and independents, and now thanks to their own words & deeds this campaign, even to many Democrats).

I'm not saying I agree with all of this — but it's why people I asked don't want to vote for her.

"This Time, It's Personal"

2008

It has been such so heart-breaking to see the Clintons' true colors revealed.

I keep coming back to *Primary Colors* (hmm?) — and recommend to all to watch (or read) again — particularly the climactic kitchen scene with Libby (Kathy Bates) when they reveal their true colors to her. That's what's happening to myself — and I imagine to so many fence-leaping Democrats these last several weeks.

It's such a total collapse of trust: her reversing her own promise and signed pledge and public statements to now suddenly be wanting to count Florida & Michigan!?; her actually saying on the stump, "You and I both know, words are cheap." (what a confession of the Clintons' rationalistic approach to life!); them playing the race card in South Carolina and *then* Pennsylvania. Are they wanting us to flash back to the 1990s . . . or the *1950s*?

This is the most disgraceful campaign I've ever seen a Democrat run, period. I've been a Dem since Jimmy Carter, and one of the big reasons I am is because our team plays fair, and is respectful of one another. We may try to out-zing each other, but there's no Willie Horton or "stealing Florida" in *our* party.

Doh!

This Clinton campaign has behaved like the worst of the Republicans — with race-baiting, trying to change the rules mid-game to suit them, and slandering decent upstanding people. It's mind-blowing that a Democrat is doing it. And *to another Democrat.* And it's such a sad, but apparently fitting, final or lasting image we will all have of this couple.

It's pillar-collapsing when heroes betray you. This couple were political gods – and to now see them day after day betray the ideals that you've lived by, and that the party embodies, and betraying the nation's future by trying to destroy this man and this moment, and betraying everything they ever said they stood for . . . I'm in a bit of shock. So —

The rallying call: *"In a heavy-weight title fight, the challenger doesn't win on points,"* as Obama put it on *60 Minutes.*

He's so right. She needs to be *knocked-out* for him to win this.

Happy President's Day!
and Year!
2008

Just think, next year on this holiday, they'll be a different President in the White House!

I wonder who it'll be?

Some good lines from the last 24 hours . . .

Ron Brownstein from *Time* said Obama is an amalgam of Gary Hart and Jesse Jackson.

Brian says he's an amalgam of Howard Dean and Sly Stone.

Mark Shields predicted Al Gore will be Obama's running mate. There's a nice President's Day vision to play with!

Joe Klein pointed out how both Clinton and McCain's campaigns were broke at one point, and only Obama has run a steady fiscal ship.

Brian says, keep in mind that Wisconsin, Ohio and Texas are all OPEN primaries to any registered voter! And the Dems are continuing to set record turnouts in every state, often by double the prior records!

Margaret Carlson said Hillary has to now convince the country that the person they've fallen in love with is really a bad person.

As the Clintons turn nasty, I think of Obama and George Bernard Shaw's advice: "I learned long ago never to wrestle with a pig. You'll get dirty, and besides, the pig likes it."

In other good news, Hillary's leaving Wisconsin! Off to her *next* loss.

Enjoy President's Day! and New President's Year!

Hillary's Lost

2008

Obama just won Wisconsin by 17 points! 58% to 41%
— another 60-40 voters decision, in another 5% African-
American state.

And he won Hawaii by even more than D.C. — 76%
to 24%!

It's not only 10 victories in a row – it's 10 blow-
outs in a row. Last night was his smallest victory yet, and it
was by 17 points.

Since Super Tuesday —

Three times he's beaten Hillary by more than 3-to-1,
getting over 75% of the vote.

Three other times he's gotten over 65% and beaten
her by more than 2-to-1.

So, in more than half the states — he's gotten more
than twice the votes she has.

The closest Hillary has gotten in the last 10
states, was losing by 17% in WI, 19% in ME, 21% in LA,

and 22% in MD. She lost everything else by 2-to-1 or worse. These are crazy-numbers.

To put it in more perspective — Hillary won New Hampshire by 2%. She won Nevada by 6%. Her "huge victory" in California – was by 10%. Last night Obama won by almost all of those differences *combined* in taking Wisconsin by 17%.

And Hillary continued her now-regular practice of not giving a concession speech. Chris Matthews called it a "courtesy deficiency." I call it sociopathic. She behaves without regard to society or others around her. She thinks she can make up her own rules and nobody will notice. She floated yesterday using a loophole to steal the voter-pledged delegates. It's psychopathic. She's getting blown out 2-to-1, but still thinks the people want her most. I'm just saying, as a friend, you need to see a psychiatrist.

Hillary's lost: her mind; her voters; her delegates; her donors; her honor; her credibility; her reputation; and anything resembling momentum. She's actually in retrograde momentum.

And meanwhile, in Houston, Obama's giving another one of greatest-hits speeches in front of 20,000 euphoric Texans dancing up through the last rafter rows of the arena.

And another great story yesterday — the first day of early-voting in Texas, over a thousand students marched 7 miles! Seriously. To vote! Shades of Selma. I know this will be hard to believe, but there are apparently some parts of Texas that screw over black people.

Hillary is losing to the voters in a big way in nearly every state in every part of the country. She's lost the media who live and breathe these candidates and can tell a loser from a champion. She lost fundraising by 3-to-1 in January

— new and final figures today: $36 million to $13. She's lost her own party — with multiple super-delegates actually rescinding their endorsements last week and embracing Obama, with more flowing his way this afternoon.

How long until she gets some psychological help? Or at least glances in a mirror?

And Suddenly, Out of the Darkness, the High Road Appears!

2008

This is huge news. Hillary's dropped the negative attacks, and she's dropped the superdelegates as an issue!

After a week of going negative didn't work in Wisconsin, rather than coming into this debate (Feb. 22nd in Austin, Texas) on the offensive looking for the knock-out punch, she's obviously changed her approach. Rather than her "words don't matter" and "plagiarism" sludge-tossing of the past week, this was much closer to the *60 Minutes* interview, even complete with her same line, "Whatever happens, I'll be fine." And she ended the debate so serenely, saying, "I am honored to be here with Barack Obama, absolutely honored."

That's as close to a white flag as you're going to get in politics. And this from the No-Concession-Speech

Queen. In fact her whole final debate answer seemed like a campaign-ending concession speech, thanking all Americans, and praying we will go forward together.

This reminded me of the Nevada debate (Jan. 15th), when we knew it was over for John Edwards, and he delivered a magnificent performance, his best of the campaign, and it was so nice to see him soar and have all of us (and him) have that be the last performance to remember his campaign by. And it seemed that way for Hillary Clinton tonight. Go out on a high note, on the high road.

And the other wonderful highlight — Hillary put an end to the superdelegate talk, saying, "I think it will sort itself out. I'm not worried about that. We will have a unified party." She's conceded the point and isn't going to try overturn the voters' decision.

This, and dropping the negative ads & approach, are huge headlines for the party, the nation, and the world.

I've been saying for a couple weeks that the Clintons *must* be able to see the writing on the wall, and it's not in their best interest to tear their party apart or their own reputations to shreds.

And I'm sure this is all driving Republicans nuts! Here it is desperation time, and the two combatants are playing nice! "Rats, foiled again!"

America Rising

2008

Tick tick, click click, time's a-wastin',
Dynasty ending in *Dallas*.
Get Smart, Eight Years Is Enough;
Voters *Touched By An Angel*
To Crown a New *American Idol* Next Week.

This may be hard to fathom, but do you realize that Hillary Clinton has never been ahead in the voter-elected delegate count (what determines the nomination) for a single minute of this entire primary?! She lost Iowa right outta the gate; she won New Hampshire by only 2% so the delegates were split 9-9; and although she won Nevada by 6% she actually lost the delegate count by 1; then there was the South Carolina blow-out; on Super Tuesday she came out with less delegates when all was tabulated; and then of course she's lost every state since.

In the More Bad News Dept.: When do you suppose was the last time in one of Team Clinton's morning briefings they could look at polls where Hillary had gone up anywhere since the prior survey? My guess is November last year.

And I assume you've heard that Obama just past the one million donor mark! According to *Politico*, in the 2004 election, 2.5 million people donated to *all the candidates combined* — that's Bush, Kerry, Howard Dean and every other candidate in the primary. This guy has single-handedly gotten nearly half the contributors as every candidate put together last time — and it's only February!

In the Veepstakes: I've been calling for Senator Jim Webb from Virginia for V.P. for the last year, and this morning the brilliant speechwriter and political strategist Bob Shrum, when pressed to give one name for Obama's running mate, sho 'nuff, clicked on the Webb. I would about die if that happened.

And speaking of dying, I'm so glad I didn't those 50 times I almost did — so I could be living for this history. The good that is America is rising again, and God willing, we'll all be around to see it.

When the actor and activist Bradley Whitford was asked about the V.P. on Friday's *Larry King* free-for-all, without any prior mentioning of the name, he said, "I would be excited about Senator Webb — he'd be fantastic." (!) And it was immediately and spontaneously "YESSed!!" by Stephanie Miller; And shortly afterwards the conservative Ben Stein said, "I think Senator Webb is a super idea. I wish we had someone like him on the Republican side." (!)

Jim Webb can out-McCain McCain!

Yeah, that's the ticket!

The Secret Obama Memo — and How He Wins the Nomination

2008

You're not going to believe this — it's right out of a great espionage novel — but just after Super Tuesday, the great veteran politico Al Hunt, now Executive Editor at *Bloomberg News*, was emailing with the Obama campaign, who mistakenly included in a dispatch to Hunt the campaign's projections for all the remaining states. But what's really amazing is how accurate it turned out to be!

The mighty Tim Russert was on the best political show on TV, *Morning Joe*, this morning (March 5th) and read out the memo's results. Back on February 6th, the Obama campaign knew they were going to win 12 states in a row! Well, except they thought they'd lose Maine 51-49, when they actually won it. But they called every other state exactly.

If this was a movie review, I'd have to write:

SPOILERS AHEAD at this point. So, stop reading if you don't want to know what's going to happen in the primary.

In their Feb. 6th projections, the Obama campaign figured they would lose Ohio 53-46 (and they did, 54-44), lose Texas 51-47 (it was 51-48), lose Rhode Island 57-42 (it was 58-40), and that they'd win Vermont 55-45 (where they again out-performed expectations in New England, winning 59-39).

So . . . how's it going to play out? In the next week: Obama wins the Wyoming caucus 60-40 (13 delegates), and wins the open primary in Mississippi 62-38 (34 delegates).

The campaign thinks he will lose Pennsylvania 52-47 (the remaining big cheese-steak, with 161 delegates), but then will win Guam (9 dels), Indiana (72), and the last big state North Carolina (115).

They will then lose West Virginia (28) and Kentucky (51),

But will win Oregon (52), Montana (16), and South Dakota (15), before losing the final caucus in Puerto Rico (55).

[Every one of those projections were exactly spot-on, except Hillary won Indiana & South Dakota by a hair each.]

The proportional delegates divvied up in states she should win: 295

In states he should win: 326.

After the Ohio-Texas Mini-Tuesday victories, NBC News estimates Hillary will gain only 8-10 delegates — leaving Obama with a net lead of around 140 voter-elected pledged delegates: 1,355 to 1,213. ie; after her "big" wins last night, she hardly made a dent in his delegate lead.

Since the campaign's projections of the prior states have been spot-on, if the rest of it plays out as predicted, he will not lose his current lead, and will probably add to it — especially since all the delegates are allocated proportionally, and he keeps his losses much closer than she does. She lost the 11 states before this Mini-Tuesday by an average of 33%. Last night she only won Texas by 3%, and Ohio by 10%.

This looks good for an Obama nomination.

And in terms of him winning over superdelegates, besides his pretty commanding pledged delegate lead, Obama is also still ahead in the total popular vote by over 600,000, and has won 23 primaries & caucuses to her 14 — with two more likely victories coming in the next week leading into the six-week primary "intermission" before Pennsylvania.

Get used to the term "Democratic nominee Barack Obama" because you're gonna be hearing it a lot this year.

BEER CONNOISSEURS
OBAMA

Powell Endorses Obama

2008

From *Meet The Press,* Sunday Oct. 19th, 2008.

[This should have happened with Tim Russert hosting —
R.I.P., see multi-voiced tribute starting on page 425 — but
this historic moment was delivered by Secretary of State
Colin Powell to Tim's colleague Tom Brokaw.]

I was so sure nothing was going to happen with Powell's
appearance on Sunday morning, I didn't even set the alarm
— was just up at that time by fluke, ready to go right back
to bed, but thought, "Well, I'll just check it out" (at 9AM),
and sure enough they didn't open with it right away. Finally
Brokaw asks him. I'm thinking this "endorsement" hoopla
is a non-event and Powell will speak kindly of both McCain
& Obama but won't endorse because he sees his role in life
as *non*-political, almost by definition of his military career.
So, Brokaw asks and I'm three-quarters ready to

go back and hit the pillow — in fact, I'm watching Powell with my hand on the remote so as soon as he dodges the endorsement question I'll hit "off" and be off myself. But before the question's even out of Brokaw's mouth, Powell is nodding Yes! He HAS an answer. I couldn't believe it!

So he starts in on this masterful unscripted riff — woke me right the hell up! Freakin' out — this is like hearing one of ol' Abe Lincoln's Inaugural Addresses or something!

~ = ~ = ~ = ~ = ~ * ~ = ~ = ~ = ~ = ~

General Colin Powell said live on the air:

"I have some concerns about the direction that the Republican party has taken in recent years. It has moved more to the right than I would like to see it, but that's a choice the party makes.

"I have especially watched over the last six or seven weeks as both candidates have really taken a final exam with respect to this economic crisis that we are in and coming out of the conventions. And I must say that I've gotten a good measure of both.

"In the case of Mr. McCain, I found that he was a little unsure as to how to deal with the economic problems that we were having and almost every day there was a different approach to the problem. And that concerned me, sensing that he didn't have a complete grasp of the economic problems that we had.

"And I was also concerned over his selection of Governor Palin. She's a very distinguished woman, and she's to be admired; but at the same time, now that we have

112

had a chance to watch her for some seven weeks, I don't believe she's ready to be President of the United States, which is the job of the Vice President. And so that raised some question in my mind as to the judgment that Senator McCain made.

"On the Obama side, I also watched him during this seven-week period. And he displayed a steadiness, an intellectual curiosity, a depth of knowledge and an approach to looking at problems like this – as well as picking a Vice President that, I think, is ready to be President on day one. And also, in not just jumping in and changing his approach every day, but showing intellectual vigor. I think that he has a definitive way of doing business that would serve us well.

"I also believe that the approach of the Republican Party and Mr. McCain over the last seven weeks has become narrower and narrower. Mr. Obama, at the same time, has given us a *more* inclusive, broader reach into the needs and aspirations of our people. He's crossing ethnic lines, racial lines, generational lines. He's thinking about how all villages have values, all towns have values, not just *small* towns have values.

"And I've also been disappointed, frankly, by some of the approaches that Senator McCain has taken recently, or his campaign has, on issues that are not really central to the problems that the American people are worried about.

"This Bill Ayers situation that's been going on for *weeks* became something of a central point of the campaign. But Mr. McCain says that 'he's a washed-out terrorist.' Well, then, why do we keep talking about him?

"And why do we have these robo-calls going on around the country trying to suggest that, because of this *very, very* limited relationship that Senator Obama has had with Mr. Ayers, somehow, Mr. Obama is tainted.

"What they're trying to connect him to is some kind of terrorist feelings. And I think that's inappropriate. I think it goes too far, and has made the McCain campaign look a little narrow. It's not what the American people are looking for. And I look at these kinds of approaches to the campaign and they trouble me.

"The party has moved even further to the right, and Governor Palin has indicated a *further* rightward shift. I would have difficulty with two more conservative appointments to the Supreme Court, but that's what we'd be looking at in a McCain administration.

"I'm also troubled by, not what Senator McCain says, but what members of the party say. And that it permitted to be said such things as, 'Well, you know that Mr. Obama is a Muslim.' Well, the correct answer is: he is *not* a Muslim, he's a Christian. He's *always* been a Christian. But the *really* right answer is: so what if he is? Is there something wrong with being a Muslim in this country? The answer is no, that's not America. Is there something wrong with some seven-year-old Muslim-American kid believing that he or she could be President? Yet, I've heard *senior* members of my own party drop the suggestion, 'He's a Muslim and he might be associated with terrorists.' This is not the way we should be doing it in America.

"I feel strongly about this in part because of a picture in a photo essay I saw about troops who are serving in Iraq and Afghanistan. And one picture was of a mother in Arlington Cemetery, and she had her head on the headstone of her son's grave. And as the picture focused in, you could see the writing on the headstone. And it gave his awards — Purple Heart, Bronze Star — showed that he died in Iraq, his

114

date of birth, date of death. He was 20 years old. And then,
at the very top of the headstone, it didn't have a Christian
cross, it didn't have the Star of David, it had crescent and a
star of the Islamic faith. And his name was Kareem Rashad
Sultan Khan, and he was an American. He was born in
New Jersey. He was 14 years old at the time of 9/11, and he
waited until he could go serve his country, and he gave his
life. Now, we have got to stop polarizing ourselves in this
way. And I'm troubled about the fact that, within the party,
we have these kinds of expressions.

"So, when I look at all of this and I think back to my
Army career, we've got two individuals, either one of them
could be a good President.

"But which is the President that we need now?
Which is the individual that serves the needs of the nation
for the next period of time?

"And I come to the conclusion that because of his
ability to inspire; because of the inclusive nature of his
campaign; because he is reaching out all across America,
because of who he is and his rhetorical abilities — and we
have to take that into account — as well as his substance —
he has both style and substance — he has met the standard
of being a successful President, being *an exceptional*
President. I think he is a transformational figure.

"He is a new generation coming into the world —
onto the world stage, onto the American stage, and for these
reasons I'll be voting for Senator Barack Obama."

~ = ~ = ~ = ~ = ~ * ~ = ~ = ~ = ~ = ~

I was surprised by *how* he approached the endorsement in the interview — that his wonderfully articulate explanation is going to appear on the front page tomorrow of virtually every newspaper in America (and many all over the world). It's not just going to be his picture and an "I endorse" — but it's the *why*:

Bill Ayers, Sarah Palin, the narrowing of the Republican party, McCain's handling of the financial crisis, how Powell's impressed by Obama's rigorous intellect and the people he surrounds himself with . . . Powell made about a dozen very solid reasons why he made his decision.

I also liked his later exchange when Brokaw pointed out it might be dismissed as one black guy endorsing another — Powell responded, "If I had only had that in mind, I could have done this six, eight, ten months ago. I really have been going back and forth between somebody I have the highest respect and regard for, John McCain, and somebody I was getting to know, Barack Obama. And it was only in the last couple of months that I settled on this. And I can't deny that it will be a historic event for an African-American to become president. And should that happen, all Americans should be proud — not just African-Americans, but all Americans — that we have reached this point in our national history where such a thing could happen. It will also not only electrify our country, I think it'll electrify the world."

Then I was pleasantly surprised how the *Meet The Press* panelists Andrea Mitchell, David Brooks and Joe Scarborough were spot-on afterwards assessing the importance of this announcement to: military families, to Floridians, to centrists across the country — that there is hardly a more respected Republican among Republicans in America — and for him to not just endorse, but to do it in this eloquent and *really* definitive way is going to be much more than a small blow to the McCain campaign.

Furthur to all that, I hereby jam: from here on out we will have a new term in politics known as "a Powell endorsement" when it is a definitive, expansive and influential endorsement — as opposed to a run-of-the-mill stand-at-a-podium-and-shake-hands endorsement.

There is already the "Powell doctrine," the "Bradley effect," a "Rovian strategy," a "Lincoln-Douglas debate" . . . real events that summarized or captured some human endeavor or political reality.

And from here on out, there will be "an endorsement" . . . and "a Powell endorsement." Does a person just endorse, or does he *really* endorse in an emphatic, considered, "large" and seriously influential way — aka a "Powell Endorsement." [see, also, update on this with "a Clyburn endorsement" on page 366 in the 2020 New Hampshire chapter.]

Where Wayward Jekylls Hide—
The Mighty Bama-Rama Rap
2008

performance poem written Sept. 2008

Like tonight is the night,
    the Barack is The Rock,
And "change" is The Word,
    and the voice has been heard,

And the heart is on drums,
    and passion's playin' bass,
And the word has hit the streets –
    you can see it in their face!

There's a choir in the chapel
    an' they've just begun to swing,
There's a band down on the corner,
    hear the chimes of freedom ring.

It starts off kinda quiet,
    an underdog in spring,
No coronation here
    from a white-haired former king.

Just a jazzy scrappy jug-band,
    eternity on tap,
And the singer in the center
    with the silky thunder rap.

The conductor of an orchestra,
    and a mighty rolling train,
Playing sweet sonatas
    and crushin' John McCain.

/ / / / / / /

The combo's on the road,
    packin' stadiums 'n' clubs;
Chopping down great big lies
    and tiny weedy shrubs.

The tour plays the heartland,
    filling all the seats,
It shines in ritzy ballrooms,
    and right down on the streets,

Where the poets strum and teachers play
    and time is on our side   *"yes it is!"*
Where colors swirl, the nuns have fun
    and wayward Jekylls hide.

/ / / / / / / / / /

Two score and five ago
    our father Martin dreamed
Imagining a whole new world
    beyond what his had seemed.

Blink your eyes and here we are
    awoken from the dream,
To find our plans were written by
    that visionary's beam.

So, . . . bless this race.
            . . . this human one,
    that comes in many shades,
Bless this space, this human one,
    inspiring in spades.

It's forty-years since Martin marched
　　and water-cannons shot,
We're still alive on the-other-side,
　　and this is what he sought.

Launching dreams from Lincoln's steps
　　arching across the sky,
Who'd a thought we'd hit the oath,
　　The inaugural bull's-eye!

/ / / / / / / / / / / / / / /

So, on to P.A., Ohio,
　　and everywhere we're not,
It's a Happy Holy Homerun
　　with everything we've got!

The band has played, the song has sung,
　　and now we're on our own,
To ride this wave, and thumb this road,
　　and take the flight path shown.

From dreams on stages, thru history's pages,
　　we're making words come true,
The choir's singin', the bells are ringin'
　　but *This* is up to you.

"Yes, we can!"

The Rose of Hope

Election Night 2008

Early morning in the Universe — sunrise over a New America.

I arose from the floor of a Harlem hotspot dreaming of something bigger than me. And right off the mat, the Election Morning Ritual of tea & subtlety, pacing & breathing, and dreaming in the bright new light of it all.

And there's the widescreen of Barack & Michelle & their girls walking into the polling booth in Chicago and taking their time to burn in the memories of casting their historic ballots.

And all over New York you could hear doors slamming on apartments and taxis as young and old, black and white went through their daily rituals — and today's quite singular one.

I realized we were getting Obama as President, at

least as Veep to Hillary, back on Super Bowl Saturday in January when I first watched will.i.am's *Yes, We Can* video. It had been uploaded only the night before, and I watched it early in the jingle-jangle morning and just lost it — couldn't watch it without getting choked up for weeks afterwards. It was so obvious then that he was ours — America's, the world's, right now's. Somehow it felt more ancient than futuristic, more traditional than trendy, more Rushmore than YouTube. And lo, it was good.

But of course there was still a helluva race ahead — first the primary against Hillary and then the general against McCain, and it did look close a couple of times, but especially starting that Monday of the Lehman Brothers collapse and McCain "suspending" his campaign and stumbling around like Henry Fonda in the woods in *On Golden Pond*, followed by Colin Powell coming out on *Meet The Press*, you knew who was going to win. In fact, I was able to post the final election results on Halloween, a full four days before Election Day — 367 to 171, and it turned out 365 to 173! — or 99.5% accurate.

I spent the afternoon getting all gussied up in my black velvet tails and Ben Franklin knickers with knee-high socks topped off with a top hat, accented with colorful Obama buttons, and everything underneath my waving homemade Obama pennant flag with a little red & white Canadian one on top. All I needed was a clanging bell and some rolled parchment.

Heading into the Election Night, for the first time in my life, I was the most popular person in Harlem! Looking like a "Hear-ye, hear-ye!" town crier from the American Revolution, I was carrying Obama's flag into battle — lighting up faces of people who still hadn't come close to learning English. Shopkeepers were waving, and mothers were pointing me out to their small children. Passing pedestrians were either breaking into huge smiles or full-out hollering, "Obama!" It was dusk on the final day of *The Nightmare From Texas*, and minorities may have been happier than anyone that the lying war sap's reign of error was finally ending.

Riding the subway through Harlem in black velvet regalia — facing beaming white smiles from dark African faces, shining and sharing across the aisle like Washington would soon be if all goes according to plan. A little boy beside me is admiring my buttons, and finally says in the cutest voice, "All Barack!" So I reach in my bag and found a button for him just before he got off. And some guy was watching me do this, and he pulled out his keys from his pocket and wound off his little Obama key-chain and handed it to me across the subway car. It's the coolest thing and I'll cherish it forever. And so I looked in my bag and found another button and hand it across to him. And there was some guy standing nearby smiling as he watched all this go down, and the guy I just gave the button to hands it to him. A crowd got on right after that and we all got separated — but within seconds all us strangers had just given each other something for nothing. America was changing right before our eyes.

Then I was off, flying between the towers of Midtown, when suddenly a-ha, a "Vote Here –>" sign for a polling station, and, decked head-to-toe in Obama, I entered most illegally (wearing campaign materials) and went beaming around. Poll site day-workers were smiling back huge hugs, and then I spotted the ancient New York State steel-levered polling machine and went over to open

the curtains and have a good gander — but nooooo — The Big Bossman spots me wearing partisan duds and nearly football tackles me the heck outta there!

So there I was — tossed back into the Manhattan rush-hour of snappy suits and swinging briefcases, big ego scowls and some big-hearted smiles.

And then aaah into the aaah of the Election Plazaaah at Barackefeller Center! People. All beaming faces. Lights. A red, white & blue skyscraper. Broadcast trucks. Giant screens. And rows of flags waving wide and high in tonight's powerful winds of change.

There were lots of people, but it wasn't crowded. And NBC had once again laid out the red carpet. Well, actually it was blue. And plush and thick, from one end of the plaza to the other — "Election Night 2008" woven into the ground that democracy's participants were walking on. And not just Americans, but thousands and millions who came here from foreign countries, like me — because "America" is so much a part of so many.

And meanwhile, I'm getting photographed more than I ever have in my life. Plus, they've got somebody dressed up like a donkey and somebody like an elephant, and for an hour the three of us become the most in-demand trio in New York. And on top of that, the inside of my coat was lined with Obama buttons that I was happily selling for five bucks. Which I never even mentioned to anyone, but people kind of figured it out. All I kept saying was, "Vote Socialist! Vote Obama!"

And a couple times I actually get challenged about being an interfering Canadian, but I quickly bounced 'em back with ol' Christopher Columbus and Thomas Paine and Alexander Hamilton as pretty cool un-Americans. And if that didn't shut 'em, I dropped Albert Einstein, Andrew

Carnegie and Madeline Albright. And if that don't do it, John Lennon, Neil Young and Charlie Chaplin usually did. You can be American from wherever you're born. [see also a longer list of Great Americans Not Born in America on page 401 in the "Dessert" section]

And waving my colorful homemade flag was doing the trick! It was like a freakin' antenna pulling in the channels. Friends were tuning in from all over. Philip the Iraq war reporter with his big pro camera weaves in documenting the stories of regular people in the eye of history. And there's Levi Asher, the online LitKicks disturber, happily dancing through the crowd like it's an outdoor Dead show. And there's the Jimmy Carter staffer Zoe Artemis waving from her comfortable perch, soaking in the immensity of it all.

And friendships are being made instantaneously all over the plaza, conversations starting without introductions. It was a family reunion and we all knew each other. And even though it was early, it felt pretty late, with everybody already a little giddy, a little silly, uncontrollably happy — and it didn't matter to anyone.

And of all excellent things, they were actually handing out plastic beer mugs! Or maybe they were coffee mugs, but I figured they'd work way better for beer. So, I copped several for the crew, and away we flew.

It was nearing time to plant the flag and hold the fort. There were two main giant screens: one for NBC, and one for MSNBC, which has been my network of choice since it came on the air about 10 years ago. And to boot, it's their side of 30 Rock that's completely bathed in Democratic blue and turns out to be the naturally livelier side of the grand plazoo all night. So, I promptly claimed 'n' maintained the screen-front fort-site!

There was a six-inch high curb running across the battlefield, a perfect distance from the screen, and it made the best forward line I can think of. Next, I was lookin' for SOUND — where some half-deaf old people can hear what's being said even while crazy New Yorkers are screaming in joy. And right along the curb line directly in front of the MSNBC screen, there was a nice big Bose speaker on a stand, squared off by barricade stanchions. So that became our solid right flank; and I was holding down the front curb-line; and our left flank was held by Gina Gershon's sister and a wall of her girlfriends who hadn't moved in an hour. "We're solid." "We're bull's-eye center." "It's a go, General." We had our private box at the theater.

Once we had our perimeter secured, there was a buffer of about 50 people deep in every direction around us — and we could just *GO!* And lemme tell ya, nobody's burners were on "medium"!

And as I kept waving my Canadian–Obama flag, along came Winnipeg-Manhattan guitarist brother Terry Derkach; and Paul, who I only just met but who's been a friend for life; and Anna, Philip's pregnant wife blessing her child who'll be born around the same time as the next president in January. And here comes Ralph the producer, and Brad the net oracle (who'd show up again in the 2020 primaries), and Anne the global adventurer. And then came somebody holding up a giant Obama yard sign as they danced and weaved through the crowd, and as the sign floated closer, sure enough, underneath it all is Nadette, an actress friend of nearly 30 years bringing suburban lawns into this uber-urban plaza.

And from our private box we could easily make runs

to the deli which you could almost see from our "seats."
The only trick was getting back through the outer ring of
the scene — excuse-me-ing through the tight outer strata
of late-comers and non-insiders, then weaving through the
gentler inner rings of patriots to our secret center where we
had enough room to dance.

And dance we did. Along came four cute girls from
England who'd flown over just for this moment and were as
funny as that other Fab Four who flew over here. Or there
was the flowing French poet who'd also flown in just for this.
Or the gorgeous Kim Basinger with the flower in her long
blond hair. Or the various Canadians who kept appearing
all night from Vancouver and Montreal and Toronto and
Edmonton. It was like all the Americans who materialized
in Ontario when we were registering people to vote with
Democrats Abroad. In fact, as the night comically revealed
itself, our encampment became *surrounded* by Canadians
— typically too shy to say anything, but when they saw my
flag, they came and stood near and felt safe. I had become
the freakin' Canadian Consulate at Barackefeller Center on
Election Night.

As Zoe & I were making what we thought at the time
was the final beer run of the night at about 7:40, we bumped
into this group of four Midwestern couples in their 40s and
50s leaving the scene. Of course we started talking and they
mentioned they're heading out to get something to eat, to
which I said, "Are you freakin' crazy?! The big moment is
coming right up and you're gonna be staring down at a tuna
sandwich?!" They all laughed as I gave 'em hell, Harry.

So, Zoe & I hit the deli, and sure enough a minute later
the whole crew of 'em came in and said, "You convinced
us." They'd just grab some road grub and head back into

Democracy's mosh pit.

Another wonderful thing about the scene was the diversity of people. Besides there being every conceivable shade of pigmentation from the darkest African blacks to translucent northern whites, there was also every body type, age, and orientation. There were turbans and ball caps, piercings and wheelchairs, suits and sandals. It was America, and it was the world.

I was talking to this bunch of Jamaicans and we were all laughing and beaming and "Yesing," and their accents were so damn thick I understood not a word! Except "Obama." Yet we were totally communicating for a good long time — our faces and hearts knowing what the other was saying all along.

And I'll tell ya, there's been a buncha times I wished John Lennon was here, but oh boy, none more so than while we're talkin' 'bout a revolution. And how this was the world playing out that he and so many other visionary people of peace have shared through sermons or songs or non-violent stands. This was the dream — and it had manifested and was dancing and cheering and wired.

It was like the night had gone into sudden-death overtime — where you couldn't leave because it could be called and be over at any moment! The best part of course was when the Dems scored points by winning a state — and a cheer went up as far as you could hear, echoing through the canyons of our spines. And for every Kentucky or Mississippi there was a playful boo, then we laughed out loud at our own silliness.

And as each state was called, just like in '04, NBC had these two giant tapestries, one Dem blue and the other Republican red, that were being pulled up the side of 30

Rock, one foot for each electoral vote won. Except unlike 2004, the blue side was climbing much higher than the red one.

Although my predictions for the presidential winner, electoral college numbers, percentage split, and Senate and House seats were all dead on or close damn to it — the one thing I (joyously) didn't get right was the time the news organizations would project a winner. I knew it could come at 8, and if not then, at 9 for sure. "There's no way we're *not* going to know before 10." But all those hours came and went with nothing.

Here's an obvious conspiracy for those who enjoy those sort of things: There was obviously collusion between the networks to all hold off their presidential projections until 11PM. They obviously didn't coincidentally all make the "call" at exactly the same time. They coulda called it a week ago, or anytime all night . . . but what the heck, the whole county was riveted until the match was sparked and the emotional fireworks set off. No matter when you tuned in or arrived at your election night gathering, by 11:00 you'd been on the edge of your seat for a while. Or, the edge of your curb, as the case may be.

There was a clock on the bottom of the screen — and although it was obvious to some of us what was going to happen when it struck 11:00:00, most in the crowd didn't know it was coming.

But after hours of good-vibe build-up, the clock ticked eleven and the screen tocked Barack — and the voices and the spirits and the hands shot up, fingers splaying, eyes blazing, thousands jumping, people hugging, falling into another, high-fiving hands so fast you never see the arms, screaming, tear-soaked faces like thousands of brand new parents — but no romantic midnight New Year's Eve couples kissing — *for just a moment* there was something even bigger than one loved one.

Some people were frozen in Buddha-still calmness, others were bent over crying and shaking. People were hanging out windows, flashbulbs were flashing from every direction, horns honking over everything, girls screaming like Beatlemania, all swirling into a roaring, deafening tornado, tossing us side to side, but hardly anyone falling down. And the cheering kept going — there was no person telling us to simmer down so the show could resume. Talking heads were yammering away on movie screens and the speakers were still blaring but we were all chanting "O – ba – ma" and "Yes we can" so loud nobody heard a word. And after one wave of peak cheering would begin to subside, another would start out of nowhere and everyone would raise their voices and arms again for no reason except the joy of it, the beyond-beliefness of everything — as new layers of what just happened were rolling through people's hearts and minds and out their faces.

For some it was a tearful release of exhaustion after sleepless nights for days or weeks or months — defenses down, fatigued openness, sleep-deprived delirium. And for others it was just a sweet gentle smile of serenity. . . . "Finally."

But so-sadly, with the networks calling it at 11:00 — that was the exact time of the last elevator to The Top of The Rock rooftop so there was no way to kiss the sky as well as all the pretty girls in the plaza.

After a prolonged evening of anticipation, the dominoes fell quickly. I lost any sense of time at this point, but it seemed like right after the projection, John

McCain was walking out to give his concession speech. As I expected, he was huge and gracious — his best speech since I-dunno-when. Poor old guy got waylaid somewhere, off into the Rovian practices of kill 'n' torture what you don't understand and ask questions later.

Everybody was in a "boo-McCain" spirit, but I knew he was better than what we'd seen in this campaign. So every time he said something particularly gracious, I'd yell, "Alight! Give it up for John McCain!" But nobody would. The crowd had followed my every cue all night — when to clap, cheer, laughing at my one-liners — as Zoe said, "You had those people eating out of your hand," — but when it came to giving props to the distinguished gentlemen from Arizona, I had zero pull.

And I just gotta say — in politics, your opponent is your enemy *only until election day;* and the moment it's over, you become colleagues again. You compete as hard as you can, or "vigorously" as Obama wonderfully called it; then we all work together. Done.

So, immediately after McCain finished his concessionary congratulatory comments to the new President-elect, the world was transported via Marshall McLuhan stacks of amped televisions to the massive gathering in historic Grant Park in Chicago where Democratic supporters had their heads bashed in by billy-clubs in 1968 — and had them blown off by words in 2008.

And once again, Obama had a beautiful stage, with a classic row of flags like those waving around the Washington Monuments and this Barackefeller rink in New York City.

And as the soul-speaker soared, the BaRock Center New York crowd was cheering like we were at the greatest Central Park concert ever. Except there was no rock star. There was not even a person in person. Just "two big screens and a politician." And we're peaking all over the city, all over the country, all over the world in a synchronized riot of joy. This is not just an American story, not just a black story, not just a Democrat's or young person's story, nor just an immigrant's story or this story — it's all of us — all North America, Africa, Europe — dancing as one, in more ways than one. It's every underdog, every book-reader and book-writer, every neighbor, everyone with hope in whatever language they speak — this Rose smells as sweet tonight.

And Obama calmly asked for our collective help, our common good. It got so quiet you only hear the people sobbing in joy in the crowd of thousands. Complete breakdowns. Some couples were now hugging like a New Year's Eve moment — and one of them is shaking and crying. We see the soon-to-be-famous tears from Jesse and Oprah, but seeing them for real glistening in the Barackefeller Lights on the cheeks of both women and men, old and young, white and black, red-eyed and helpless, weeping uncontrollably — there wasn't an unblurry eye in the house.

"This is our time to reaffirm that fundamental truth, that out of many, we are one; that while we breathe, we hope. And where we are met with cynicism and doubts and those who tell us that we can't, we will respond with that timeless creed that sums up the spirit of a people: Yes, we can."

And your cells and limbs harmonize with the words, and you're "Yes!" And Joe Biden walks out, and *that* gem finally kicks in – "Oh my god! Joe freakin' Biden is Vice

President!!"

And as the guests began to leave, I stayed and shook hands or winked into their dazed eyes or stood for a picture next to their ear-to-ear smile as they passed from the plaza womb out to the New World of New York tonight where strangers were stopping strangers just to shake their hand.

As we were leaving the light and into the night, my final image was of the giant blue column still climbing up 30 Rock, and the whole plaza bright and glowing . . . like it should be.

Meanwhile the streets were all a half-hour-after-midnight on New Year's Eve — laughter echoing through every canyon, girls holding hands and skipping down the sidewalk, old shopkeepers watching everything from their doorways.

Terry Derkach and I whirled around the corner onto Sixth Avenue and Boom! Right into the Midwestern crew we talked into staying at 8:00! And it was now a whole lot more than a few hours later. The well-put-together folks we'd met were now red-faced and joyous with their glasses listing crookedly, their hair a shambles, shirt-tails flapping, just a puddled mess they were, and as soon as they saw me rounding the corner they dropped their bags and ran over with giant bear-hugs of joy, thanking me profusely for encouraging them to stay. And the leader goes, "Hey, wait a minute," and rushes back to his bags, and another guy says with a beam, "You're gonna get something special." And sure enough he comes back with this high-end print of an almost 3-D painting of Obama & Biden that will beam from my walls forever.

And after a boatful of giant hugs, off they sailed into

the glistening New York Sea as Terry and I floated on down
the Avenue of The Americas, following The Great Invisible
Forces to . . . . Times Square.

As we whooshed around the corner smack-dab
into the Square's trash & vaudeville — it was barricaded
streets, shut-down sidewalks, battalions of uniforms, and
eight lanes of traffic racing through the center of it all! The
massive crowd had dissolved down to a nice loud throng
— so we fit right in! — bolting directly to the center island
— the core of the core — ground-to-sky screens all around
— Obama's ears 8 Miles High — a constant roar — traffic,
different speakers blasting different speakers, and a very
high cheers-per-second ratio.

cue: *Dancing In The Streets* — loud.

And my Canadian flag's immediately attracting a
flood of delirious Canucks, some from the city I just left,
some from places I never heard of. And again it's the
celebrity camera flash-flash of my town crier top-hat 'n' tails
hailing in the news in Times Square routine.

All heck's broken loose — for a moment it seemed
like old New York — people having a good time and no one
interfering. *Signed, Sealed, Delivered* is being belted out
by a sidewalk ensemble well beyond any concerns over
harmony. There's a thousand Lady Libertys with one arm
raised holding torches of camera-phones broadcasting
beacons of freedom's light to the rest of the world. It's the
first time New York's been like this since the Rangers won
the Stanley Cup in game 7 at Madison Square Garden, when
all the cars on Seventh Avenue were caught in the human
flood, and the streets for blocks around became an instant
street party — and you could walk up the avenue between
rows of cars high-fiving both drivers and passengers from

their open windows.

It was like that all through Times Square, except it seemed every car was coming *from* an Obama party, not just arriving at one! It wasn't random drivers caught up in some random New York street party, but every person in the city *was in on it.* Or at least every person who was awake and outside. The few Republicans here were long since safe behind their security systems, and anyone who was alive for the last few hours couldn't help hearing and seeing and feeling the emotional and literal fireworks shooting off of every streetcorner in New York.

It was Fourth of July. It was Beatlemania screams still echoing outside Ed Sullivan's Paramount Theater. Not only was every car smiling like a cartoon, and every driver too, but there was a person sticking out of every sunroof that went by — and people leaning out the side windows to high-five the Times Squarers as they drove through the piazza. And if you weren't honking your horn enough and got stuck at a light, brothers reached in your open window and honked it for you. And not only were *people* chanting as they marched, a fire truck went by honking out "O – ba – ma" on its horn in time with the crowd, and the young Irish cops were doing stand-up routines for the crowds and working the passers-by like the best street comedians.

I talked to one of the officers in charge who said there'd been no problems at all over the entire city all night.

Nice, eh?

New York, I love ya! So much like the big blackout night five years ago — happy positive vibes flowing everywhere. It was Woodstock without the mud. It was a sunrise without the hangover. It was a White House without a Bush.

And word filtered up that Union Square was overflowing with people, and St. Marks Place in the East Village had broken into a spontaneous street-long block-party, and it was clear this was not going to be over anytime soon.

And it was so gawdamn global — the giant screens were flashing crowds of people in Paris and London and Rome and Rio and Sydney and Toronto and hot-damn, summer in the city! The back of my neck feelin' all goose-bumpy.

It was great that we were not dancing just cuz it was some date on a calendar, but because of something worked for by people the nation and world over — and because of all the changes this will bring, from the smallest of human exchanges to the speeches of kings — it's "a transformation of civilization" as Neil Young was currently singing it — it's the hundredth monkey cracking the coconut for milk — an evolutionary step in our species — a turning-point that'll be taught long after we're gone.

And it's happening now. If you can read this, you've got your invitation. *We* are the cells that are multiplying. *We* are the lucky ones that made it across the river to The Promised Land. *This* is a moment all people will wish they lived through. And that this is even bigger for *the world* than it is for America.

It *is* our time, as he kept saying.
Live it or lose it, as I keep saying.

~ = ~ = ~ = ~ = ~ * ~ = ~ = ~ = ~ = ~

And a wonderful P.S.:

The next night, a bunch of us went to the best band in the land — Phil Lesh & Friends — and at the beginning of the show, the 68-year-old bandleader came out and Deadicated the show that night — something I've never seen any Grateful Dead member ever do . . .

Phil on stage: **"Two days ago, we lived through and participated in a turning point in history, as important as anything that we've seen in our lives. And I bet everybody in this room was a part of that in some way. So, I want to dedicate this show tonight to that uniquely American spirit, which just rose up, at the perfect moment, with this man, and this movement, and these people. So, here's to you!"**

Followed by chants of, "U.S.A., U.S.A., U.S.A.," at an underground Grateful Dead concert in the core of Manhattan!

Obama
Inauguration
Adventures

The following are the Inauguration Dispatches that were composed on the ground in D.C. and sent out via email distribution lists. Although both my website (BrianHassett. com) and my Facebook account (Brian.Hassett.Canada) were up and running by January of 2009, not all that many people were using either yet. But they went "viral" before there was a word for it because people were forwarding the Dispatches all over their work and friends email lists. I ended up meeting and becoming friends with a bunch of people I'm still friends with to this day because they found their way onto these distribution lists. And they were lists plural because there were limitations to how many people you could send to in one email.

I ended up sharing an apartment a block from the famous Deep Throat parking garage in Arlington Virginia where Bob Woodward would meet with their contact who had just been revealed to the world a couple years before we were there as Mark Felt. He lived to see Obama elected, but missed the inauguration, having just died in December. And sort of strangely karmically and wonderfully I was sharing the space with the Woodward to my Bernstein, who I'll call Deep Mitch. The two of us had been infiltrating places we weren't necessarily supposed to since the early '80s, and now here we were pranking the pinnacle of politics and each sending out our dispatches.

My daily reports, usually written in the overnight to be sure they'd landed in people's in-boxes by the morning, spawned the spontaneously riffed title of this book, as well as ending up in the climax of Woodstock producer Michael Lang's concert memoir.

Thursday, January 15th, 2009
Barackstock coming on Sunday

Hey Homies of the Brotherhood of all that is Cool!

The "Mission Inauguration" — Shucks-&-Awww Ground Operation has Commenced.

Other than Tuesday's 11:30 – 1:00 swearing-in coverage, this Sunday's concert will be your best chance to enjoy the Inaugural jazz without being there.

2:30PM — The Welcoming Event – **"We Are One: The Obama Inaugural Celebration at the Lincoln Memorial"** — Obama & family WILL be there. HBO is producing.

The official lineup so far — Bruce Springsteen — Stevie Wonder — Bono (and maybe U2) — Sheryl Crow — John Mellencamp — will.i.am — John Legend — Herbie Hancock — Beyoncé — Shakira — Mary J. Blige — James Taylor — Garth Brooks — Usher — Josh Groban.

Plus — Martin Luther King Jr.'s son, Tom Hanks, Jamie Foxx, Denzel Washington and Samuel Jackson will be among those reading historical & inspirational passages.

More as it develops.

Friday, January 16th, 2009
We're Gonna Sing

Checkin' in from Yasgur's Farm,
Maggie's Farm,
Obama's Farm.

Just got the physical ticket to the inauguration in hand and
I'll be right up front for the swearing-in on Tuesday.

Going On The Road in a few minutes to Baltimore for the
Whistle Stop tour — the train tracks, *Festival Express*,
my grandfather George the CPR engineer, the *Dream
Tracks* Indian book with Teri McLuhan, the hopping trains
back in the 'Peg to get around town — all clickety-clackin'
into one.

Barack and Joe ridin' the rails,
from Constitution Hall in Philadelphia to Constitution
Avenue in Washington . . .

and Brian & Mitch are Jack-&-Nealing in the salt-streaked
Blue Bomber Cruiser
lookin like it's burned white through re-entry
from driving like lightning through the salt-dusted blizzard
roads,
chasing history's trains
and America's future.

~ = ~ = ~ = ~ = ~ * ~ = ~ = ~ = ~ = ~

The HBO stage at the Lincoln Memorial is just Gorgeous
and HUGE!
This is SO Woodstock —
in the 21st Century.
It's entirely custom designed and built for this one concert,
with camera booms swooping,
and dozens of Jumbotrons rippling the images across the
Reflecting Pool
to America,
and the world,
this one, short, creative human fireworks celebration.

So right.

And now.

As a species, we've done some things right.
And there's Lots of work ahead,
But for a moment,
We're gonna sing.
surreally,
on Christmas Eve in the Universe.

Saturday, January 17th, 2009
The Baltimore Report:
Bama Sightings and Concert
Rehearsal

I saw The Man in Baltimore today!

Woo-woo!! Goo-goo ga'chooo-chooo!

He & Michelle and Joe & Jill went up the hill of steps at the small old-world town hall square in front of City Hall with maybe 30,000 people cheering them on. He talked a lot about the history of America and how the great works that prior Americans did need to inspire us to rise to that in our own lives, and collectively as a nation.

He came across so comfortable — staying a long time afterwards shaking hands and hanging and waving and being very calm and kind to people.

The guy's in the middle of this Whistle Stop whirlwind and about to start the hardest job in the world in the middle of two wars and a recession, and he's genuinely buoyant. He instills confidence. And earnestness. And honesty. And friendliness.

I talked to a couple different women in the crowd who had been at Martin Luther King's "I Had A Dream" speech at the Lincoln Memorial in '63 — and one of them remembered that "scrawny nasal singer with a guitar." Afterwards, the streets in every direction were like a Grateful Dead parking lot with happy people selling just about anything you could think of with some image of Obama on it — toy trains for the Whistle Stop tour, toques, posters, postcards, baby clothes, flags, car window flags, every possible article of clothing from jackets to underwear, every type of glassware for the kitchen, wooden flutes, bobbleheads . . .

Baltimore is the third city I've been to (after New York and D.C.) that was completely jazzed and transformed by the joy, pride and hope that this guy brings to people's hearts. You could hear "O – ba – ma" randomly hollered from car windows. And groups of strangers started to chant, "Yes we can," for no particular reason, and then laughing that they'd all done it together.

~ = ~ = ~ = ~ = ~ * ~ = ~ = ~ = ~ = ~

We drove back from Baltimore and went straight to the Lincoln Memorial on the National Mall for the concert rehearsal, joining maybe a hundred people there in the below-freezing night.

And who should be playing as we walk (and then run) up but U2! *Priiiiiide, in the name of love.* And City of Blinding Lights, Obama's campaign and his favorite U2 song, which the band had debuted live outdoors at the foot of the Brooklyn Bridge in New York City. Bono's strutting around like Mick Jagger, and bassist Adam Clayton's wearing this huge hooded parka that made him look like a Neil Young Road-eye from the Rust Never Sleeps tour.

148

Then James Taylor came out and did three takes of his beautiful, long *Shower The People* you love with love, with John Legend, Jennifer Nettles and others really stretching it out vocally into some transcendent channeling chant off the final refrain. [and P.S. — that third take was even better than the Sunday show!]

Then Garth Brooks ran though a couple takes of a 3-song medley that includes bye bye Miss *American Pie*, that's gonna blow the roof off Washington tomorrow! The guy's such a born entertainer. He had this whole choir of kids come out and just *lift* it. There were about a hundred of us in a space designed for millions, but he was giving it like we were the world.

Afterwards, I've never been much of a Garth Brooks guy, but he came over to a backstage barrier where we were hanging and talked to every single person, signed anything for them, posed for pictures. I hung with him for a half-hour or more, taking pictures for fans, and being a sidekick for his asides. I also talked to him for bit, asked him how Don McLean was doing — he said, "He's doing great. He's too stubborn to have it any other way." I told him I'd seen them duet at his show in Central Park, and he was, "Ah boy, you sure hit the big ones!" After he had talked to everybody and his handlers in the background were sighing, "Thank gawd! Let's *gooo!*" just then this whole bus full of people suddenly arrived. "Hey, Garth!! We're from Texas!" they're yelling as the whole busload herd of them ran up to him waving their cameras.

Party on, Garth.

Sunday, January 18th, 2009
Democracy is Something you Do

There was a joy today that I've rarely felt before,
and it came after the big concert on the Mall
biking around the Washington Monument and the Capital
Dome
with all the families of America,
whether they were foreigners just arrived,
or descendants of slaves,
whether in new full-length leather coats,
or mama's cloth rag from the attic,
whether they squeezed the family in the car and drove up
from Atlanta,
or flew in first class from Boston for the day,
everyone was united in their love and passion for
Democracy —

and how it's not something you have,
but something you *do* — as Granny D taught us.

And these people and this spirit
is what's on display for the world to see in Washington DC
right now.

There's kids running up the steps of the Capitol
and jumping for joy that they are where they are,
trading off cameras to send pictures home.

Today, it was all about the kids
in each of us
being ignited.

It's the families — the fathers and mothers shepherding
their herds,
that was powerful.

Bono singing *Pride*, in the name of love,
from Martin Luther King's stage,
and will.i.am's riffing vocal rap
and Sheryl Crow's grooving on Bob Marley's *One Love*,
and Stevie Wonder taking us to a *Higher Ground* in that
climactic jam,
and John Mellencamp's "Ain't that America?" that I kept
singing all afternoon
biking through the shining rainbow faces of America,
or the soulful duet of *A Change Is Gonna Come* by Bettye
LaVette and Jon Bon Jovi — *that stole the freakin' show* . . .

and of course Barack's Amazing speech of beauty, strength
and brevity.

    All that was powerful . . .
    But it all came down to families,

    of relations or not,
    of natural-born Americans
    or not,
    who recognize how great
    voting
    and voting for Hope can be.

    And we're all the living proof
    we need.

Monday, January 19th, 2009
The Day That Could Never
Happen

Brothers and Sisters of the Universe,

The final and official stage of our National Transformation
is here —
And all of us are taking The Oath
to be more understanding of others
and to help each other as ourselves.

And masses of Hopesters and Democracy-loving Americans
have made it to the mountaintop, running like water
through the streets, which are all closed to cars this glorious
day. There's t-shirt and button vendors lining every
riverbank; giant rows of port-o-potties winding through
the trees like a Christo installation; and packs of police and
fatigue-wearing National Guard everywhere — but not a
single arrest is ever made.

The *high* temperature tomorrow is predicted to
be *maybe* 32 degrees –
so, feel the freeze when you sees
those couple million standing there in majestic dignity (as
MLK called it).

After it's over, Obama and everyone on the podium will walk back inside the Capitol Building where the new President has lunch with the members of Congress.

As usual for this kind of moment, I highly recommend hitting "mute" on your TV as soon as it's over so you can let it sink in and form Your Own opinions —
You saw it for yourself; the talking heads will still be babbling about it years from now.

At 1:20-ish, a large helicopter will rise up from the other side of the Capitol building and ex-President Bush will fly the hell out of our lives. It's a very cool visual moment — the peaceful hand-off of the leadership of the most powerful country in the world.

At 3:45-ish the parade begins — as President Obama rides in his new tank Caddy (nicknamed "The Beast") from the Capitol Building along Pennsylvania Avenue to the White House.

Live it or lose it.

Scrumptiously & surreally.

Tuesday, January 20th, 2009
Inauguration Day

Blissfully Ravaged in Democracy

There'll never be anything like this again in my lifetime.

The greatest moment of my life? Probably.

And I got to spend it all with my best poli-warrior buddy, Mitch!

He always "got it" — and we fully *lived* Clinton's election and inauguration — but as great as all that was . . . this was transcendent, beyond words.

It's changing history — besides everything else, a major nation elected a minority to lead it — and as it was happening, every single one of the million people I met were Beaming with joy. In terms of a crowd euphoric, the only thing I ever heard of that was like this was Woodstock in '69. And that changed a lot, but this was Woodstock in the seat of power. Jimi's *Star-Spangled Banner* was the prelude, and a scant 40 years later, here's that scorching soul of new thinking actually overtaking the reigns of government. As Barack put it in his speech, "This is the meaning of our liberty and our creed, why men and women and children of every race and every faith can join in celebration across this magnificent mall; and why a man whose father less than 60 years ago might not have been served in a local restaurant can now stand before you to take a most sacred oath."

Rollin' in to the apartment after nine hours of freezing frost I looked like a guy stumbling down off Everest — white parched lips, face scorched red from freezing, but liquid eyes blazing. The thing I missed most in the tranquil heat of home were the screams of joy I heard all day long.

Until I began to warm up and come to, the only words my frozen hands were able to write were —

"blissfully ravaged in democracy"

So, please excuse if this isn't polished scripture — but the levee broke and emotions runneth over. I know you have your own wonderful memories of this day and what it all meant, but here's a tale of the day everything changed from someone who was there . . .

*

I left the apartment in Virginia at 9:30AM by bike. It was 22 degrees — *without* riding into the wind. Starting out in the carless streets of Rossyln and crossing the scary-empty Theodore Roosevelt Bridge it was like living through one of those end-of-the-world movies. Not only were there no cars, but all the people were already at "the show" (or yet to come) and it was just me and the wind. I finally got to the closest point they'd let me ride my bike by about 10:15, worked the miles of snaking security line, and was inside the gates by 10:45 for the 12:00 ceremony.

My ticket was for the Blue South field which was off center, but after seeing the freeform mayhem once you were inside the security zone, I figured I could wing it, and weaved and excuse-me'd toward the dead-center, and in no time was right in front of the stage!

And then the whole show went down, which you saw on TV. Part of the fun of being there was all the running commentary everyone was making, like me yelling, "Dr. Strangelove" at Dick Cheney in his wheelchair, the comical booing of Bush, and the choruses of "Na-na-na-na, na-na-na-na, hey hey-hey, good bye." It was all in good fun. And of course I just loved Aretha singing, "Let freedom ring!" And that beautiful orchestral piece by John Williams, with Yo-Yo, Itzhak & company elevating us like the wind into heaven. And my new-favorite, Reverend Lowery, closing the show with the poetry of Amen. And of course Barack's speech. But you saw all that for yourself.

*

The Party at the Podium

When the official program was over, the fun really started. Just as I figured, everyone started to leave. Once again I was happy I grew up in Winnipeg and could handle a little cold, and I just climbed over the fence and walked straight up to the podium. Security was over. The new President and everybody had gone back inside the Capitol building — there was nothing to "secure" anymore. So I just breezed right the heck up there and started the party.

Those who were really touched by what happened were still sitting there aglow. A few others, like myself, had shimmied up on the energy waves. I just kept riding them till I was right below the podium with the music stands and walls of camera bleachers on either side. It was just a gorgeous party — and it went on for hours. People from all over the country and all over the world were handing each other their cameras, laughing, and ouing and awing. And looking out at the crowd from the Capitol Hill and seeing people all the way to the Washington Monument horizon — what a sight! What a moment. There was no one there who will ever forget it.

Then the Marine One helicopter rose up from behind the Capitol with the now-former President on board, and once again without a shot being fired, the most powerful nation on earth changed its leader — and elected a member of a minority. We gotta be doing something right.

*

I could've lived in that party for the rest of my life. And
in fact I think I will. Everyone was SO happy, beaming,
radiating, loving, friendly. Any which way you turned was
another amazing picture: Straight up at the glowing Capitol
dome. Looking out at the masses of people as far as the eye
could see. Looking into the blissful faces right beside you.
Looking up at the deep rich red, white & blue flags draping
the brilliant white Capitol. The sun peaking in and out from
behind clouds in a bright high-noon sky with flags flapping
a frame. Overwhelming beauty.

Cell phone service was way-intermittent — but messages
were coming in from Canada, New York City, Pennsylvania,
California, as well as from friends in the crowd trying
to find me. To attempt to be a better antenna, I headed
down to the now vacant Mall, and to my favorite general's

monument, Ulysses S. Grant majestically on a horse right at the foot of the Capitol, looking straight down the Mall — I was communing with the big guy. And right in front was the Capitol Reflecting Pool, frozen like a Canadian pond, with one person skating on it, and scads of Southern kids running and sliding on the first ice surface they've ever seen.

It's an easy grounding spot for people to find me, and Democracy-loving road warrior Nadette from New York City (the only person I knew who made both the election night at Barackefeller Center in NYC *and* the Inauguration in D.C.) pulled it off, and so up we rambled back to the Podium Party, and Lord knows it was still goin' on.

Brian and Nadette in a post-Inaugural glow

*

And after another hour of New Years Eve hugging and
doing unto others, I walked over a few feet to where you
could actually look all the way from the Capitol down
Pennsylvania Avenue to the White House — all cleared off
and waiting for a parade! And then Boom! — suddenly a
roaring stream of blue motorcycle cops rode past to my
right. A loud cheer went up from a crowd far away. Some
flags start marching past. A band was playing. *The parade
is starting!"*

I asked a cop — "Was that Obama that went by right in
front?"
"No, there's a couple of bands first, then him."

Oh my God, really?

Everybody said you can't do both. It's either the parade or
the Inaug.
But I'm right there. For both!

The whole thing is — I was still on the Capitol grounds.
Everyone coming for the parade was crowded on the other
side of the Avenue. But I was on the nearly empty roadside
where the cars were pulling out from the front of the
Capitol!

And suddenly there were the press flatbeds shooting
backwards — and there was Andrea Mitchell reporting from
the back of one of them!

Andrea Mitchell at work

"They're coming!" I realize. "I'm right here!"

The Beast in motion

And then Boom! — there he is! There's "the Beast" — the new nuclear-proof Cadillac — and there's Michelle waving at me from 20 feet away! And there's the kids sitting facing their parents and waving and beaming out the windows! And there's Barack on the other side! I'm right freakin' here! This is the whole Big Parade Moment that people lined up for since 7AM!

Not only did I see the swearing-in beginning of this Presidency right up front, but I'm standing on the curb as our new President drives by on his Inaugural trip to the White House!

This was God's gift.

I had put so much into doing the swearing-in right, I had no plans or hope of seeing the parade — and yet here I was a few feet from the family sedan!

All sorts of other amazing, touching, life-giving moments happened with people of every age and color, it would take a long night of beers just to scratch the surface, but this was The Moment — God's glowing gold bow on the gift of the Inauguration, after a day of freezing, weeks of planning, months of campaigning, and a lifetime of volunteering in Democracy — and this is the thanks I get!

*

Take what you've gathered from the day, or let contemporary historians nudge you, but I just wanted to share one person's experience of participating in Democracy.

This will be on postage stamps and coins a hundred years from now. And no matter where you were, you lived to see it. Thank your Spirit source.

And now the rest is up to us.

Inauguration Addendum

As these real-time dispatches made their way around the world, one of the recipients was the great writer and editor Holly George-Warren, who was working at the time with Woodstock producer Michael Lang on his memoir of the festival.

The guy who envisioned and produced the concert that changed everything used my words *on the climactic page of his long-awaited book* about the festival — in the Jimi Hendrix slot, as I like to think of it.

Forty years later, the *Wall Street Journal* would refer to Obama's inauguration as "Washington's Woodstock." Experiencing the joy in coming together with a million celebrants on the Mall in Washington, a writer named Brian Hassett put it this way: "As it was happening, every single one of the people I met was beaming with joy. In terms of a crowd euphoric, the only thing I ever heard of that was like this was Woodstock in '69. That changed our country a lot, but this time Woodstock was in the seat of power. Jimi's 'Star-Spangled Banner' was the prelude, and a scant forty years later, here's that scorching soul of new thinking actually overtaking the reins of government."

From *The Road To Woodstock: From The Man Behind The Festival* (2009) by Michael Lang with Holly George-Warren.

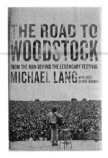

Some Favorite Moments from the Campaign

2012

Some Favorite Moments, Classic Quotes and Lasting Images of the 2012 Campaign, roughly in the order they happened ...

— The ever-increasing availability we all have to unlimited polling data, particularly at RCP (RealClearPolitics) and Nate Silver's FiveThirtyEight.

— The sharing of funny images and insightful articles on Facebook — like having your own customized clipping service made by friends from all over the world.

— Looking forward to 11PM for Jon Stewart's take on the last 24 hours.

— Michele Bachmann getting laughed out of the primary by voters in Iowa and going home after one contest.

— Newt Gingrich's classic, "It obvious to any thinking, independent observer that I'm going to be the Republican nominee."

— Rick Perry's live debate "Oops."

— Every time comically crazy Herman Cain said "9 9 9."

— Gingrich's "moon bases."

— Everything Rick Santorum said, period.

— Mitt Romney's live television mid-debate classic to Rick Perry — "I'll bet you $10,000," as he reached out his hand to really do it.

— Or his oblivious — "I like being able to fire people."

— Or his accidental honesty — "I'm not concerned about the very poor."

— Or his sense of reality — "Middle-income families make around $250,000 year."

— Or his — and I'm not making this up — "I'm not familiar precisely with what I said, but I stand by what I said, whatever it was."

— Him trying to be witty answering a voter's question about unemployment: "I'm also unemployed."

— And being in England when he told the country they were not very well prepared to host the Olympics that year and seeing him become a running joke on the tabloid covers and cartoon pages for the rest of the summer.

— The New Orleans Musicians for Obama concert at Generation Hall near the French Quarter with the Nevilles, the Meters, Dr. John and half the town's players.

— Donald Trump cementing his reputation as a wholly demented buffoon.

— Romney's pollster's "We're not going to let our campaign be dictated by fact-checkers."

— Missouri Republican Representative Todd Akin's "Legitimate rape."

— Senator McCaskill: "This Akin guy is so far to the right he makes Michele Bachmann look like a hippie."

— Mitt Romney's you-can't-this-stuff-up — "I love this state. The trees are the right height."

— And of course Lindsey Graham's classic "We're not generating enough angry white guys to stay in business."

— Clint Eastwood talking to an empty chair.

— Then his later comment to Extra, "Anyone who asks me to speak at a political convention is an idiot."

At a Democrats Abroad debate-watch party in Toronto.

— Jon Stewart's tag line for his Republican convention coverage in Tampa: "The road to Jeb Bush 2016."
— Bill Clinton's hour-long improvised speech at the Democratic convention in Charlotte.
— Watching any and every appearance by The Big Dog after that — seeing the master back in his element.

— Obama's "Don't boo. Vote."
— The whole priceless week of Romney's "47 percent" — saying half the country's on welfare and will never vote for him.
— Mitch Potter's "Nostrahassett."
— V.P. nominee Paul Ryan getting booed to his face at the AARP convention.
— Watching Ryan getting challenged by Chris Wallace on Fox and saying he doesn't have time to explain how their tax cuts add up.
— David Letterman's ongoing refrain "Just don't vote for him" after Romney would never appear on his show.
— Hearing that sensationalist drug addict Rush Limbaugh blubber, "If Romney doesn't win this election it's the end of the Republican Party."

— The Democrats Abroad's debate watch parties in Toronto.
— Joe Biden's classic — "Malarkey."
— Obama's gracious mid-debate trap — "Please proceed, Governor."
— Romney's pandering fail — "Binders full of women."
— And debate host Bob Schieffer making fun of Romney, cutting him off to end the final debate with, "I think we can safely say we all love teachers."

— Bruce Springsteen on the trail and on the stage.
— Katy Perry's form-fitting ballot and "Forward" rubber mini-skirts.
— All the early voting numbers.
— Indiana Republican Richard Mourdock's "When a pregnancy occurs during rape, it is something that God intended to happen."
— Tina Fey's "If I hear one more grey faced old man with a two dollar haircut explain to me what rape is, *I'm gonna lose my mind!*"
— Romnesia.
— David Axelrod's "I'll shave off my mustache that I've had for 40 years if we lose any of Pennsylvania, Minnesota or Wisconsin." [he never had to shave]
— Republican Governor Chris Christie's embrace of Obama.
— Watching Obama's poll numbers rise as Sandy's waters receded.
— Romney's Jeep-jobs-to-China doubled-down final desperate lie-filled ad.
— Joe Biden's "It's Daylight Savings Time tonight. This is Mitt Romney's favorite time of year ... he gets to turn the clocks back."

What a year and campaign it was!

Restoring my Faith in Democracy

at

Democrats Abroad
Primary Debate-Watch Party
Toronto

April 2016

Attending the Democrats Abroad debate-watch party in Toronto this week reminded me how we are so much better than the memes and mean comments you see on social media or news opinions every day.

"Democracy isn't something we have — it's something we do," as the great Granny D put it.

In a couple roomfuls of a hundred or more American Democrats in Toronto — which was split about 2-to-1 for Bernie supporters — we just had a helluva party.

There was no animus, no hatred, no division. Yet it was like a sporting event with supporters of both teams in the room. I never heard a "boo" all night — but I did hear applauding and cheering for both candidates, and in fact saw Bernie supporters applauding Hillary comments, and Hillary supporters applauding Bernie answers. It was a bright-eyed manifestation of how I see and experience politics.

Maybe it's the anonymity of being online — of being isolated in one's own world — that's a factor in some of the unfortunate things that are said and passed around.

But it was my experience, being in a room full of ex-pat Dems from all over America, that we actually got along. Quite well.

I engaged in I-don't-know-how-many wonderful conversations and mid-debate joke riffs with Democrats strongly in favor of one candidate or the other. There wasn't a bad word exchanged between any of us all night during nonstop back-and-forths between people 100% committed to opposite sides.

It was the greatest thing I could ever hope to experience — I mean, in a Democratic primary sorta way.

The smiles, the joy, the energy, the engagement, the understanding, the knowledge that these people have — it's like legend tells us Congress once was — people of different philosophies respectfully debating the issues before them. Imagine!

I just saw it play out among Democrats one border removed.

I started talkin' to this couple, and a first question often is, "So, where're you from?" And they answered Chicago. Apropos of little, I say, "Oh! I was just there for the 50th anniversary Dead shows!" And they lit right up!! And as we riffed along the tune, eventually the guy tells me he was at Winterland for the shows where they shot the *The Grateful Dead Movie.* (What?!) Of course he bought a copy of my book and now weir all besties for life.

And there was another brilliant moment where I was sitting in front of this guy who looked a lot like Bernie and was supporting him, next to a woman who didn't look unlike Hillary ... and was supporting her. And I just listened in awe to the two of them riff the light fandango — smart as hell — SUPER friendly rapid-fire back-&-forth. I never understood that Carville–Matalin marriage — but here I was listening to it play out right next to me. With Love. And Respect.

It reminded me of Bernie saying, "Hillary Clinton

on her worst day is a hundred times better than any of the Republicans."

In this hastily-called gathering in Toronto, with Americans from California to Florida to New York to Kansas, we celebrated the hell out of both of the candidates, taking over multiple rooms of a former mansion in maybe the coolest bar in downtown Toronto — and it was a love-in! We applauded, cheered, fist-pumped, toasted, laughed, high-fived — and the room was *totally* split. And it was the most contentious debate of them all!

We Dems Abroad have the same energy at presidential debates in the fall — but to see us all doing it in April in the thick of a close primary — so . . . together — it was a beautiful thing.

CTV News and the local CP24 news crews were there with camera crews, and the bartender and I were laughing about how hardly anybody in this massive multi-floor establishment was watching the hockey playoffs or baseball games on the other TVs — and that a cable *news* channel was causing the loudest cheers and thickest crowds in the joint!

Democracy isn't something you have — it's something you do.

And boy — were we doin' it up in Toronto.!

These kinds of engagements are happening all over America, and all over the world.

Connect with any Dem / Bern / Hill group of your choice — but get out and join them.

Live this.

This is the 9th Presidential primary I've been involved in — and it's the most wildly crazy unpredictable beyond-fiction one ever.

Get out and have as many public experiences of this as you can. Get involved.

All the way through the election.

I love being a Deadhead. I love being a Prankster. I love being a Beat. And I love being a Democrat.

The core Democrats Abroad crew in Toronto —
l to r: Ed Ungar, Julie Buchanan, Bennett Moase, Karin Lippert &
Yours Unruly

Bernie Sanders rally – April 27th, 2016
Photo by Jeremy Hogan

Front Row at The Revolution

2016

It all started waking up on New York et al primary election day at Ken Morris's house in Cleveland the day after we pre-scouted the city for the upcoming Republican Implosion. I mean, Repugnant Convention. There were three different messages in my in-box about a just-announced Bernie rally tomorrow in Bloomington — where I just happen to be heading for a major Merry Prankster reunion.

A month ago I had hipped the Wizard of Wonder, who was hosting these blooming festivities, that a Bernie rally might happen when we were all together, as Indiana was the only state on the primary calendar that week. Sure enough. Boom! It's the one day before we would all decamp to the site of the three day Acid Test.

Merry Pranksters are pretty much all Berners, and I told them when I arrived that tomorrow would basically be — just get-up-and-go. Doors open at 5PM, and it's in this smallish but gorgeous old 3,000-seat theater. We've all seen Bernie's arenas-full of supporters, and Bloomington is a giant Greenwich Village, an Austin, an S.F., a packed and passionate town of progressives on the prowl. So this venue was gonna be *way* too small and this was gonna get crazy. Gotta be there first thing.

True to my woid, I jingle-jangle in the morning maniac music, believe me, but then the ol' Gets Things Done brain kicks in and I get the hell out of Wonderland and over to said site.

As I arrived near it around 11AM, the car in front of me was from Missouri. Then a car cuts in at an intersection from Florida . . . and we're all in this super-slow-mo line to the only parking lot on the Indiana University campus — and I'm thinkin' — this does not look good.

But The Spirits were with me, and I bolted around the parking lot that I got to know when I was here with John Cassady and Walter Salles for the Midwestern premiere of *On The Road*, [captured vividly in my 2018 *On The Road with Cassadys*] and sure enough there was an open spot right in the key corner closest to where I was going. Boom!

Outta the car quick-as-a-bunny, and power walk to the Auditorium, which I also knew cuz it's the building right in front of the theater where *On The Road* premiered. And this morning there were all these steel fences for the incoming crowds, which was actually separated into two lines, going around either side of the central plaza in front.

Everyone who arrived, starting with the first person at 7AM (!) had lined up on one side, and there was maybe 50 people in it as I'm arriving at around 11:15. But the remarkable thing was, there were about six people just starting to sit down at the very front of the other empty fenced-in line. These two hip chicks, Taylor and Allie (known for the most beautiful eyes this side of Zooey

Deschanel) had figured out that this line was equal to the other line, except nobody was sitting in it yet! I came up just as they're plunkin' down, and they shared the lowdown of how this was gonna go down — how the gates were gonna open at the same time in both lines — 'cept there was nobody here but us! Boom! Done! I'm the 7th person in line for Bernie in Bloomington!

Then a few other people arrived and pretty soon we had a pretty cool little crew in this 8-foot wide steel-fenced pen of a line, and we've got the whole front of it to ourselves. Of course I start talking to these friendly Berners, and I'm tellin' 21-year-Zac beside me how I'm in town hanging with the Merry Pranksters, and how they helped form The Grateful Dead, and how I'm expecting a bunch of them to come to the rally in full costume. But he's never heard of any of them, or Ken Kesey or anything. Super smart guy, computer programmer er sumpthin, he called it Informatics, but I might as well have been tellin' him Civil War tales.

But then all of a sudden these two 19-year-old freshmen girls say, "Are you talking about the Grateful Dead?! We like them." And then one of them holds up Bob Dylan's *Chronicles*! Like — *she's got it with her in line!* And she's taking *a course* in Bob Dylan! Which is coming right on the heals of her "History of Rock" class! Kids these days! And her friend is sitting there reading *Naked Lunch*!!

I pulled out a couple copies of my *Hitchhiker's Guide to Jack Kerouac* book to show them, and they freaked out. And while they're sitting there reading them, the Dylan girl, Eliza, gets on her phone and I figure I've sort of lost her attention pretty quick, but then a bit later when she gets up and hands me the book back, she says, "I just ordered it." (!)

And then at some point, Jim Canary & I got
together — the guy who preserves Kerouac's original *On
The Road* scroll — and he tells me about this huge exhibit
happening in Paris later this year and that I really must go
to. Here we were together again riffin' Jack at the very place
we first met — the world-famous Lilly Library as it was co-
hosting the *On The Road* premiere. [see, also: the *On The
Road with Cassadys* book]

And then somewhere in here the freakin' Secret Service showed up! Word probably got out that Hassett & Canary were in the same place at the same time.

Or maybe it was that presidential candidate — cuz the next thing you know they're hauling in metal detectors.

And ol' Zac sez — "They can't be very secret if it says 'Secret Service' right on their shirts."

And in this rainy, stormy weather these bastards later confiscated everyone's umbrellas as we entered! — like the Secret Service couldn't handle a freakin' umbrella attack.

And all this other stuff was goin' on, including these college kids playing cards. I mean, with physical 52-card decks. They asked me if I knew how to play Euchre.

(!) They're all digitally wired and haven't watched a TV show on a TV in their lives and have phone screens the size of bread loaves — but were sitting there playing with playing cards! Two different groups of them!

And then there were the light-saber kids fighting around the fountain . . . and the official Bernie merch tent was set up out front with unquestionably the coolest political buttons and shirts that have ever appeared on a campaign trail, including this Grateful Dead dancing bear who was first created for the legendary chemist Owsley "Bear" Stanley . . .

And they set up a big screen and speakers for the overflow crowd outside — with the coolest slogan — "IN for Bernie" . . . using the abbreviation for Indiana . . . all while the line continued to form, all around the fountain square, then all the way down the street, then around the far corner, and down the hill, and back up the far side, then around the tennis courts, and people were *still* arriving! I'm guessing maybe a tenth of them got in.

And I kept wandering around on my observational roamabouts . . . then would circle back and hang sumore with our killer crews at the front of the line . . . and we were having this debate about what would happen to all this Bernie energy should he not get the nomination. Will they stay inspired and mobilized and work to elect like-minded Democrats to the House and Senate and continue to steer the party to its proper place on the left? . . . or will they Bern out and fade away. I'm concerned it's going to be the latter, and I challenged all of them to not make it so. But sad proof that I may be right about the lack of involvement was when the Bernie volunteer coordinators came by trying to recruit volunteers from the hardest of the hardcores at the front of the line, not a single person ever responded to two separate appeals for help. Mind you, it *was* finals time on campus.

After nearly six hours of having the most sidewalk fun I'd had since hanging outside Abbey Road Studios for an afternoon, they finally opened the gates and we dashed up the stairs to the indoor security phalanx — the whole airport security empty-the-pockets / metal detectors / magnetometers wand-scanning routine, including making you hold any buttons you were wearing in your hand to show them (?!) and then as soon as you're thru that, it was this kind of crazy "festival seating" rush of democracy-loving kids that flashed me back to KISS concerts in the mid-'70s — where as soon as we had our ticket torn at the door — ahhh, simpler times — we ran like hell for the front of the stage. But here we were doing it for a presidential candidate!

I love life.

Eliza and her two friends had come through one of the metal detector shoots right at the same time I did, and — "Oh, Great! Hey! Ha! Ya made it!" as we're laughing in giddy joy, running to the promised land. The ushers had been sending the first arrivees into the theater to the far side aisles, and as I came in I could see there was absolutely NO ONE down at the front of the stage yet. (!)

I don't know how the hell it went down exactly in the flash of the moment — but I noticed the direction lady usher at the top of the center aisle got momentarily distracted, and I just blew right past her and zoomed straight down that muthrpuckin center aisle, and BOOM! — Dead center, just like I did at Radio City when I snuck into my 2nd ever Grateful dance in 1980. DONE! And Eliza kept right up with me, and ZOOM! We all made it! Front row center! I grabbed the aisle seat, as is my wont, and they fell in right beside me, and voila! **Front Row at the The Revolution!**

And then it was the whole pre-show hang . . . in a comfy-seat in a poor-man's Radio City. Over the PA they blast Neil Young's "*Rockin' In The Free World*" — not once, but twice! And this fellow Winnipeg Kelvinite is fist-pumping the air to the Beat, knowing that everyone behind me looking at the stage can see this energetic arm punching out the rock that is the core of this revolution.

They also played Simon & Garfunkel's "*America*" ... twice, refraining the great visual ad from earlier in the campaign; and Willie Nelson's "*On The Road Again*" which always evokes Kerouc to this booksmith, as Eliza's telling me about seeing Willie and the now late-great Merle

Haggard together in this very venue just a few months ago.

Then somebody texts her that they just saw her on CNN, which, since we were sitting next to each other, might mean I just had my five seconds of fame right there and I missed it.

On one of my many walkabouts, I checked out the media row along the mid-house horizontal aisle — and, I know it was the day after Bernie's devastating New York loss, but still . . . there were rows of empty reserved seats where there were supposed to be reporters.

Shortly before showtime, they brought in five rows of people to fill the bleachers behind Bernie's podium. I'd seen the bunch of them gathered in the lobby on one of my reconnaissance rounds, and they told me they'd simply been picked out of the crowd as they came through the lobby. I was there when they were taken through the back door into the theater, and there was absolutely no arranging of them according to age or race or gender. It was just in whatever way they filed through the door, with no manipulation of who sat in the front row, or right behind Bernie, or in what pattern of faces.

And while on one of these scouting missions, a middle-aged woman came walking down the aisle toward me, looking at me kinda strange, and said, "Are you one of the Merry Pranksters?" (!)

I don't know how in the hell this world works, but it sure works fast!

There were two warm-up speakers — the main student organizer; and the head of the Dems in Indiana, who was a middle-aged black near-Baptist-preacher who did a riff on how he wasn't into Bernie at first. But

187

then he looked into his history of fighting for the little guy, "And I started to feel the Bern," [big cheer], "Then I learned about his position on banking reform, and then I was *definitely* feeling the Bern," [bigger cheer]. And he does about ten variations on this, and then – "I saw him winning 17 states and having the longest line for any event in I.U. history, and now I'm feelin' the Bern *all over!*" he says as he shivers 'n' shimmies to crazy cheering.

And finally, about nine hours after I left the house this morning on this mission, The Man appears! White hair and all!

No teleprompter, just a variation on a campaign speech he's been giving daily for the last year. The only time he'd look down at his notes was, for instance, sharing the specific stats and names of businesses from Indiana that've moved to China or Mexico since certain trade deals.

I kept thinking of his "speech" as "a performance" or "a show" because it really was one. Including a lot of audience participation. He had the place in the palm of his hand from the standing ovation when he first walked on stage.

The guy has it down. There was either a laugh or an applause line roughly every minute of the nearly 90 he talked for.

And I must say it *was* a helluva speech — a colorful articulation of pretty much every Progressive position. And in most cases, I'd like every one of them to be the Democratic platform. Sure wish I could have caught a Hillary speech right after this to compare & contrast.

And speaking of Hillary, at the first and every subsequent mention of her name, a loud boo instantly arose from the assembled. By about the fifth time, it had become a joke, and people were booing and laughing at the same time at our goofing on our cue.

Bernie's got the timing and delivery of a professional comedian, and has a lot of sure-fire laugh lines that have prolly worked in every city he's appeared. Of Hillary not releasing her quarter-million-dollar speech transcripts — "Getting paid that much, that must be a pretty fantastic speech! That must solve all of America's problems." (laughter) "That must be *some* Shakespearean prose!" (bigger laughter)

"And then there's my good friend Donald Trump," (laughter). "My wife and I were never invited to his wedding." (bigger laughter)

"Trump has come up with a whole new way to deny climate change. He thinks it's a hoax . . . created by the Chinese. (laughter) I would have thought he'd think it was caused by Muslims or Mexicans." (bigger laughter)

"I have a major announcement to make here tonight. I am now going to release the transcripts of all my Wall Street speeches. Here they are," as he dramatically throws an armful of nothing in the air. (big laughter) "They never offered me $225,000 for a speech. I've got my cell phone on. I'm just waiting for a call from them." (bigger laughter)

But this also kind of manifests one of the problems with his speech / campaign. Members of Congress are prohibited from accepting money for speeches or any kind of appearance. He keeps saying it like he's some pure guy — but since he left Vermont, for the last quarter century he's held a job that prohibited him from giving paid speeches. There was this and a lot of other holes in many of his two-paragraph-long diagnoses of our ills and how we would fix them. That's definitely a downside I can see his non-supporters seeing.

On the other hand — he rattled off more real and important things that need to be changed — and at least *some ideas* of how to fix them — than any other candidate I've heard over the last year: including passing a law that if a corporation needs a bailout, the CEO is prohibited from getting bonuses; and that marijuana should be reclassified as a schedule 2 drug, and not in the same class as heroin. (big applause on campus)

And he talked powerfully about our incarceration problem — and how we have the most imprisoned people of any nation on Earth — spending $80 billion a year to keep 2 million Americans behind bars. "Criminal injustice is a crime in America," he Ginsbergianly put it. And of course this gets another standing ovation.

He talked about how we're the only industrialized country to not guarantee healthcare for all its citizens, and how seniors are having to split their pills in half because they can't afford them, and this whole very real plight of the uninsured elderly brings Eliza beside me to tears.

Women are making .77 cents on the dollar that men are . . . public colleges should be free like they were when he went to them in the '50s and '60s . . . we have money for wars but not inner cities . . . immigration reform must also include Native Americans . . . we need to live with nature and not destroy it — because it will destroy us . . . (and at this point I can hear Eliza's friend sobbing her eyes out) . . . we should be making solar panels mandatory on all government buildings . . . and every one of these points got a separate standing ovation, by anywhere from 10–100% of the audience.

At one point during a smidge of silence, what sounded like a 5-year-old girl, squeaked out, "I love you, Bernie!" that got a huge laugh and more applause.

And the whole thing built to this sermonistic climax — "Families looking out for each other always trumps greed. Love trumps hate." —> into a jumping-up standing ovation.

This was John Lennon as a politician — which I never realized until I sat in front of him for a whole Sermon on The Trail. What a religious experience. Certainly delivered, received and perceived like a prophet.

Even by me — a political pragmatist. This guy's special. I really haven't seen this before. **He's got Jesse Jackson or Obama's oratory skills, albeit in a completely different style; combined with a Lloyd Benson or Joe Biden maturity; a Ralph Nader or Jerry Brown philosophical approach; an early Howard Dean or Gary Hart fervor; an essential Paul Tsongas or Bob Kerry sense of humor; and a Bill Bradley or Dennis Kucinich appeal to college students.**

It's quite a blend. And I love a good blend.

[see, also: Dead, Grateful]

The speech ended, and people flooded the front of the stage because he walked forward and not to the wings. And I was right there, "on the rail" as my live concert practitioners call it — and the whole front-of-stage area suddenly packed with people rushing in to feel the Bern, not unlike the joyous sardine end of any great rock concert.

Bernie came down into the orchestra pit and walked

the wooden rope-line barrier, and I got to shake his hand at a nice slow long pace, giving him the double hand wrap around his one, and looking right through his glasses into his eyes, telling him, "Thank you for what you're doing."

And within moments I was singing, "*I shook the hand, that shook the hand, of Abbie Hoffman and Charlie Chan.*"

And right after he passed and heads back up the stairs and waves a final farewell, the guy we were hanging with in our front row foursome is bawling his eyes out! Apparently Bernie not only shook his hand but gave him a bit of a hug, and the guy's totally losing it, sitting and shaking face-in-hands on the orchestra pit divider, with his girlfriend consoling him, and I'm like, Whoa! This *is* Beatlemania! Or Berniemania.

That made it all three out of the three people sitting next to me being overcome with emotion to the point of tears.

It really was that good. I wonder if three out of three people next to me at a Hillary rally would be moved to tears?

And in the **It's-Not-A-Real-Adventure-If-You-Don't-Get-Chased Dept**.:

As I was looking at my three new BFFs in their hyper-dramatic state, this security woman who told me earlier that pictures was prohibited for some insane non-reason, and I just kept taking them anyway, was standing along the side wall with the other various cop types, and suddenly she was leaning over the orchestra barrier into the open space of the pit about 15 feet from me, with two tall white uniforms behind her.

"Excuse me, sir," she says loudly right to me, leaning out into the open pit to catch my eye and pointing full-arm directly right at me, and like she was coming for my camera.

Those were the last words I ever heard anyone say to me for quite a while . . . . . and they're still echoing.

I'd had my eye on the wall-hanging Blue Meanies who had their eye on me as I was, clandestine as I could, shooting the hell out of the show with my you're-not-supposed-to-use-it camera. I knew there was every chance they were gonna come for me at the end . . . and at minimum erase the pictures — or maybe worse.

But there was *no way* I was gonna let *this* night end badly!

Without saying a word of goodbye to my linemates, I grabbed my coat from the seat, and booked it up the aisle, with a kinda slight Groucho crouch to make myself smaller. I got half-way up and hit the back end of the exiting crowd that were snail-inching their way out. I lingered and pretended like I was just gonna hang there in the line for a while . . . feeling their surveilling eyes and approach behind me; and as I know so well — do *not* turn around and look behind you. Pretend like you don't know they're after you. Then after a few seconds fake-out delay in this aisle, I cut over left through an empty row to the next aisle, and snailed along with those people for a few seconds, again acting that I was just naturally slowly leaving, not running or anything, suddenly stuck in the cattle cluster. Then I broke and cut through another empty row, now getting to the nearly last aisle, which is fairly open, and speed-walked it to the top of the audience bowl, and

Boom! — spot the lower hidden exit in the dark, bolt down those steps cuz now I'm in an unobservable tunnel, through those doors into the lobby with hundreds of other departing Berners. Again — *don't look back* to any other exit where they might be coming towards me, but power-walk through the lobby to the nearest exit to the outer lobby, and finally see the nighttime darkened glass doors, with one last line of black uniformed Secret Service staring us down as we leave. I listened for walkie-talkies going off — "Stop that long-haired guy in the jean jacket!" — but I heard / saw / felt nothing, and just blasted past the bullet-proof vests into the blooming raining Bloomington night, heart racing a thousand miles an hour, and heart beating even faster for democracy.

Republican National Convention

Part 1 — Arriving in Cleveland

Saturday, July 16th, 2016

Lesson One going into the convention war zone streets
of Cleveland — as hipped by my poli-Adventure-brother
Mitch — "If you hear fire crackers, don't assume they're fire
crackers. Get behind cover."

Roger that.

Mitch and I met in 1983 through him being a music
reporter in Winnipeg and me managing one of the top local
bands he loved. What usually happens with relationships is
— they stay in the realm they were formed. He and I shared
that rock 'n' roll crazyworld ... but gradually discovered we
were both history buffs ... then ... hardcore politicos. We've
spent a thousand hours talking politics in person and
over the phone from Winnipeg or Toronto to New York
long before the internet signed in! I was calling him with
payphone reports from D.C. during Bill Clinton's first
inauguration — a quarter-century ago. Then we roomed
together within eyesight of the Lincoln Memorial during the
week of Obama's inauguration — he making his newspaper
deadlines, me making my email dispatches (which you
probably read just a few pages back) — and now here we
were together again — 30-something years after our first
crazy Prankster Road Adventure began.

I love Cleveland! And have had nothing but a good time here since I first hit it with John Cassady to go to The Grateful Dead show at the Rock 'n' Roll Hall of Fame . . . a Grate Adventure Tale you can read in-depth in one of my Beat Trilogy books – *On The Road with Cassadys.*

So the Rock Hall has always been my touchstone in town and the obvious first place I went to get grounded with the newly-landed gentry of Republican delegates — with the minor modification of the streets being filled with police and skies buzzing with surveillance helicopters.

I started talking to a nice couple from Kansas who'd just left The Hall and were beaming in the beauty of it all. We riffed a soaring jam on the Beatles, Elvis, the Stones, and how great the museum was.

I just got back from a month in Greenwich Village and Woodstock, and before that nearly a month with the Merry Pranksters in Wonderland, so I was quite used to strangers stopping strangers just to shake their hand, as Robert Hunter put it about people who get the Grand Prank of Life and are surfing the ripples of light. It's the enlightened people, as I see it, that one should soak in by the lifetime.

Then suddenly this seemingly lovely Kansas couple, obviously mistaking me for someone else, segued from Elvis on Ed Sullivan into, "Mike Pence is a great V.P. choice. (!) He adds a lot to the ticket. He's got a lot of experience and has been fighting for all the important stuff for a long time."

And I suddenly realized – "We're not in Woodstock anymore."

Kansas is in the house.

On this sunny Saturday leading into the convention
— downtown was a ghost town. And it's not that the streets
were blocked off — it's cuz all the locals had been scared off
by predictions of crowds and mayhem.

And speaking of dead roads . . . this town is a freakin'
poster child for the decimation of the infrastructure in
America! With the Repugnant Congress blocking anything
that's good for the country in hopes people will blame
Obama, and a Repugnant Ohio Governor toady who goes
along with their plan, a lot of sidestreets here are like
driving through a war zone after a bombing. There are pot
holes you could hide a keg in.

The best news from the first day's recon — besides
learning that my shuttlecraft bike is *The* Way to get around
town — was that the coolest single block in all of downtown
Cleveland — Positively 4th Street — was just *out*side the
massive security perimeter. (!) This one short narrow old-
world pedestrian alley has nothing but bars & restaurants,
feeling like the French Quarter or Greenwich Village or
North Beach.

And who should I find occupying my new favorite
street, but my old favorite news network.

I can tell this is going to be the block I'll be spending
some considerable time.

I wonder if ol' MSNBC is outside of the perimeter,
like me, because they weren't credentialed for this
auspicious embarrassment?

In other news — I talked to local cops, state police,
& Secret Service, and even in their buzz-shaved heads and
starch-stiff uniforms they were as friendly to this longhaired

biking freak as could be; even told me I could ride my faithful bike Ranger on the sidewalks!

I don't intend to be storming the Bastille or jumping any fences, because they've deputized an army of out-of-state cops and cleaned out their jails for miles around and are prolly just itching to fill the new vacancies, but all the ones I talked to were as friendly and helpful as a concierge in a 5-star disaster.

But for now it was time for this cowboy to get back on the horse and ride off into the sunshine.

Part 2 – The Going Gets Weird

Repugnant Convention

Sunday – July 17th, 2016

Even with the overlay of three police officers just being killed during racial unrest in Baton Rouge, the streets of Cleveland remained calm, pleasantly controlled and festive. Locals were celebrating summer, delegates are being feted at the Rock 'n' Roll Hall of Fame, and the police are being applauded.

Positively 4th Street was the obvious go-to strip — and may end up looking more like Mardi Gras by week's end. But as the convention began, it seemed like there were more journalists and police here than people to protect or report on. I mean, they're so desperate for anyone to talk to, they're even talking to me!

And a beautiful thing was that the few protests I'd seen so far were stressing Love — and would make John Lennon proud.

"Love can Heal what Hurt Divides" said the words of the prophets written on the cardboard signs. Or there was this great billboard of Donald and Ted Cruz on one of the main streets downtown . . .

I was just digging on all the people, the political buzz, and the architecture. In the 1930s, that Terminal Tower here was the fourth tallest building in the world!

And all the best political reporters in the country were here. I got to spend some time talking about writing with one of the journalistic pillars in American poli-letters, the *Washington Post's* Dan Balz. And like the natural consummate reporter he is, he ended up asking me more questions than I did him.

Dan Balz and the author at the end of Positively 4th Street.

The *Post* converted a bar/restaurant on 4th Street into their social headquarters for the week. Wonder if they let in subscribers?

Furthur along the block-long road, the multiple MSNBC studios were in constant swing from anchor to anchor, guest to guest, show to show.

The 7:00 / 8:00 turnover from Chris Matthews to Chris Hayes.

I even got in a little walk 'n' talk with CNN and radio host Michael Smerconish who I've long loved for his honest, logical, centrist, non-ideological way of thinking and interviewing. I told him about Jon Anderson being on his show years ago. "The singer from Yes!" he exclaimed, brightening right up. As I mentioned how he riffed "Smerconish" in an improvised song on air, Mike goes, "Boy, you've got a good memory!"

Hanging with Smerch on Positively Fourth Street.

But the best reporter I talked to all day was Mitch Potter from the *Toronto Star*!

We finally got together about 9PM . . . and did nothing but power-riff politics until 2 in the morning.

And then began another day in poli-paradise . . .

Part 3 — The Party Kicks In

Repugnant Convention

Monday, July 18th, 2016

Bizarrely and somewhat depressingly, I started my day by visiting the nearby site of the Kent State massacre in 1970.

When people talk about how bad things are in our country today — at least the National Guard aren't shooting unarmed student protesters on their campus.

The university has done an amazing job of honoring the fallen, with the spots where each of the four died permanently cordoned off, and interpretive signs all over the area that walk you through each step of that terrible day, plus an entire museum dedicated to it that's reverential, tasteful and effectively rendered. It brought me to tears. And I can't have been the first one — because they have boxes of tissues for viewers in the film room.

Then holy shit — what a first convention day in Cleveland! This town is throwing *A PARTY!*

For starters, the cops and all levels of security have obviously been well prepped in social interaction and are being so freakin' nice!

At one point, 'round midnight, I needed to know if a certain exit from the Quicken Arena perimeter was the only one, and I went over, and this Secret Service agent spent five minutes figuring out the answer for me.

Unreal.

I've seen police forces here from California, Michigan, Texas, Georgia . . . and there's *armies* of them!

After three days at the core of it, tonight, once, I heard the only cross words spoken between two people. It was between a local and a Republican supporter. And frankly, the guy on my side was out of turn. He was just taking out his anti-Repugnant anger on this one guy. But I've been around *thousands* of people already, maybe tens of thousands, for *days*, and have only heard this one angry exchange between any two people.

How many huge political gatherings can you say that about?

I had a lengthy discussion with the Deputy Police Chief about all things security, and at the end when I asked if I could get a picture with him, he asked politely if I minded if he put his arm around me while we took it.

Which was followed by hanging with leading alternative presidential candidate Vermin Supreme.

Where there had been few protesters during the weekend leading into the convention — even though the town was already as full of delegates and reporters as it would be during the convention — by Monday all the characters and costumes were out in full color.

Code Pink outside the Red Zone.

This is full-on Prankster protesting by committed Groucho Marxists. Abbie Lives! indeed.

This is not a rocks and Molotov cocktails crew — it's more your flowers in the ends of gun barrels crowd. The convention and city have become a giant art show with installations all over town — both official and un.

I mean, at times I couldn't tell if I was hanging with Pranksters or protesters.

Or exactly whose convention I was attending. At one point I said, "I think there's more Democrats in town than Republicans."

Part 4 — Love & Hate

Repugnant Convention

Tuesday, July 19th, 2016

As the crazy circus rolled on around the coronation of the bigot as the Repugnant "standard-bearer" after years of less obvious assholes — the playful sense of humor of many sensible and silly Americans was still on display in places.

Multiple Upright Citizens Brigade Theatre-type groups were staging sketches and singing songs on the streets all over town.

And another group brought hundreds of tennis balls to bounce around to protest the convention banning them (!?) . . . while allowing people to open-carry guns on the streets.

But cops outnumbered protesters about 10-to-1 —
in a strategy known as "overwhelming force" — so nobody
even *thinks* of doing anything wrong.

There's been nothing I've seen resembling actual
violence or real threats by any civilian in Cleveland, but
the cops have been over-hired with our tax dollars and get
all dressed up in their hot 'n' heavy Play War gear every
morning, and after a couple days of smiling and playing
nice, they were now ready to crack some heads and kick
some ass.

What was once a cool, friendly, welcoming scene had
devolved into an over-policed aggressive unfriendly vibe.

You know who Robert Smigel is? He created the *TV
Funhouse* cartoon shorts on *Saturday Night Live*, and the
puppet character Triumph, the Insult Comic Dog, and he
and I spent some time together at a Kerouac event at St.
Mark's Church in-the-Bowery many years ago where he

absolutely killed making fun of us as Triumph. *Really* funny guy.

He's been out on the campaign trail keeping it light at Trumpenstein rallies — for instance, saying to one heavyset Drumpf supporter, "I think he needs to build a wall between you and McDonalds," which made even the guy laugh — and doing his level best to keep people smiling during this ugly period in American history.

For the convention, he organized a comedic parody of a protest at the Public Square, one of the designated gathering places in town, with such inflammatory protest signs as — "Make Memes Great Again!" and "God Hates Morning People."

But the cops obviously missed the joke. The Square was filled with nothing but Smigel fans, curious bystanders, and a bunch of official (and non) reporters with cameras. Again, maybe because the cops felt like they had to do *something* since there were 50 million of them just standing around in the 80 degree sun, they called in reinforcements and systematically cleared the entire square, pushing people back using bikes, riot gear, and barking voices.

On the stage was a satiric comedy routine. A gag. A goof. A spoof. But they brought in the armed forces. Although they didn't fire, it was still painfully reminiscent of the peaceful protests at Kent State — authorities in uniforms not at all understanding what was happening in front of them — and overreacting.

They got all dressed up for war and had nothing to do. So they did something.

And a very strange subset among the assembled were both young and older mostly males walking around filming what they were seeing and narrating their "reporting." If you overheard them, they were describing things as though everything in front of them was terribly nefarious, and disaster about to strike. They story-told their reality as a death trap, and damn they were going to have their cameras rolling when Armageddon hit in the next few seconds.

But besides even the cops and camera kooks, the strangest of all buzz-kills downtown were the Jesus freaks with their bullhorns yelling at everyone. These bloviating blowhards sounded like judgmental fascists telling everyone else they weren't as good as they were. They've gotten *The Bible* about as wrong as some Muslims have gotten the *Qur'an*. It's no wonder so many people are turned off religion these days.

As a Christian friend of mine said of them, "Welcome to the U.S. 'Christian Right' ... aka anti-Christ."

Me, I'm not losing my religion. I know there's still beautiful people like this doing nothing but spreading the gospel of Love . . .

Part 5 — "This is a Shitshow"

Repugnant Convention

Wed. & Thurs., July 19–20, 2016

When I tried starting this story after coming home on the final night around 4 AM . . . all I found when I woke up this morning was —

"Republicans are loons . . . ."

But boy, this was just the greatest time! Sheesh! It was like the 4th of July ... *for a week!* As I said before — now I know why they're called political *parties!*

Somehow the definitive moment for me was dancing at night in the fountain at the Public Square, led by a master drummer named Freedom who I just became friends with a couple days ago.

It was right before Twitler's speech on the final night, and security had successfully secured the week, done their job and it was effectively over, and Freedom picked right up on that freedom and started a tribal, festival-like, Grateful Dead dance party at the very heart of the city. Just one of the many people I met who I'll be friends with for life.

Another definitive moment was experiencing Twitenstein's speech on Positively 4th Street, which ironically was being broadcast to the city by the very non-Republican MSNBC.

You might read into this that Fox didn't want to set up a giant screen viewing area to broadcast their sociopath's words to the city. But MSNBC thought — *people need to hear this!*

Fourth Street was the hot spot in the city and the go-to place for everyone not in the arena. The street was packed from one end to the other — and what was striking was how *un*enthusiastic and non-responsive the crowd was. The prop poobahs inside would cheer and applaud each line on cue, but outside it was mostly falling on dead ears . . . in a street full of Republicans . . . and with people like this who thought *this* was a good idea . . .

The night *should* have been like being in the crowd at a home team's victory — like Cleveland just celebrated last month with their Cavaliers basketball team bringing the first national championship to the city in 50 years — but the gloominess felt like a home team *loss*. The silence was deafening as the applause track from the arena played to nonplussed indifference. In Cleveland. To Republicans.

These conventions are like the Woodstock of politics. Every star in the political world is here, there's days and nights of non-stop "shows" on multiple stages all over the festival site (city), and people are partying like there's no tomorrow. Which, in the case of every level-headed Republican, may be true.

But prior to the big night, there'd been a couple more days of fun in the sun with some of the smartest political reporters in America. Since MSNBC had taken over Positively 4th Street, a bunch of them were around, including *Morning Joe* Scarborough and his soon-to-be bride Mika Brzezinski; the kick-ass campaign reporter Hallie Jackson; and my personal favorite, *Meet The Press* host Chuck Todd.

Instead of smiling I was busy telling Chuck how he was Tim Russert's living legacy. And boy did he appreciate that.

Meeting all the different *Washington Post* writers, I had the excellent entry line with, "I'm a big fan and longtime subscriber …" which always seemed to buy me extra time and a genuine connection. These guys who can stay so focused and get the story with new angles and insights and deadlines day after day, year after year, impresses the hell out of me and makes me laugh every time I see someone dismissing "the MSM" or the *Post* in general just because Jeff Bezos bought it. That guy saved one of the great literary institutions in America — and made it *better*, not worse, by turning it into a high-functioning, easily interactive online read as print edition sales steadily declined. There are a ton more op-ed writers there now than there used to be — a lot more diversity and styles and viewpoints — and there's more bylines on big stories than there used to be. These are the signs of a healthy and thriving journalistic enterprise and we are all the better for it.

The *Post*'s brilliant Kerouacian Dana Milbank On The Trail.

And in the Appearances-Can-Be-Deceiving Department:

From his countenance on TV, I always thought David Frum was some depressingly dour frump. But he was the friendliest, *funniest*, most talkative, interesting, coolest guy I met from the Republican side in Cleveland. It just goes to show — people aren't always what they seem.

Us two fellow Canadians had a long walk-n-talk and I told him how much my strong-minded mother loved his strong-minded mother Barbara when she was the host of the national *Journal* every night on the CBC, long before America ever had a female news anchor.

And he told me how Cleveland seemed like a perfectly preserved Toronto from his youth in the '60s and '70s — a lakeside city with wide roads, open spaces and great old-world architecture.

I knew he'd been a speechwriter for George W., and that he was a smart Republican at a convention nominating an illiterate dimwit, so I gently broached whether he was a supporter or not, and he riffed an op-ed on-the-spot ripping the amoral a-hole a new one. And for the first time I sorta felt bad for good-guys like Frum who were having their party ripped from them.

A couple of wayward Canucks Frum the old country.

And speaking of wayward Canucks riffing stories on the spot in a recast Toronto . . . once again Potter & Hassett were On The Beat and On The Road writing the stories above the fold.

We had beers in the garden and jams in the dark, riding the rainbow of an epic arc that stretched from the prairies to nights with Jerrys, and now had us caught in a land most fraught with the death of civility as it yearned for tranquility.

With Brother Ken we rocked a trio overflowing with bursting brio, that took to the streets like joy-chasing Beats in search of the pearl in this political swirl.

Three authors of their own Adventures in the afternoon
sun-speckled wild

And like any red-blooded male, I made sure I talked
to *The Daily Beast's* Olivia Nuzzi. My old girlfriend was
Italian, and ever since the Renaissance they've had a pretty
good handle on beauty. She was part of exposing the whole
Anthony Weiner story — whose exposure caused exposés of
epic comedic importance.

We talked about I-don't-know-what and I don't
really care.

Another smart young political reporter – Olivia Nuzzi.

One of my favorite types of people are serious brainiacs who are smart enough to know to be happy. And the *Post's* Chris Cillizza is one of those.

CNN & the *Washington Post's* Chris Cillizza.

Other journos and playas seen on the scene but unsnapped — Rick "Google" Santorum; *NBC Nightly News* anchor Lester Holt; former RNC Chair Michael Steele; Obama's Special Advisor Van Jones; the *Post's* always-dapper Jonathan Capehart; *Politico's* bespectacled Mike Allen; *Mother Jones* writer and breaker of the Romney 47% story David Corn; Campbell Brown & Dan Senor; Republican strategists Mike Murphy, Barry Bennett, Jack Kingston and Alex Castellanos; Howard Fineman, Roland Martin, Ron Fournier, Joan Walsh, Tucker Carlson, Samantha Bee, and Frank Luntz – the guy who got Chickenhawk Bonespurs III to say of war hero John McCain, "I like heroes who don't get caught."

One thing I found for sure — every writer or senior Republican operative I talked to all week saw the same thing. Many of them used the phrase "This is a shitshow," and the party chairman of one of the largest states in the union put it simply — "We're fucked."

Plagiarism, disconnection, disloyalty and dictatorial were the words I heard that summed up each of the four days in sequence.

I've been in a lot of crowds at a lot of awe-inspiring large-scale events over the last 40 years and know what happy fans act like. A lot of the delegates and others leaving the arena looked like they were walking out of a funeral. They should have been dancing in the streets after their team just put on the greatest show on earth . . . but they were stumbling as though they just wanted to get home and bury their head.

However Faux Noise or this Repugnant Party try to spin this celebration of a clownish fascist, they've been taken over by an intolerant illiterate racist, who they voted into their captaincy themselves. History will not look kindly on this coronation in Cleveland.

But I will forever look kindly on my Beat brother Ken for not only hosting my 24-hour madness all week, but being an A-Team Adventure Buddy — and cameraman-in-a-pinch!

Ken, Freedom & me, in the fountain in the Public Square, 10PM Thursday night.

Election Night 2016

New York City

It was such a beautiful fall Tuesday in New York.

We were all in such a good mood.

But in retrospect there were some early warning signs I'd rationalized and dismissed: The tollbooth clerk I had a happy election exchange with but when asked who she was voting for answered, "I don't tell people that." Or the random middle-aged poor guy in the New York deli who volunteered, "I like Trump. That guy tells it like it is." Or the two women in the Democratic heart of NBC's Democracy Plaza wearing "Trumplican" t-shirts. Or the young cool-looking hippie-rebel dudes outside Trump Tower spending their days holding up pro-Trump signs. Or when I left my Beat buddy's apartment in Brooklyn in full Democratic regalia on election day, not one person responding positively — *so* unlike walking the New York streets in Obama gear in '08. Or when I was leaving the Port Authority Bus Terminal for the Hillary victory party at the Javits Center some construction worker type guy said as I passed, "I pray to god you fuckin' die."

Another sign was when I asked a Clinton campaign worker in the afternoon about the evening's planned fireworks over the Hudson and he told me they were TBD. Then around 8:00 I was talking to a high-level security coordinator straight out of Scorsese Casting and he told me they'd been canceled.

It still didn't dawn on me.

Just to set the scene — it was glorious. I got to the Javits Center about 3:00 — and by 5:30 was outside with thousands of fellow Democrats at a block party on closed-off 11th Avenue next to the glass-ceilinged building.

Oh and a funny thing — during my pre-scout the day before, when I saw how small the main room was inside the Javits and learned there would be a big outdoor party scene, I also noted how there were no seats or benches out there. So when we were inside the airplane-hanger-like holding pen I spotted a woman pushing a cart stacked with folding chairs, buttonholed her, asked if I could have one, and managed to talk her into it! "Okay, but don't tell anyone where you got it." So now I was the only guy in a crowd of thousands with a chair! Then when we went through security, I folded it up and carried it with me! When we were going out the door to 11th Avenue and I still had it, a cluster of cops were looking at me and the only woman in the bunch said, "Hey you can't take that outside." And I said, "Yeah I can — they gave it to me to use." Ha! So now I was outside with the one & only chair on the avenue!

Another funny thing was, the party space was this long rectangle — 4 or 5 blocks of 11th Avenue — and the first to arrive went to the stage that was about 7/8ths of the way down. It was positioned sideways towards the cordoned off camera risers on the sidewalk, so there was only a small area in front it — which was of course immediately sardined. But those of us who arrived first went to the little area just beyond it that very few people ever knew was there and we had all this whole space to ourselves — oddly right next to the reporter's pen.

I went straight to the boom camera operators and

226

told them how I needed the chair, and they let me fold it up and put over their barricade whenever I wasn't using it.

I could see the images from the boom cameraman's monitor that the crowd was subways-at-rush-hour packed all the way north from the stage. But those of us who broke on through to the other side coulda played frisbee back there!

Then it hit me — this very Javits Center was where I first raised my hand and became an American citizen! (see the 1996 chapter earlier in book)

And now a woman was becoming President in the very place where my mother's dream for me came true — and where her dream of women's equality was finally shattering the last glass ceiling!

At 7:00 they turned on the giant two-sided movie-theater-size screen that faced both up and down the avenue — and suddenly we collectively had a news feed with blaring audio. They started with CNN, and every 10 or 15 minutes would flip between that and NBC, ABC or CBS. So it was kind of like being at home except some omnipotent hand was holding the remote control.

It was around this time my old Prankster friend Lucy popped in and beautifully colored the evening from here on out — including her psychedelic perspective and big-picture grounding much later when the storyline changed.

Prior to election night, with the polls looking good, I was so convinced Hillary would win 322–216 that I drove nine hours to be at the party. I only qualified my optimism by saying, "I'll feel better when I start to see the first actual numbers come in around 7 or 8:00." And of course that's precisely when things started to look less than positive.

End of the day I only got 5 out of 53 calls wrong
— FL, PA, MI, NC & WI

I was interviewed by a ton of news organizations over the course of the night including *Time*, the *Guardian*, the *Boston Globe*, *Newsday* (by two different reporters), *W* (the fashion mag), the *Daily Beast*, the *Boston Daily Free Press*, *Fortune*, Chinese, Czech & Norwegian television, Italian & Portuguese print press . . . and just like in full regalia in '08 for Obama at NBC's Democracy Plaza, had my picture taken about a million times.

"Democracy isn't something you have, it's something you do," as the great political folk hero Granny D put it. Politics is not a spectator sport. And just as I was active and visible in person and online throughout the year of the primary and months of the general — election day & night is not a time to blend in but rather to dress up and rise up!

And talking to the hard working journalists of all stripes from all over the world who were out there racing against deadlines to get the story, I thought again about the ridiculous "mainstream media" haters from donald trump to the Berners who parrot the meme that everyone who's a reporter is part of some grand imaginary global conspiracy. Many of the press haters are the same people who consider themselves too "smart" to vote for Hillary Clinton or think that "it's all rigged." But of course most of them have never been in the presence of a Congressperson or working journalist in their lives — yet they know everything about the professions — and sound a lot like the Republican running for president.

And here we were surrounded by journalists — from print to television to web-based, from 20-somethings to septuagenarians, from New Jersey to China, from the time I arrived until the time I left around 1AM — all working their butts off to capture the moment and story.

Another of the early warning signs that things weren't going well came around 9:00 when a reporter asked me how I was holding up considering what was happening. "Why — what's happening?" I thought. I didn't know the depth of the bad news, so I improvised an answer about Democratic-leaning precincts not reporting yet, but could tell by her reaction that she knew something I didn't.

And another crazy part of the night was — the few people who got inside Javits figured they had the catbird seat. But the funny thing was, nobody including Hillary ever spoke to the crowd in there, and all the people like Katy Perry, Chuck Schumer & Andrew Cuomo who made appearances at the event did so at our little stage outside (!), which was broadcast onto the giant screens both inside and out. And being in the secret little enclave just beyond the stage, I was about 10 or 20 feet from all of them all night.

Senator Chuck Schumer

But even without us knowing the final outcome like I think some of the speakers already did, there was a distinctly perceptible inauthenticity in their voices as they said, "We're going to win!" to flag-waving cheers.

The information on the big screen was trickling in piecemeal. The newsdesk projections were regularly overridden by the speakers on the stage, and the hard numbers on the bottom of the screen were often blocked out by the closed-captioning, and I choose to Adventure without a phone to the internet, so it was hard to read the trajectory. But the numbers I managed to catch were not taking the upward turn they needed to be taking. Suddenly we were seeing 95% of Florida counted and Hillary was still behind by a bunch. Same in North Carolina. And PA.

All the states that I figured Trump would win, had already been called. But all the Hillary states were still "too close to call" ... and she was behind in most of them. There would be CNN's dramatic drumroll signaling a projection coming and I'd stop answering some journalist's question to listen ... and it was ... Connecticut! A state that's usually called at about 8:01 for the Democrats wasn't being "won" until 10 or 11 at night. And Florida was still about 100,000 votes in the wrong direction. And Virginia still wasn't locked up! And Trump had broken 200 electoral votes and Hillary was still lingering at about 109 or something.

"This isn't happening. . . . This can't be happening. . . . There's just no way." — as the numbers on the screen continued to not add up. "It's just not possible." But the crowd had quieted down. In fact, it was actually thinning out. "This isn't good."

The environmental journalist from *Grist* I'd been talking to was absolutely ashen. Other reporters along his fence line were calling out for me to come talk to them — wanting the raw grieving parent quote. I shook my head silently "no" and kept my face away from them — and went instead to my buddy Manuel from Switzerland who I'd met in line about eight hours earlier. He was solemn but sanguine — no horse in the race. But he was a calm familiar face and became something of a grounding touchstone.

I finally embarked on a recon mission around the site at 11:30 or 12 — for the first time braving the sardine crowd. But by now there was a single narrow one-body-wide path along the outer rail where a person could just squeeze through the football-field-length crowd stretching up the Avenue — and then it was open space to 40th Street, which was blocked off by a wall of dump-trucks to keep the bad-guys out.

I stopped at the porta-potties for a much-needed jazz cigarette break that was supposed to be the celebratory cigar after the victory but was now medicinally deployed. "I gotta change my way of thinking, make myself a different set of rules," Dylan started singing in my head. And just as I stepped out of the door a ways down the row, cops were beginning a sweep search of the johns starting at the far end! I felt like the guy stepping out of the Port-O-San in the *Woodstock* movie. "Outta sight, man!"

By the time I headed back through the crowd, the narrow squeeze-through path had grown wide enough to walk your dog. There'd been a steady flow of sad-faced souls streaming from the stage to the exit. When they'd passed over this same pavement in the opposite direction hours earlier they were in the opposite mood — from a celebratory birth day to a grieving funeral in a few hours.

When I got back to my grounding chair and Swiss

brother and tried to grasp reality, I felt like Mia Farrow in unscreamable horror in *Rosemary's Baby.* "This is really happening!"

Then one of the TV commentators said, "This is one of the biggest upsets in American political history."

Yeah, . . . see, now . . . that didn't help.

The crowd was thinning by the minute. What was once 5,000 people, was down to less than a thousand. Sometimes the big screen news channel would momentarily cut to the Trump event at the Hilton uptown and they were all partying like we were supposed to be — chanting, "Call Florida! Call Florida!" They were loud and crazy — and we were subdued and cold. "This ain't right." Having seen Victory Parties from both sides many times, I knew how this movie was gonna end.

Now what?

I sat in that chair for a long time unable to come up with any place in New York I wanted to be. I had no krewe anywhere. In fact, the only person I knew who was On The Beat was my Beat brother formerly known as Levi Asher ... who was already getting on a train home.

And that's just what I thought of doing. Getting the puck back to Canada. This town was already not feeling friendly before tonight kicked in. Now it was gonna get downright ugly. And I looked ridiculous. This was gonna be one helluva "walk of shame" home tonight — with a top hat and 97 buttons for the losing team. And there was nowhere to go. But home.

Trump was at 244. A state or two away from crossing the 270 victory line. Some people on both the screen and in person were saying there was still a chance. I didn't wanna walk out of the moment and miss the greatest comeback in history. I'd wander to the exit starting to leave ... then, "Holy shit — it's not over." . . . "Yeah ... get out of here ... this isn't happening." . . . "You'll regret it the rest of your life if you leave and she comes back and wins." . . . "The streets were really ugly already and I need to get off them before the hounds are unleashed." . . . back & forth until finally I split. And Swiss Manuel sent me off with, "You deserve your beer now," knowing my Canadian soul had been pining all night.

Some girl from some internet news station in China stopped me just outside the gates for one last interview. I agreed to a couple of questions, and while I was answering one of these same guido construction worker guys like the one who prayed I would die earlier, stopped behind her and glared at me with his arms flexing and his eyes bugging out like he wanted to punch the shit out of me right there. And as he lingered in red-eyed seething hate . . . I keep riffing for my life to the good people of China.

"It's pronounced 'Gina.'"

I'd only reached the borderline of the outside world — and this fist-clenching goombah was what it had already become.

Then it was out into the darkness of Port Authority Hell's Kitchen where the street lights were still blown out like it was the '70s — with nothing but scary nuthin-left-to-lose street people lurking in nightmarish midnight shadows. And I'm all velvet tails and Gatsby top hat with a coatful of buttons that say "mark"!

It was like leaving a Dead show in some strange city — where all night you're surrounded by people like your offbeat crazy colorful self . . . and then wander into

234

some ever-darkening streets that ain't like the world you're coming from at all.

And this is New York. This is my town. This is my home. And it's gone. First it was that rabid rat Giuliani — whose nickname in town was "Saddam Hussein." Then Joe Bruno ending rent control. Then the complete corporate Disneyfication of the whole city. And now the redneck racists have won the championship. They don't have to be polite no more. "It's clobbering time," The Things were saying.

And then right at this bizarre point ... well, as I had been answering the *Newsday* reporter Emily Ngo's question if I thought this result would happen, I said something like, "No. ... I'm not religious ... but there's *something*," and I looked up into the low lit-up clouds above Manhattan. "There's something. And whatever it is, I didn't think it would let this happen. There's just no way." And she was nodding and *so* getting it.

Whatever that thing is — he or she or it took the wheel at this point and I just went along for the crazy ride:

A split-second before swiping my card at the subway to head back to artist Aaron Howard's studio I heard a cop inside the station tell someone the A/C/E lines weren't running. So now I had to walk from 8th Avenue right through the madness of Times Square to get to the 6th Avenue lines. And I'm decked head-to-toe in losing Democrats — walking into "the crossroads of the world" where donald drumpf was now the proud flag-bearer of fuck-you.

But halfway there, this young blond-haired Swedish couple came walking towards me under the bright lights of 42nd Street — he wearing a blazing brand new blue

Henrik Lundqvist Rangers jersey — and as I smiled he said, "They tell everyone this is 'the city that never sleeps' — but everything is closed!" And he's right. New York is now a cartoon of its former self and it sucks. But I'm still a New Yorker, and we take pride in our city and don't want anyone to not have a good time, so suddenly it's my mission to do right by my Swedish Beat brother Johan Soderlund, and for all the great Swedish hockey players, and that admirable recycling-leading, socialist-leaning country whose whole vibe and color scheme I love, so I escorted them to O'Lunney's, the very first bar I ever looked into the window of in New York City — but this involved walking through the packed throngs of madness in Times Square, which is ABC's headquarters, where they'd built an outdoor studio for the night.

And it was just packed . . . with very dark energy . . . and I think of what this was like at this same time eight years ago . . . and *man* is it different! If not for the Swedish couple I never would have seen the contrast between Times Square when it was like the Rangers winning the Stanley Cup on Obama's victory night versus now with George Wallace realizing his racist dream.

Continuing to 6th Avenue I looked in car windows and saw women blankly staring in stunned shock. "This isn't good." Walking south down dark 6th Avenue looking for a deli beer to merge with my coffee cup prop, some guidos — and don't get me wrong, I *love* Italians, and was effectively happily married to one for six years — but there's a whole ugly side to that culture that was coming out on this day in spades, as I'm sure they'd love to phrase it. And as I walked down the shadowy Avenue in the abandoned 30s a few of them got out of an SUV and were eyeing me with this vicious "I wanna fuckin' kill you" look on their faces.

Once on the subway — take 2 — the train somehow skipped 14th Street where I needed to transfer and suddenly I was at West 4th in the Village — my home stop for my first eight years in Manhattan. For some reason I'd been transported to my old home base. "Why are the Fates putting me here?" I was happily headed to Aaron's and maybe the highway to Canada an hour ago. And now two different transportation alterations brought me to my original New York "home."

Greenwich Village post-trump. At least I knew I was safe in heaven alive (to riff on that great Village-mate, Kerouac).

Of course I went straight to the Kettle of Fish, but for once it was not a happy place. Even the owner's home state of Wisconsin hadn't gone our way. And it also wasn't a political hotbed like it had been when Norman Mailer ran for mayor and used its former incarnation The Lion's Head as his campaign headquarters.

So I continued back into the streets — where people were in shock. We just looked at each other and made the tiniest gestures of acknowledgment. As another Beat brother Tim Moran observed the next day — there was a silence on the streets not heard here since 9/12. Or as another New Yorker put it: 9/11 = 11/9.

I thought of the night the Mets won the World Series in '86 when I hosted a huge party right there on Washington Square North and how we poured into these same streets full of dancing screaming singing joy as we were supposed to be in right now. But tonight tumbleweeds and depression were blowing down Fifth Avenue.

When I finally got to the L train platform, a 20-something German girl was sitting on the stairs staring into the distance freaking out. When the train came, a middle-aged woman was crying uncontrollably. When we got to the next stop, two different groups of young politically-centric people got on — and immediately merged into one. When they saw me pouring another Heineken into a coffee cup, they toasted me and offered brandy from a flask. And at the end of the car ... two homeless people slept.

Whatever-the-hell happened tonight ... you're probably sleeping in a more comfortable bed than a subway car. As bad as you think things are, you're alive, you have people who love you, and a million blessings all around you, and you're functioning, and can still make a difference.

You can still be kind to strangers, you can still do the work you were put here to do, you can still be "a warrior" as Ken Kesey called us fighters, and you can still be part of the solution.

Van Gogh didn't topple a government, Abbie Hoffman didn't die in vain, John Lennon never remained silent, and neither should you.

This is the only shot each of us is going to get on this run,
So may as well leave the bleachers, and Get Things Done.
If you wanna ditch the darkness and dance in the sun,
I'll see you on the field where it's way more fun.

The Ballad of The Profiteers

You're suckin' on / your money's teat
When nothin's left / for folks to eat
You're livin' high / down on Wall Street
Crushin' dreams / beneath your feet

How come it is / and why it's not
The biggest thieves / are never caught
When all you are / is what you bought
And what's inside / just ain't a lot

You're singin' the Ballad of the Profiteers
Sailing a yacht on a river of tears
Scorchin' the Earth for all these years
You're the skill-less, soul-less profiteers

You don't make a thing / 'cept for money
You don't find anything / to be that funny
Your only friend / is a hired bunny
And you're drownin' *alone* / in your milk & honey

Selfish is / as shameless does
And profits are / your only buzz
You cast aside / whatever was
You have no love / and all because . . .

You're singin' the Ballad of the Profiteers
Sailing a yacht on a river of tears
Screwin' us all for too many years
You're the skill-less, soul-less profiteers

You'd push your mother / down a hole,
If it added to / your bankroll;
You're all fluffed up / like a perfumed troll
That thinks it scored / The Golden Goal

Life don't start / on Monday morn
It began on the day / when you were born
When you looked outside / with so much scorn
Then skipped the dance / with The Golden Horn

cuz ...
You're singin' the Ballad of the Profiteers
Sailing a yacht on a river of tears
Fuckin' us over all these years
You're the skill-less, soul-less profiteers

repeat as needed

Introduction
to This Year's Battle

by
Kenneth Aloysius Morris

Wow! Brian Hassett is finally putting out the Big Book of Politics. Wow! ... again!

Of all the things he & I have connected on in the past several years — Kerouac, the Beats, Kesey & the Pranksters, the sixties, music — then there's politics ... POLITICS!!!

It's that red button subject we can never shake, especially in these trying times that test men's souls. And as Allen Ginsberg proved when the talk has to be the walk, nothing is as important as politics when one wants to be understood, when one wants passions to be law, and when change (however slow) has to be dealt with. Allen knew a line must be drawn in the sand in order that certain inalienable freedoms should be preserved. And in his and our lifetime — battles for gay rights, dissolution of censorship, marijuana legalization, preservation of the arts, amongst others — a proactive & energetic front must always be vigorously maintained 24/7, 365. Otherwise, the idiots run the show and pass policy. Certainly this is no way for a poet to remain above the fray? Ha.

And for many of us entering the last third of our lives, and those who have lost more than won in this game of politics, we remain steadfastly passionate, skeptical yet positive, defiantly pragmatic, with that built-in "never suffer fools" defense that allows for continuous battles to educate, advocate, and grind "grass-roots" for the policies & candidates that appeal to our heads & hearts.

One thing Brian Hassett and I have consistently espoused is the idea that democracy is always a participatory sport. Citizenship demands your input. And that means politics. And that means voting and working on campaigns and never missing an election. And that means staying educated about candidates, policy and events that influence campaigns, and keeping others informed.

I cannot think of a better guide, storyteller and raconteur to provide more than enough recollections, anecdotes, larger-than-life personalities that explain politics, and will keep it interesting, always amusing, and never boring. Sometimes it takes an expatriate (Canadian) to offer new insight into the machinations of the everyday that is politics. Think of a new century Alistair Cooke, without the accent & formality, with more tie-dye & flowing locks, to unlock the real joy of a ride that us political junkies enjoy.

Enjoy The Hassett Ride. It's never a disappointment from my "Gets Things Done" compadre & Brother.

2020

Vote Blue No Matter Who

"Vote blue no matter who."

What beautiful poetry to start the year. Some put it — "Any blue will do," . . . or "Vote blue, do not renew" — but however you wanna rhyme it, it's music to our years.

For me, picking a candidate in the primary is like choosing something on a menu at a great restaurant. You're gonna like whatever you order. And there's no sense in getting upset about a tablemate making a different choice.

Of the 26 candidates who ran for the Democratic nomination, I immediately went for **Elizabeth Warren**. Forgetting about playing pundit and trying to game out who could slay the Trumpenstein monster — when I just closed my eyes and pictured who I'd most like to see behind the Resolute desk in the Oval Office cleaning up this mess, it was Gets Thing Done Warren. She's articulate and energetic and smart and I've loved her in every interview I'd ever seen her do over many years, going back long before she ran for the Senate. She took on the predatory lending of the big banks, which I think is the worst mass crime committed in America in my lifetime — these soulless unregulated profiteer banks conning poor people into mortgages they knew they couldn't maintain just so they could take their homes for their own profit and ruin millions of families lives and dreams forever. I wanted all those bastards in jail for life — and so did this feisty kick-ass woman.

Plus, she was the person who came up with the idea of a Consumer Financial Protection Bureau, and when Obama & Company made it happen, the repulsive Repugnant Senators were so scared of the little firebrand who actually wanted to make a difference and protect poor people from criminal predators, they wouldn't allow her to be appointed the head of the very organization she caused to be founded. So what did she do? She ran for Ted Kennedy's old seat in Massachusetts that had temporarily and embarrassingly been filled by the vacuous former model Scott Brown. Warren whooped his ass in 2012 and put Ted's old seat back in Democratic hands, and put herself in the Senate with the very pricks who had denied her her rightful job as the head of the agency.

There are few people in Congress who are as well versed in the details of financial legislation — and nobody who is as passionate and clearly communicative when talking about it. She embraced many of the same ideas as Bernie Sanders that I liked, but didn't come with the angry wacko Bro baggage of cultish supporters. She seemed perfect and obvious, and it was a woman who almost won for the first time last election. Well, Hillary did win the most votes, of course — in fact the most votes ever cast for any Presidential candidate in American history not named Barack Obama — but wouldn't that be something if we could nominate a woman who didn't come with *Hillary's* baggage!

Plus, once she got into the race, she reminded me of *me* on stage. Wiry – energetic – pacing around – boppin' up and down – could barely hold her own exploding energy together. And she kinda looks like my mom! And has her same kind of take-no-guff, stand-up-for-herself, take-charge personality. So, with all the candidates in the field, she seemed like the obvious first choice to me. And then she took off in the early polls! She even, for about a day in October, passed frontrunner Joe Biden into first place in the RCP average! Was I gonna continue my recent streak of backing winners after backing in my first four presidentials Gary Hart, Jesse Jackson, Paul Tsongas and Howard Dean? I got behind Obama early and enthusiastically in 2008, then Hillary in '16 — was I actually gonna pick three primary winners in a row?! All of her speeches and all of her TV appearances were killer — she's smart and funny and knowledgeable — and she had this catchphrase of "I've got a plan for that" that sounded like my kinda candidate. She was a lot like Paul Tsongas — another Massachusetts Senator — in how she actually put her plans in writing. This is the kind of person I want to be president.

And in all the early debates she never took the bait to attack another Democrat and was riding majestically above the fray. Then she had that great answer in a town hall to some guy in the audience asking, "Senator, my faith teaches me that marriage is between one man and one woman." And she responded, "Then just marry one woman. I'm cool with that." And after the whoops died down, she added, "Assuming you can find one."

BOOM!

And I love that she held one of her biggest rallies in

my former front yard — with 20,000 people in Washington
Square Park — on the edge of where I was born as a political
person at the Gary Hart rally in 1984. Edgar Allen Poe,
Mark Twain & Eugene O'Neill all roamed there, the Beats
hung there, Bob Dylan, Pete Seeger, John Sebastian &
countless others played there, labor union and suffragette
protests took place there, Obama held one of his biggest
rallies there in 2007, as did Bernie in 2016, so it holds a
sacred place in the cultural / political history of America —
and her going there was harmonically in the continuum.

Everything was falling into place for my nominee . . .
until the December debate when out of the blue she started
attacking Mayor Pete Buttigieg over some fundraiser he
attended in a "wine cave" — suddenly thrusting that term
into the national consciousness. It was so uncalled for and
out of character for her. And it went against everything
I liked about her. It was petty, mean, out of place, and
misguided — and Mayor Pete slayed her with his comeback
pointing out he was the only non-millionaire on the stage,
and that she shouldn't be "issuing purity tests that you
yourself cannot pass."

The air kind of went out of the balloon for me in that
moment. I'll vote blue no matter who in November, and
campaign like hell for whomever the nominee is up to then,
but after that debate moment I no longer had a candidate.

I've liked **Bernie Sanders** more on the stump
since he came back from his early October heart attack. He
seemed lighter of spirit, easier to laugh and quicker to toss
off a one-liner. He's massively popular, especially among
my friends, and has got more total campaign contributors
than any presidential candidate in American history (over

5 million at press time) — but I just feel like he's yelling at me all the time — like I've done something really wrong and my dad is letting me have it. For 45 minutes. That the quintessential curmudgeon Larry David plays him on *Saturday Night Live* is perfect and telling.

I don't know what kind of an epiphany he had after the heart attack, but he seems like a changed man — as much as a 78-year-old can change. And damned if his poll numbers didn't start to go up!

He has regular rational supporters who calmly say that he's their first choice, and of course they'll support wholeheartedly whoever the nominee is. But sadly there's also the rabid Bernie Bros & Brats who scream at everyone that they alone know everything cuz they saw it on a meme and if they don't get everything 100% their way they're gonna burn down the country and blame it on Hillary Clinton. Adult level-headed Sanders supporters need to be stepping up and tamping down the tantrums their less mature cohorts are throwing — because Bernie's only giving it lip-service. The problem's so obvious that *SNL* wrote it into a February 2020 sketch with Larry David saying, "I don't know how or why it happened, but I'm the king of an army of internet trolls called Bernie Bros. Could I stop them in their tracks? Of course. Should I? Yes. Will I? Meh."

If Bernie extremists spend 2020 the way they did 2016 joining with Republicans tearing down Democrats, we may very well end up with the same horrific result in November. But if Bernie can keep up his Incredible Lightness of Being and win more people over and get the worst of his frothing supporters to stop behaving like trump cultists, maybe something good can come of this.

I'll vote blue no matter who, but I'm concerned about

him getting the nomination, because, to riff on a Romney-ism, there are *binders* full of opposition research on him that have never been utilized. Trumpovich got himself impeached trying to stop Joe Biden — he wasn't trying to stop Bernie Sanders. A GOP strategist I greatly respect, Rick Wilson, author of *Everything Trump Touches Dies* and *Running Against The Devil*, and who, along with George Conway, Steve Schmidt & others, formed The Lincoln Project, a group of Republicans working as hard to defeat the sitting Racist-in-Chief as any Democrat, said in a January 2020 *Salon* interview that "Bernie Sanders is Donald Trump's election insurance. He is every cliché ever in the history of the free shit movement. Republicans will turn Bernie into the worst

caricature you've ever seen. He is the scary old socialist figure of their nightmares. But in this case, it's not fake. He's actually that guy. He's got an unbelievably thick oppo file. They're salivating over this guy. I still talk to guys in the mafia, the Republican mafia, and they're working their hardest to make sure Bernie's the nominee. They *want* Bernie to be the nominee. Bernie will lose every single state south of the Mason-Dixon Line, no questions asked, including Florida. And you can't lose Florida."

So there's that.

My concern is that he wins Iowa and New Hampshire, then starts to lose, including big on Super

Tuesday, then his cultist wing goes on a rampage that it's all a conspiracy because *they* like him therefore everybody else must, and 2016 will start all over again. Their zealotry does not bring in a single new supporter to Bernie's camp — it's a counterproductive circle jerk sneering at everyone else. It's such a crime that this candidate's life's work may forever have in the first paragraph of his biography these hate-spewing conspiracy Bros.

And then there's Mayor Who? I mean, **Mayor Pete**. No, I *do* mean Mayor Who. Who is this guy and where did he come from? I know — South Bend, Indiana — but what a wonderful come-outta-nowhere story it is for him to validly earn his way into the top tier of candidates in a field full of nationally known figures. Like Liz, he's articulate and thoughtful and can think on his feet, and is personable, and seems kind, and I agree with him on just about everything from prison reform to raising the minimum wage to getting rid of the electoral college to repealing the Repugnant 2017 corporate tax giveaway. Maybe he can even be the gay guy to break the ceiling like Obama did for African-Americans. But he's 37 years old. I'll enthusiastically support him if he wins the nomination, and he's sure made a name for himself and will probably be a factor in the Democratic Party long after I'm gone, but I have a hard time putting my chips on the young Mayor of South Bend as the guy who's going to bring down the monster in the White House. I can't see the blue collar voters we lost in Michigan, Wisconsin and Western Pennsylvania coming back into the fold to vote for a gay 30-something small town mayor for President.

In the Wild Card Department:

Former 3-term New York City Mayor **Michael Bloomberg** is actually a very philanthropic guy (the #1 in the world in 2019 according to the Chronicle of Philanthropy) and we're gonna be reading his name a lot in 2020. In the 2018 midterms he gave $110 million (!) to 24 House seats he figured had a chance of turning blue — and 21 of them flipped! He gave another $38 million to Everytown For Gun Safety to fight back against Murder Inc., aka the NRA. He's a staunch environmentalist and knows climate change is all too real. He was the United Nations' official climate envoy for years, and partnered with Jerry Brown on America's Pledge working with American businesses to meet the Paris Climate Accord goals. He's shut down fossil fuel plants, and bankrolls the Sierra Club's Beyond Coal campaign. When he was Mayor of New York City, he and Bette Midler started an initiative that ended up planting one million trees throughout the five boroughs.

The 9th richest person in the world didn't get in the race until November because he was planning to simply help the primary winner. But when no clear frontrunner emerged, he jumped in late. He's already committed to keeping a staff of 2,400 employed (and counting, and all with full benefits) through November to beat Trumpov in 2020 whether he gets the nomination or not. The dude puts his money where his mind is. I'm not saying he will, or even should, get the nomination — but he's going to be a major player in 2020.

He was a lifelong Democrat who only ran for the Republican mayoral nomination because he could get it — then governed as a Democrat. I went into his campaign office during his first mayoral campaign, and after looking around with some hesitation, finally said a staffer, "I've never been in a Republican's campaign office before in my life." And the three people sitting behind the table laughed and said they were all Democrats and never had either.

Michael Bloomberg may actually end up being the difference in the outcome of 2020.

Yep.

The guy who made a global fortune analyzing financial data has created his own private political data analytics firm called Hawkfish that by all accounts is the most advanced in the world, and he'll be using it to help us beat Twitler — a person he dislikes even more than you do. Hawkfish is an umbrella entity that does everything from advanced analytics for ad placements and voting demographics to content creation and messaging. Through November he's going to use his database science, obvious political savvy (see what he did in 2018), and a General's strategic read of the battlefield to deploy ads and ground game personnel and whatever other resources he's sees as needed in the places he sees them needed. He was 21 for 24 in the 2018 House seats he worked. Plus he has the money to do things neither the DNC or any of the candidates can afford to do — like running ads during the Super Bowl.

Hillary and the Dems were historically disastrously unstrategic and unaware in 2016. Hillary's "never visited Wisconsin" will be forever tattooed to her and her campaign. That race should never have been lost to a sociopathic neophyte — and it was everything from messaging to vision to ground game that she and her campaign couldn't do remotely right. So, whomever Dem voters nominate, there's going to be a separate campaign being waged by somebody who can afford to wage it. And it wouldn't take much to do it better than Hill & the Dems did in 2016.

And then there's ol' **Amy Klobuchar** from Minnesota, the state that is most like my native Manitoba — Midwestern practicality and politeness, with a quirky sense of humor, a strong work ethic, and an appreciation for nature. She'd been dropping hints about running for a long time, and as much as I like her having all the Minnesota qualities I mentioned, I just didn't think she had the stage presence or "vision thing" to catch on.

I'm loving the Democratic Party's debate inclusion criteria — and how its entry minimum generally ticks up one percentage point for each successive debate. If you've been campaigning for a year and are at 2% in the polls there's no reason you should crowd the stage with the candidates who can garner at least 5 damn percent. It's not too much to ask.

That Klobuchar is still making the cut as Iowa and New Hampshire get underway is a happy surprise. She stands for basically every bedrock Democratic principal but without the pie-in-the-sky Free Ponies For Everyone baloney — as befitting her Midwestern practicality. I love that she does not attack other candidates, and is sometimes the adult in the room on the debate stage. People keep citing her as a solid VP choice, and that seems right to me. But I'm not sure if she has the tenacity to rip the heart out of The Orange Beast. She seems to have echoes of her fellow Minnesotan Walter Mondale — solid, middle-of-the-road, honest — but she doesn't have that natural star quality of grabbing the microphone and taking over a room. She's sort of the *Twenty Feet From Stardom* candidate.

254

And even further from the stardom spotlight is the improbable campaign of **Andrew Yang** — a guy *nobody* had heard of a year ago. He's probably got the best sense of humor of any candidate in the race — which may explain why some of the funniest dudes in America like Dave Chappelle and Norm Macdonald have endorsed him. When he first appeared on *The Daily Show,* Trevor Noah opened with, "Of all the candidates I've seen on the trail, you seem to be having the most fun," to which Yang said, "That's a very low bar you've set," and Trevor's face hit the desk laughing.

He's a natural in front of a crowd and really knows how to work a room from stage — exactly what I was saying Amy isn't a natural at. He started out with some crazy plan to give every American adult $1000 a month for life, but has since gotten much deeper on Medicare-for-all, and is big on using more efficient technology to combat climate change and to institute automatic voter registration, and like Klobuchar and all the others he's a basic bedrock Democrat, and like a successful CEO he's also a problem solver. As a Yang Gang friend of mine, Brad Verebay, said, "I respect the way he approaches a problem. He's the only politician I've heard that zooms out far enough to see the roots of problems. I want that kind of brain in the office." And like all the candidates I've mentioned above — Andrew Yang is going to be a permanent fixture in the American political landscape going forward.

And that brings us to **Joe Biden** . . . the frontrunner since he declared in April. I remember on Obama's first Inauguration Day on the drive from the Capitol to the White House, people-person Joe jumped out of the limo and ran over to the crowd along the sidewalk with the biggest grin on his face, shaking hands like mad! Justin Trudeau in Canada is sorta the same way — he just loves meeting people and goes down into the subway and greets commuters just for the hell of it. I thought watching Joe's actions that day — "This guy's gonna be the most popular Vice-President in history!" I don't know if he was or not, but he was sure a smart choice by Obama, or, "a big fucking deal," to put it in his words.

History will forever record Biden as the highest ranking government official to publicly come out in favor of same sex marriage when he just blurted it out on *Meet The Press* one Sunday (May 6th, 2012) — and then the Prez followed his Veep three days later.

He often gets slammed by those on the extreme left for not being "progressive" enough, but he now stands for many of the same things Bernie, Liz & most others do — eliminating private prisons and mandatory sentencing, overturning Citizens United, preserving a woman's right to choose, protecting the environment, expanding Obamacare not destroying it, expanding Medicare, decriminalizing marijuana and voiding prior convictions, increasing taxes on corporations and the ultra rich, and so on.

And something must be said about cherry-picking individual votes on different bills passed by Congress. 1) the political climate for what's possible to get something through Congress changes as history unfolds. And 2) a bill may have something in it that you or I oppose, but it may also have something in the same bill that you or I support. That's the nature of writing legislation and passing legislation, and how government works. You see it in every election cycle where some candidate gets attacked for some vote at some point in their history, but there could be a lot of stuff in that same bill that the attacking person actually supports, and the time it was passed is now a time long passed.

"Don't Ask, Don't Tell," signed into law by Bill Clinton in 1994 is a great example of this. It's now sometimes criticized for not being accepting enough of gay rights, but in 1993/94, it was a positive breakthrough for gay rights. Prior to that, for all of U.S. history, anyone found to be gay in the military would automatically get an undesirable or dishonorable discharge. This bill stopped that. Officers couldn't ask, and as long as soldiers didn't "tell" they could continue to serve honorably. With this in place, and as our society continued to evolve on the matter, eventually the bill got challenged on the grounds that soldiers should be able to "tell" and be themselves, and by the time Obama was President it was repealed and gay soldiers could serve openly. So, when someone's been serving in government as long as Joe Biden has (nearly a half-century) there are going to be moments where something that was done decades ago seems wrong today, but it was right at the time, and it's the natural evolution of societies and governance. Abraham Lincoln initially resisted outright emancipation of "the colored race" before he wrote his famous Proclamation. Marijuana was illegal everywhere in the U.S. when The Beatles first admitted they smoked it — and now it has anywhere from outright to partial legalization in 47 states. Our society and governance evolves, as do our candidates for elected office, and ancient individual votes should not be held against someone any more than ancient essays in alternative newspapers should.

My concern is that Biden may be more Walter
Mondale / Mike Dukakis than Barack Obama / Bill Clinton.
And is it just me, or do Joe and Bernie seem too old
. . . and Pete and Yang too young? Do I suffer from Perfect
Candidate Syndrome like so many other Damn Democrats?
Am I being sexist for not embracing more age-appropriate
Midwestern Amy? I don't know, but Biden would be 78
when he started the hardest job in the world, and Bernie
would be 79. That would be nearly 10 years older than the
current sociopath and the prior out-of-touch conservative
blowhard Ronald Rayguns.

So I circled back to Liz — and there she was on TV
smiling away, bright eyed and feisty tailed, articulate and
fired up, talking about responsible taxation of billionaires
and corporations, and citing the Women's March the day
after Pussy Grabber was inaugurated, the largest single
protest rally in all American history, and how women
showed up in 2018 making it the highest percentage
Midterm turnout in over a hundred years.

And I looked again at Bernie and remembered how
he won swing state Wisconsin over Hillary by a lot, and
Michigan by enough. Those are the very states we need to
win back, and in 2016 they chose the radical socialist over
the conventional Hillary/Biden. And then I see him rising
in the polls, and how every article from on the ground in
Iowa and New Hampshire tell the same story of him having
by far the biggest and most enthusiastic crowds of any of the
candidates.

And I circle back around to Joe being frank and
candid and sometimes funny answering town hall questions
with nuts & bolts answers about closing specific corporate

tax loopholes to pay for free community college, and reminding people for his entire career he was listed as the poorest man in the United States Congress, and how he's released the last 20 years of his tax returns if you don't believe him — and just watching him interact with voters one-on-one he reminds me of how Bill Clinton was so comfortable with rank & file citizens, how neither of them were born silver spoon millionaires. And I'm reminded how this average Joe is just a damn decent man.

There's that old political truism that people want a presidential candidate they would feel comfortable sitting down and having a beer with — and gawd, I'd love to do that with any of these top three. Or Amy or Pete or Andrew. I'm not sure if Mike would be much of a party, but sometimes appearances can be deceiving. As I recounted in the 2016 Repugnant convention section [part 5] the seemingly dour David Frum was the most animated fun guy when he was off camera. Maybe Mike's a real pisser when he's off the clock — he does have a real skill at dry comic delivery from the stage when he wants to.

Despite these ugly times perpetuated by an ugly man in the White House, we are living through a glorious period in human history, politically and otherwise.

It's so much easier to learn so much more about every candidate and every issue in 2020 than it ever has been in history — and you don't even have to crack a book. But I'm glad you did this one. No candidate is perfect just like no human is perfect. And the history books paint beautiful portraits of JFK and Lincoln and Jefferson . . . but that was before every news article and opinion piece ever printed about them was instantly accessible on a rectangle in your hand.

People talk about how Facebook and Twitter are such big factors in the election, but I find myself using YouTube even more. With its Filter option, you can put in any candidate's name and just see what they've been up to in the "Last hour" or "Today" or "This week" or whatever. You can see them actually talking an hour ago, not just some meme or 140 character postcard or some basement blogger's rant.

And now a word about The Whole Primary Thing . . .

There's long been a debate about whether to change the order of the first four primary states. I understand the argument — Iowa and New Hampshire are too homogeneously white and not necessarily representative of the nation as a whole — but both are swing states, and there's an important advantage to doing the first contests in smaller states where money is less of a factor, and on-the-ground connecting with voters is how you win them. But the screw-up in Iowa counting their caucus votes in 2020 may have put the final nail in them holding the lead-off position.

Nevada & South Carolina have been third & fourth the last three primaries, which adds a Western state with an Hispanic population, and a Southern state with African-Americans, so that seems reasonable and logical. Maybe the Western state could be switched to neighboring Arizona — more of a swing state but with a similar diverse demographic — and maybe it should be North Carolina in the South cuz it's more of a swing state and the Dems always lose South Carolina by about 15 points so I don't know why we spend so much time and money there. Both would be better spent laying the foundation in a state we might actually win.

Or another idea I thought of — for each presidential primary we decide the first states and order is based on the closest contests in the previous election. Based on 2016, you could pick any four out of — Michigan (0.23% difference between Trump & Clinton) – New Hampshire (0.37%) – Pennsylvania (0.72%) – Wisconsin (0.77%) – Florida (1.2%) – Minnesota (1.52%) – Nevada – (2.42%) – Arizona (3.55%) – and North Carolina (3.66%).

If the Democratic nominee loses in November — twice in a row to an insane pathologically lying illiterate racist — then the party needs to look at making changes in how it comes up with a nominee and runs a general election.

For starters, we gotta get rid of **these stupid caucuses!** There are only 3 of the 50 states still doing them in 2020 (thank god) — Iowa, Nevada & Wyoming. They have NOTHING to do with our democracy. Americans don't vote for ANY elected official using a freakin' caucus system. Most people do not have multiple hours to spend sitting (or more often, *standing*) in one. And the people who do — retirees, students and the unemployed — are unfairly represented over people who can't afford babysitters, or who work evenings, or who have better things to do with their time than arguing with their neighbors about politics for hours on a freezing Monday in February. The people who participate in the Iowa caucus — or any caucus — are not representative of our voting citizenry and should not be used to determine a party's general election nominee any more than playing badminton.

In 2016, Iowa declared Romney the winner and Santorum 2nd, which basically ended the latter's surge. Then a week later they reversed the results and Santorum won but by then it was too late to save his campaign.

It really seems like Iowa being the first state may now be a part of history.

Another major change that's legislative and not up to the Democrats alone is **automatic voter registration**. Sixteen states and the District of Columbia already have it, and it should be everywhere.

Anybody can opt *out*, but everybody is automatically registered when they renew their driver's license or register with any number of other government agencies. The current address is automatically attached to the name; there's no voter registration forms to fill out or renew; it saves states money rather than having a separate department and system just for voter registration; it's more accurate because it's got the person's most recent legal address and info; it makes voting go smoother & faster at polling sites on Election Day; and it's been a huge success in the states where it's been implemented. Oregon saw voter registration quadruple, and Vermont's went up 62%, according to the Brennon Center for Justice that monitors this stuff.

It's worth noting that progressive Democratic-leaning states are where this logical fair simple democratic system is in place. California, Oregon, Washington, Nevada, Colorado, Illinois, Vermont, Massachusetts, Rhode Island, New Jersey, Maryland and a few others all have it now. It's pretty illustrative of how the two parties feel about people voting. Democrats want everybody to be able to vote; Republicans and their Heritage Foundation-type cronies want to make it harder.

The Repugnant Liar-in-Chief actually said publicly, repeating insane ultra-fringe conspiracy bullshit as one of his 18,000-and-counting lies he's told since taking office — "People get in line that have absolutely no right to vote, and they go around in circles. Sometimes they go to their car, put on a different hat, put on a different shirt, come in and vote again." (!)

And then there's **mail-in voting**. Colorado, Oregon and Washington all do it very efficiently already. States don't have to rent locations and hire massive numbers of staff at polling sites; it eliminates everything from waiting in line to human error to the weather or a virus affecting turnout; and creates a paper trail for every vote. Seems like a no-brainer, but one party opposes it. Can you guess which one?

And then there's **gerrymandering!** Don't get me started! Gerrymandering is when state legislatures redraw House districts to benefit their own party by roping as many opposition voters as they can into a single district and then slicing up the whole rest of the pie for themselves. To be fair, both parties have done it, but again you can guess which one does it more and wants to keep it.

The term, if you don't know, came from Massachusetts Governor Elbridge Gerry, who, in 1812, approved a state Senate district in the shape of a salamander — which prompted the term "Gerry-mander."

Also, we're all pronouncing it wrong. Elbridge Gerry and his family pronounce the last name like "Gary" not "Jerry." In fact, the decedents still say it that way. What happened was, the term caught on in political reporting in the early 1800s, and because this was before radio nobody could *hear* the word, and people read it in print all over the country and pronounced it "Jerry," and by the time it got back to Massachusetts, there wasn't much the Gerrys could do about it.

> And parenthetically, speaking of language,
> you know how political discourse is
> particularly coarse and crude these years?
> Many think that back in the olden days
> it was much more civil. But it wasn't. In
> all the 1800s elections I've read about,
> the newspapers were full of extreme
> commentaries and biting cartoons.
> There have always been the comedic
> equivalents of Bill Maher or Andy Borowitz
> or Tom Toles drawing or writing for the
> newspapers all over the country — as
> well as the most vicious op-eds you can
> imagine. So, yeah, it's bad now, but it's
> not like politics were exactly saintly back
> in the day.

Sadly, even with a disparaging "gerrymandering" moniker, the ugly practice has progressed to an absurd extreme. This isn't accepted or practiced to the American degree in any other democracy in the world. Where I currently live in Canada, the population of my town grew in the last census, meriting a second district. So what did they do? They just drew a straight line through the center of town.

Everyone should be aware of this problem and support anything in your state to end it. Only five states have thus far turned the job over to nonpartisan commissions — California, Washington, Idaho, Arizona & New Jersey — and five states only have one district/ Representative so there's no districting — Montana, Wyoming, North & South Dakota, and Vermont — so if your state's name is not in those two groups, your democracy is being stolen and you oughta be pissed off about it and support whatever local candidate wants to fix it.

There are a few national organizations that are working to reform these laws, like the Campaign Legal Center and FairVote, but the Supreme Court gutlessly failed to step in and rule on it in two cases challenging the obvious crime against democracy in Maryland and Wisconsin. Now is the time to raise your voices and actions to get reforms in your state before the next redistricting in 2021 (after the 2020 census). Know where your local state representatives stand on this matter and vote according. And loudly. Between 70%–80% of Americans polled want this fixed so it's not that radical an idea to talk about with your friends.

And besides gerrymandering and the electoral college, something else the nation builders of America got wrong as evidence in the 21st century shows — in the Senate races of 2018, Democrats got 20% more votes (58%– 38%) yet lost two seats while the Republicans gained two.

In the last three Senate cycles — therefore counting all the votes for all 100 current senators — Democrats got a total of 125 million votes, and Republicans got 100. By that metric, the Dems should be holding 56 seats to the Republicans 44 — rather than the current 53 – 47 for the Republicans. In both the most recent Senate races, as well as the Senate as whole, the American voters' will is not being represented.

And the same with the presidency, as I'm sure you know. The person who is currently "President" actually got *3 million less votes* than the person he was running against. In fact, Republicans have lost the popular vote in six of the last seven presidential elections. This is not democracy.

In The Illustrative Joke Department:

What do you call "the popular vote" in other countries?

The vote.

As Ezra Klein points out in his 2020 book *Why We're Polarized*, the Supreme Court has now had two appointments in just this term by a person who lost the vote of Americans. So — all three branches of government — the Congress, the White House, and the Supreme Court — are being run by the party who lost the popular vote in elections.

That should be a wake-up call for all of us — particularly on the left. We need to come together and stop the in-fighting and embrace our diversities. As Klein also points out so accurately:

> "Democrats are a coalition of liberal whites, African-Americans, Hispanics, Asians and mixed-race voters. Republicans are overwhelmingly dependent on Christian voters. Democrats are a coalition of liberal and nonwhite Christians, Jews, Muslims, New Agers, agnostics, Buddhists and so on. . . . Winning the Democratic primary means

winning liberal whites in New Hampshire and traditionalist blacks in South Carolina. It means talking to Irish Catholics in Boston and atheists in San Francisco. It means inspiring liberals without arousing the fears of moderates. . . . To win power, Democrats don't just need to appeal to the voter in the middle. They need to appeal to voters to the right of the middle. If Republicans couldn't fall back on the distortions of the Electoral College, the geography of the United States Senate, and the gerrymandering of House seats — if they had, in other words, to win over a majority of Americans — they would become a more moderate and diverse party."

He goes on in a *New York Times* January 2020 op-ed:

"A democratization agenda isn't hard to imagine. We could do away with the Electoral College and gerrymandering; pass proportional representation and campaign finance reform; make voter registration automatic and give Washington, D.C., and Puerto Rico the political representation they deserve. But precisely because the Republican Party sees deepening democracy as a threat to its future, it will use the power it holds to block any moves in that direction."

And he goes on to point out that, following current

population trends, by 2040, 70% of America's population will be in 15 states.

> *"That means 70 percent of America will be represented by only 30 senators, while the other 30 percent of America will be represented by 70 senators.* It is not difficult to envision an America where Republicans consistently win the presidency despite rarely winning the popular vote, where they typically control both the House and the Senate despite rarely winning more votes than the Democrats, where their dominance of the Supreme Court is unquestioned and where all this power is used to buttress a system of partisan gerrymandering, pro-corporate campaign finance laws, strict voter identification requirements, and anti-union legislation that further weakens Democrats' electoral performance."

This is what we're facing.

And by "we" I mean everyone on the left. If we continue to factionalize and fight within our family rather than uniting and accepting that there can be Catholics and atheists within the same collective, Bernie supporters and Biden supporters, Michael Bloombergs and Tulsi Gabbards, DNC loyalists and independents — if we don't see ourselves as all part of the same expansive open inclusive assemblage of left-leaning Americans,

we are doomed to a future, both immediate and long-term, of an extremist right-wing minority dominating the laws imposed upon us all.

If you think trump's good for the country, and the 2016 election results were just fine, and the senate impeachment trial was handled responsibly, and Brett Kavanaugh is the kind of person you want to see on the Supreme Court, then by all means keep tearing down anyone on the left that you disagree with. But if you'd like to change the sinking Titanic direction of this great country, it might be an idea to remember where the problem lies and who your teammates are, no matter the specific shade of blue of the jersey they're wearing.

We need as many people rowing towards the future as we can get.

Fun & Loving on the Campaign Trail 2020

A Prankster's Primary

The obvious thing to do was — go to New Hampshire! It's not too far from my current CentCom homebase outside Toronto, and I'd done it once already during the historic 2004 campaign when I was all wrapped up in the Howard Dean campaign. [see 2004 section starting on page 67]

New Hampshire is a fantastic state for a whole bunch of reasons. It's New England, which, along with the West Coast, are my two favorite parts of America. It's the land of writers for a reason. It has history. And gorgeous architecture —from the big ornate Victorian and Tudor homes to the grand granite turret municipal buildings. And it has a really small population — barely over a million in the whole state. The biggest town, Manchester, is only 110,000 people, which is half the size of the small town in

Canada where I live. In fact, it's so small the whole state still only has one area code!

I figured in early January I'd already missed my chance — that every hotel room in the sparse state would already be booked by the many campaigns and the masses of media — but on a whim I emailed my good Kerouac friend there, the Reverend Steve Edington, who's been basically running the Lowell Celebrates Kerouac Festival for about 25 years. Nashua was where Jack's family lived before they moved 20 miles down the road to Lowell where Jack was born & raised. His parents, brother and daughter are all buried in the Kerouac family plot in Nashua. The town is built at the confluence of the mighty Merrimack and smaller Nashua Rivers, the former of which is also the central artery of Lowell and Kerouac wrote about it in every book set there. So I got in touch with my ol' Jackster homie, and sure as heck he had a home for a me!

I got there early — on Monday February 3rd, the day of the Iowa caucuses — knowing all the candidates and media would still be in the Midwest and I could get grounded before the circus came to town. I also thought maybe I could rack off seeing one of the smaller candidates not ensconced in the distant farmlands, and sure enough, **Deval Patrick** was appearing at the Nashua Public Library five minutes away! In fact, of the first eight candidates I went to hear, the furthest I ever drove was 20 minutes!

When I got there early like I always do for things of this nature, there was a New Hampshire Democratic Party meeting going on where they were discussing all sorts of issues from polling times and water pollution to how the gas tax was no longer bringing in enough revenue due to better fuel-efficiency and hybrid cars, and this was when I first encountered the ritual of arriving at a primary rally that would repeat itself at every one I attended for the next week.

There are staff and volunteers at the door who "check you in" — meaning you sign in with your email and cell phone number. One of the incredible things was — before you even got home from any rally you'd already received a message thanking you for coming and giving you some bullet points of the candidate's essence, and letting you know about other events, and how to sign up as a volunteer, and of course a button to click to contribute. Once you've signed in, they'd give you a button or sticker to indicate to the rest of the staff that you had indeed registered. It was a pretty slick operation.

Deval Patrick, the former two-term Governor of neighboring Massachusetts, is a smart, compassionate, former South Side of Chicago kid who was the first in his family to ever go to college, and graduated from Harvard no less.

In a room full of Democrats (well, about 50 by the time some left after the meeting) Deval spent the first 20 minutes with his stump speech then 40 minutes answering questions. This appearance structure would repeat itself with slight variations on the time split at every rally I'd attend, except for Bernie, who doesn't take questions or do a meet-n-greet. The candidate/performer (see, also, the 1984 Gary Hart chapter) delivers their set piece, then the fun for them is the improv of the questions. Deval was asked about how growing up on the South Side of Chicago informed his approach to politics (it made him stand up for himself, understand being the poor, and learn to build consensus), why he didn't get into the race sooner (his wife was diagnosed with cancer, but was now in remission), and how he could stand up to trump (because he succeed making Massachusetts better in all the ways trump hasn't in Washington).

After it was over, Deval just hung out at the front of the room and talked equally casually with a flaming transvestite with wild hair and a plaid-shirted truck driver with a thick Boston accent. I marveled at his ease of discourse, his genuine smile and warmth towards others, and his gentle playful nature. He looked over at me listening to him talk, and I must have had a pleasant visage as he smiled right at me while answering other people's questions.

He'd already talked about strengthening environmental regulations and enforcement — my #1 issue — so I asked him about marijuana, something that is still in flux in America, though his home state of Massachusetts had just full-on legalized it. He told me it was time to fully do that nationally, that he hadn't always been for it, but that the nation had evolved to the point where it should be. I like candidates who evolve as the nation does. It shows growth and open-mindedness and flexibility of thought.

Deval was super friendly, with an easy laugh, and when I asked for a picture together — the first of 9-out-of-9 candidate 2-shots I'd score — I stuck my hand out towards the camera, he blurted out, "Oh, how dramatic!" and we both laughed. This guy's alright with me.

After our time together, a young New England woman named Kennedy came up and asked if I would like to attend the big upcoming Democrats dinner on Saturday night as Deval's guest. I would go on to meet people from every other campaign except Tom Steyer's, and it was Deval Patrick's that was the most inviting and friendly to me. I went into New Hampshire a Liz Warren supporter and circled around the field and got to like every candidate and campaign, but the one that really reached out to me was Deval Patrick's, and not my beloved Liz or anyone else.

It made me think of the Brett Hull / Team USA story. The hockey player son of legend Bobby Hull was born in Canada but grew up in the States and was a dual citizen. Canadians have bitched for decades that he chose to play for the American team, but when he was first eligible for an international tournament he contacted both Team Canada and Team USA to let them know he was available. Team Canada never even got back to him — and Team USA asked him to join immediately. And this BH suddenly identified with that BH. I wanted to play for Team Warren — but they never asked me to join. Team Patrick signed me up as soon as they met me. So I will forever think very kindly of this man and his campaign.

~ = ~ = ~ = ~ = ~ * ~ = ~ = ~ = ~ = ~

The next day — Tuesday, February 4th, the day after the Iowa caucus vote-counting debacle — I pulled off three rallies — Biden, Tulsi & Amy.

The order I caught the candidates all week was in direct correlation to the order they appeared in Nashua. The whole primary in New Hampshire is the New Orleans Jazz Fest for politicos! All the best performers are playing all day long, every day, for a week! And the only challenge is figuring out which stage you wanna be at. :-)

For this 12 noon Joe Biden rally I got there at 11. This is key. Always arrive an hour early, wink-wink, jot a note.

There were already about a hundred people in line and I was busy making friends with everyone around me when across the frozen tundra came strolling the beaming face of Reverend Steve! It was the first time I laid eyes on my old Beat Brother in the primary palace. He was volunteering as a Canvas Captain for the Biden campaign, meaning he coordinated other volunteers in their door-knocking efforts for the Democratic frontrunner.

This was the morning after Iowa and the official results weren't known yet, but we knew ol' Joe didn't win. Yet everyone was in a positive mood. It was a smidge chilly, but a bright blue sky sunny day, and everyone was lining up for democracy in the optimism of the unknown — like the red carpet before the Oscars when everyone could still be a winner.

TV news crews with cameras and print reporters with
notebooks were wandering the line interviewing random
people, and eventually a stunning beauty pageant queen
with a camera crew in tow approached me. I asked where
she was from and she answered Boston as though I was
asking for her phone number. Allowing myself a follow-up,
I learned she was from Fox News and the on-air *Bombshell*
face made sense. She was sparkling her eyes and batting
her lashes at me in a routine she probably used every day
but I was happy to fall for.

Her name was Golly Fine — I mean Molly Line — and
even though she was a fox from Fox she was fully jamming
on what this abnormal Adventurer was on about, and we
talked and riffed about all sorts of things with the cameras
rolling. I later asked if it would air and she said it's all just
sent back to the news center and they decide what to do
with it. Not having a lot of friends who watch Fox, I never
heard if they ever showed it, but we had some fun in the
sun.

The best part was — she asked if I was happy with
the Democratic field, and I said, "Yeah, we're lucky," and I
reached out my left arm all the way. "We've got everybody
from Tulsi and Bernie," I said looking at my distant hand,
then extended my right all the way out the other way,
"To Biden or Bloomberg," and there I stood like a classic
Brian arms-extended photo for the rolling camera of Faux
Noise, holding the wide rainbow spectrum of Democratic
candidates, with me in the middle, which is pretty much
where I come down.

The rally was held in the big gymnasium of a Girls Inc.
building, a national organization founded back in the Civil
War to help girls and young women reach their potential.

As I got in, the third and final row of seats was empty, so I went right to the dead center directly in front of the microphone with the big "Biden – New Hampshire" placard in front of it.

And suddenly I was back in the big league political fray! A row of news cameras along the wall behind me. Political hats and shirts and buttons everywhere. Political talk in the air. Almost everyone was still undecided. And almost everyone had already been to a bunch of other rallies and planned to go to a bunch more.

I spotted the bald head of tall John Heilemann wearing a casual blue pullover and weaving throughout the crowd, taking it all in, snapping pictures of the assembled. Heilemann co-wrote *Game Change* about the 2008 campaign and currently hosts Showtime's ongoing political documentary series *The Circus* with Mark McKinnon and former hippie Alex Wagner, and I've heard enough inside tips to know Heilemann's somebody I'd wanna hang with off the record and off the clock. We like the same music and smoke the same cigarettes, as it were. I was happy to see him here at this first post-Iowa event cuz I wanted to make sure we got in a good hang somewhere, and maybe meet his *Circus* cohosts, so this was already starting out like the political all-star show I figured it would be.

There were about 300 people in the room, including a battalion of yellow-shirted "Firefighters for Biden" along one wall, and mostly grey-hairs filling every seat. In fact, except for the young volunteers, I only counted 6 people under 30. I know they are the lowest turnout percentage of any age demographic in any election — and it proved to be the case at every rally as well.

With Aretha singing *Respect* and The Beatles *Come Together* as pre-show music, Biden came out to a rock star ovation and was the same gracious, polite man you see on TV town halls and interviews. He's very empathetic to people's problems. I'm sure that's why he got into public service in the first place. Whatever votes he may have taken in some distant political climate, he cares about people. He talked about lots of not-famous citizens and the struggles he's gone through with them. He was born with a speech impediment and has worked his whole life to overcome it. And because of the kind person he is, he's been mentoring similarly suffering people for decades. And he's a guy who wears his compassion on his sleeve. And his face reveals it.

One thing that was a bit disturbing was the presence of teleprompters. When I was much younger, I always wondered how these candidates could come out on stage and riff these long talks without any notes, and they were so well sequenced and funny, and then I learned it's cuz they're out doing it every day! And like a stand-up comic, they practice the lines in front of an audience and morph the riffs by reading reactions. But this is frickin' February, and Biden got into the race back in April last year — so how the hell does he not have his stump speech memorized by now?

Which also sorta segues to another disturbing observation that ol' Joe has a bit of a tendency to forget what he's saying in the middle of a sentence . . . which is always punctuated quickly after the silence with, "Look folks, ... " and he jumps off into whatever else he can think of.

But one bizarrely cool thing this 77 year old grandpa does is frequently sprinkle "man" into his dialogue like you're listening to Dizzy Gillespie or something. He so often seems like a patently unhip old geezer, but man, sometimes this cat sure can swing!

Then at some point the talk was interrupted by a screaming protester. I don't get these guys. For one thing, I've never heard one who actually made any kind of point or sense. It's not like they stand up and start loudly making some good case for their issue — they're just screaming some slogan or incoherent babble. I was maybe 30 feet away from the guy, and I don't have a clue what he was yelling about. Pretty soon the audience started chanting, "We want Joe, we want Joe ..." to drown him out, and then some barrel-chested firemen surrounded him and escorted him out the back door to great applause. To which Joe responded like a pro — "This is why I'm running. We have to stop this kind of disrespect and anger."

And then — oh God. Right after this was over . . . Anybody know the crazy overly enthusiastic Jake Byrd "super-fan" character (played by Tony Barbieri) on occasional segments on *Jimmy Kimmel Live!*? Well, his real-life counterpart was there out front before this started, going up and down the line trying to engage people in his Biden-fanaticism and even trying to get them to sign a petition or join a fan club or something in this unintentional comedy routine. Well, lucky me, when we got inside, he came and sat right next to me! — directly in front of his obsession's podium! And as soon as the protester was turfed and the room was beginning to settle back to normal, this comic figure started yelling out really loud — "That's what Nancy Pelosi said! That's what Nancy Pelosi said, Joe! With trump, all roads lead to Putin!!!"

It was *completely* out of context to anything that was being said, and the guy was not angry, just crazily enthusiastic and right outta his cuckoo's nest, and coming directly on the heels of the yelling protest man, it sorta froze the room, including Joe, to where all eyes turned, and he just wide-eyed, "What?!" then did the Catholic cross on his chest ... and the room laughed.

After it was over, as I was leaving, I saw ol' Golly Fine again, and we shared a big smile, and she said with an eye-locking prankster's twinkle just about the coolest thing anybody said to me the whole time I was in New Hampshire —

"Enjoy your Adventure!"

I mean — she *got* it, just from our little talk together. She didn't say "Enjoy the campaign" or "the primary" or "your day" . . . she *got* the entire essence of what I'm about — what I *am* — in our few minutes of riffing.

I was interviewed by the *Washington Post* (twice) and

USA Today and the guys from Sweden I'll tell ya about later, but this Foxy Lady from Fox freakin' News of all things was the one who got the bullseye point of *this* story better than anybody else I spoke to in ten days.

"Enjoy Your Adventure"

That should be the title of every book I've ever written!

~ = ~ = ~ = ~ = ~ * ~ = ~ = ~ = ~ = ~

When Joe & I met post-speech — my hair got tussled cuz it was kind of a madhouse.

The other candidates all had organized meet-n-greets after the show (speech), but Joe just sorta wandered over to the rope line and started talking to someone, then just kinda started working his way along the line, very impromptu.

A bald Secret Service type guy came out immediately. I saw him on the side of the stage earlier and he looked so much like the strategist Steve Schmidt, I thought it was him.

Joe picked me out with his eyes in the second row — I wasn't right on the ropeline.

I'm sure my visage reflected positivity. And he looked over two people's shoulders and stared me right in the eye and said, "What's your name?" reaching out his hand. I was kinda caught off guard, but ... "Brian. . . . I was at your first inauguration."

"Yeah, so were a lot of people," he said, but not dismissively, rather, celebratory.

"I hope to be at your next one," I smiled. And the

other people in the thick crowd kinda moved aside as though he and I knew each other or something and gave us space. And by this time a staffer had shown up next to Joe, so I handed him my camera, and Boom!

I was now 2-for-2 actually meeting a candidate and getting a picture with them. And this guy was the frickin' Vice President!

And then in the never-ending excitement that is New Hampshire in primary season — the next event started in less than an hour . . . and was a five-minute drive away! — back at the same main central downtown public library as Deval was last night — for **Tulsi Gabbard!** From the former two-term Vice President and primary frontrunner since he got in the race — to a retiring anti-war Congresswoman who's never polled above 2% in a year on the trail!

And right from the git as you walked up there was some friendly young hippie dude with a big smile and an funky arrow pointing to the library door. This is not a Secret Service event with a wall of TV cameras — this is a Dead show with pot smokin' peaceniks! And speaking of Dead shows — as soon as I got to the room I recognized people from the last rally! There are bona fide tour heads in this racket! But they're all active participants in democracy.

And in the homemade spirit of the home-cooked food in the Shakedown Street parking lot, Tulsi's mother had baked a bunch of her special family recipe Hawaiian toffee, and they were giving away free doses to get you in the mood as soon as you came in the door!

Tulsi, to me, has come across as a bit of crackpot — from her pimping absurd conspiracy theories to her very first answer in her very first primary debate slamming Obama and Clinton as she attempted to win the Democratic nomination. Does she even know what in the hell contest she's trying to win?! But in person she was warm and wonderful.

She begins every rally with "Aloha," the Hawaiian term for "Hello," which also means love, peace, respect and compassion — and as she points out, it always brings a smile to people's faces.

As much as I'm suspicious of her constant appearances on Fox Noise where she's always ripping Democrats, in person she's almost like a shamaness in her gentle calm demeanor — sort of a Buffy Sainte-Marie meets Ram Dass.

Also like the Dead, she does a shit-ton of live shows — 115 town halls in New Hampshire alone! And she's also good at improvising. She really only did about a 15-minute talk — mostly about foreign policy and stopping wars — and then just opened it up for nearly an hour of freewheeling questions.

She began her opening remarks with, "How many people here wake up thinking about foreign policy every day?" The correct answer, of course, was no one. But some enthusiastic audience members trying to play along raised their hands. "Wow! I'm impressed," she said to the people who blew her point, then went into her very logical anti-foreign-wars riff which came across so much more reasonable in person with five or ten minutes to flesh it out than in the one-minute debate or interview answers we usually hear. She went into the *Washington Post's* recent release of "The Afghanistan Papers" that exposed how we're still spending *four* **billion** *dollars every month* in Afghanistan right now. (What?!) "So, for the hour that we are here today," she says, pointing to our little library room, "That's five and a half million dollars." And then she went into how the government lies to us about what victory is — by not defining it — while simultaneously denying all services at home from cleaning up contaminated water to paying teachers.

And I felt for the first time this funny phenomenon of

thinking while listening to candidates speak, *"I gotta vote for this person!"* It would play out multiple times over the next week, but Tulsi was the first who sparked it. She was damn right about prit-near everything — and this was a candidate I walked in there taking about as seriously as a street corner conspiracy kook. But when she had the time to calmly explain in her tranquil Hawaiian way her full worldview in paragraphs and not soundbites it suddenly made poignant sense. She's just an awful campaigner — for a former soldier she has terrible aim. If she would have used her debate stage time to make these same points rather than personally attacking specific Democrats, she could have won people over rather than simply making enemies both on stage and off. She has a great argument to make — hell, even trump makes it about the stupidity of waging distant & expensive wars for no gain — and was born with the camera-friendly vessel to deliver it, but for some misguided reason she chooses to spit venom at every Democrat around her rather than make the winning case that she was this afternoon. Consequently, there were only about 100 people in the room and one camera crew. But with her looks, demeanor and message, there should have been another zero at the end of both those numbers if not for her firing at the wrong targets.

Like many of the candidates would do, she hung around after her talk, and unlike other candidates, she squatted down to be at eye level with little kids, and hugged fellow returning veterans. When we got a couple minutes together I told her, "Thanks for being the voice for so many of us," and "If John Lennon was alive you'd be his candidate."

"Oh Wow! Thank you for saying that. I'm a huge fan."

~ = ~ = ~ = ~ = ~ * ~ = ~ = ~ = ~ = ~

Later that same Tuesday the week before New Hampshire's election day I went to **Amy Klobuchar** in the gym at the Nashua Community College. There was a long wide line stretching down the long hallway with a bunch of friendly volunteers greeting you as soon as you arrived, getting your digits for their database and giving you a green "Amy for America" button.

I hate standing in lines anywhere for anything. Time is too valuable, and whatever's at the front of it needs to be run more efficiently. But during the primary it was one of the most fun things to do! Happy, friendly, upbeat, well-versed volunteers are walking up and down the line, engaging anyone who wants to talk about the candidate or anything else political. And the people in front of and behind you are all proactive explorers wanting firsthand empirical experiences to supplement their vast reading. Some voters are issue-based and want to hear how a candidate addresses education or climate change or whatever is their go-to concern. Others want legislative experience and to assess with their own eyes whether a candidate is confidently well-versed in the ways of governance. Still others want someone with the fire in their belly to take on trump and beat him. And much like the candidates meeting voters at the end of their rallies and learning firsthand what's on their minds, I was surveying the electorate from the admission lines. Voters have all different reasons for supporting a candidate — all valid — and every person who goes out of their way to drive to a rally on a cold February night to wait in line then wait in a chair for a single person to stand at a microphone and talk for an hour is the kind of person who *should* be electing our leaders.

This was the first time I met *an army* of volunteers so numerous and passionate and wild-eyed beaming I thought they were Beatlemaniacs! One was a friendly smart black girl from Florida named Jazzy. Whadda name! She was part of a Political Science program at some university down there, and the whole class flew up to New Hampshire for the week and got involved in whichever campaign they wanted. These are the kinds of things that give me hope for our future.

There were about 400 people in the college gym, and other than the volunteers, I counted 3 under 30. A pattern was emerging. If the college Poli-Sci students gave me hope, the general lack of engagement by the youth across New Hampshire reinforced that young people are just (sadly) not engaged in the process of democracy. Yeah, some are in the Bernie movement, but writ large it's still old people who have learned the responsibility of engagement and actually voting.

Another manifestation of this divide were the red-shirted AARP people that took up a front row of one of the sections at every rally I attended. They got there early and sat unmissably in front of every candidate's line of vision with their huge "AARP" white lettering on their bright red shirts, their petition clipboards for lower drug prices in their hands, and were ready to jump in with a direct question if the opportunity arose. I got to know their leader Mark, and he had a Pranksters' twinkle & happy bubbling energy. **And that's one of the beautiful things about these Primary Moments — feeling the same positive energy from a 20-year-old black girl and a 70-year-old white dude within a few feet and minutes of each other**.

And speaking of interracial shared joy — this was at my third "show" of the day and once again I flashed on this being the New Orleans Jazz Fest for politicos! Just today, there were 21 different candidate appearances in the area from 9AM to 10PM — and the only challenge was picking which stage you wanted to be at!

Beforehand, the campaign was playing mostly Minnesota's own Bob Dylan over the PA — and afterwards they blasted Prince — two musical giants who've both sold hundreds of millions albums and proved that universal voices do indeed come from the breadbasket of our land. Being a Midwesterner myself, where we like to cite my fellow Kelvin High School alum Neil Young, and city-mates Burton Cummings & Randy Bachman, I can relate to both the power and pride of our sensible voices reflecting on the distant coasts. And that's what Amy seems to be doing without the help of an electric guitar.

Her stump speech was full of Midwestern down-home anecdotes, but also the dry comedic sensibility that's run from Mark Twain to Garrison Keillor to David Letterman to Jim Gaffigan. "My father was married three times, but we won't talk about that right now." Mentioning some meeting at Mar-a-Lago, she asides, "Were any of you there?" And bringing my homeland into it, she noted how "Trump even blames Canadian Prime Minster Justin Trudeau for cutting him out of *Home Alone II*. Who does that?!"

But she also talked Midwestern Practical, and how she won 42 counties that trump carried and is the only candidate in the race who can win rural votes, and how she took the lead on over a hundred bills that passed through Congress. The campaign passed out American flags on the way in — a nice touch — but it also made for some great flag-waving visuals during high points of her speech.

I talked afterwards to somebody who grew up with Amy's family in Minnesota who said she seemed tired. When I got home, I learned she didn't get to New Hampshire until 4 in the morning after the all-night Iowa caucus vote-counting debacle. If tonight's funny, sharp, light-of-foot person was Amy *tired*, boy — what must she be like at full steam?!

When she finished her speech, she did what Elizabeth Warren has turned into a primary staple — the post-debate "selfie" with the candidate. For the most part, these should really be called "2-shots" since they weren't taken by either "self" in the photos but rather by a third person, but like so much with language, once a word catches on there ain't no changin' it. Hamburgers aren't made of ham, pineapples aren't apples and don't grow on pine trees, and selfies aren't always taken by a self.

Amy's campaign has got it down to a science. There are *six* staff members who make it make it tick like clockwork. The first two coordinate the line so everyone doesn't mob the stage. A third gives you instructions at the bottom of stairs to the stage and tells you be quick and exit down the other side. A fourth takes your phone or camera and hands it to the fifth, the photographer. And a sixth person hands you back your camera and points you to the stairs off stage. It's quite the operation!

Despite them wanting it to all go zip-zam-zoodle, I tend to write my own rules, and when I got up there I riffed with the boss about how I was an American but grew up in Manitoba, and how they were really each other's cross-border twin, and in that way she & I were related. She loved it.

~ = ~ = ~ = ~ = ~ * ~ = ~ = ~ = ~ = ~

When the primary first got underway in early 2019, the question then — and which remained for many all the way through was — Can the candidate beat trump? Removing myselfie from the punditry class, I closed my eyes and pictured each candidate behind the desk in the Oval Office putting out this trumpster fire, and the person I most wanted then (and still do) to have that job is **Elizabeth Warren**.

This rally on Wednesday, February 5th, was in the same gym at the Nashua Community College as was Amy's the night before — except it didn't have a curtain closing off a third of it. This had the biggest crowd by far of any rally I'd attended — at least 500 people including standing room along the walls — and it was the youngest, the most diverse, and most gender equal rally yet. It was also the biggest press pool by far, with a wide riser full of cameras and a big roped-off press section with three long rows of work tables behind.

As I came in — the luck of the Irish — they had been holding out the front row for some reason, but the second I got into the quickly-filling venue and started snooping the front for the best seat, one of the organizers asked if I'd like to sit in the front row!

BOOM!

Before "the show" they were playing *The Big Chill* soundtrack, or at least a bunch of songs from it. And Diana Ross, and Neil Diamond. But it was far from just a Boomer audience. I was sitting with a 21-year-old actress, Bebe Wood, who was excited to be voting in her first election, and a 30-year-old who supported Liz while her boyfriend was voting Bernie.

Age has become something of a storyline in this election, and proof that 70 is the new 40. Just *attending* three rallies in a day (as I did yesterday) was exhausting. I don't know how these 70-somethings do it. And it also makes me less than sympathetic when people sit at home and do nothing but type vitriol towards others about how terrible some candidate is. Even if I disagree strongly with someone running, I deeply respect how they're sacrificing their lives and health to seek public office.

To prove this point of vitality, Liz has a great showbiz entrance — remember, that's how I got into this whole racket — where she's introduced from the stage, then comes *running* to it from the far back corner door of the gym!

And the whole time she's on it, she bouncing like on a pogo stick in sneakers, allowing her natural exploding energy to consume her, prowling back and forth like Mick Jagger, and expressing herself with the energy of a little kid excitedly telling you her latest discovery. What a bundle of good and high energy she is. In fact, with all her arm waving and bopping around, she reminded me of footage I've seen of *me* on stage doing one of my theatrical readings!

And there I was in the front row, just a few feet from her for the whole hour-long talk where she told a lot of personal stories, including that she was a late baby in her family, as was I in mine. Her mom called her "the surprise," and she got one of her many laughs from the crowd. She talked about being the first in her family to go college, and passing the bar to become a lawyer. "I practiced for about 45 minutes." Another laugh.

She tells a story about when she was a kid and the toast in their old toaster oven caught fire and ignited the kitchen curtains and nearly burned down their house. And now when you buy a toaster oven that can't happen — because the Consumer Protection Safety Commission mandates basic safety regulations on home appliances — and how that kind of basic safety for products was what was behind her forming the Consumer Financial Protection Agency which now protects Americans against predatory lending and other attempts to fleece the unsuspecting.

She talked about pulling the party together, and how both staff and volunteers from both the Kamala Harris and Cory Booker campaigns have come over to hers. And looking around the room, it was the most ethnically diverse of anything I'd seen in New Hampshire so far.

For the second half Q&A — she did something cool I've

never seen before. When people were waiting in line earlier, they passed out raffle tickets to anyone who wanted to ask a question, then pulled the numbers from a hat on stage. It was so playful and democratic and added a little audience-interactive drama to the proceedings of a political talk.

Hearing her answer questions with, "I've got a plan for that," and getting a big whoop of acknowledgment from the crowd was like playing the hook of a hit song. "So, here's the thing ..." "I know how to fight and I know how to win." She's got a bunch of 'em. And she climaxes with her go-to single — "Dream big, fight hard" — repeating it over and over like Jesse Jackson's "Keep hope alive!" For a skinny little white girl, she sure got soul.

Afterwards, in what the history books will write about her campaign, was her patented "selfie line." Being right in the front, I got right in the front of it, also cuz she said she could only do it for a few minutes and had to catch a plane back to Washington to vote that afternoon to impeach the orange Trumpenstein.

If Amy Klobuchar's operation was the Rolling Stones, Elizabeth Warren's was the Chuck Berry original. She invented this shit. Not only did they have the Instruction Person, the Take The Camera Person, the Take The Picture Person, the Pass the Camera Back Person, but they also had two or three people offering to hold your winter coat so the picture looked more natural, and another person with a clipboard seeing if you wanted to sign up for a volunteer shift. And they made it all fun.

When my first choice candidate and I got our moment together after supporting her campaign for the last year, I told her she looks like my late great mom, and she beamed back, "Oh, what a nice compliment, thank you." And I told her she reminded me of me on stage in the way she paces and bops around, and she said, "Hey — we make a pretty good team!"

Snap!

~ = ~ = ~ = ~ = ~ * ~ = ~ = ~ = ~ = ~

Following Liz's gym-filled Democratic love-in, that evening I went to the weirdest rally of the trip — **Bill Weld's** — who was challenging Twitler for the Republican nomination.

It was held in this huge, ominous Stephen King–meets–*The Sopranos* former shoe factory building in the old industrial neighborhood of Nashua. You got the eerie feeling some weird shit went down in this building over the years — then I found out it was also where they made caskets for the dead!

After the fairly packed rooms for Biden, Amy & Liz,

it was off-putting to walk into this large wedding reception style banquet room, and there were maybe 30 people in there, 10 of whom were the red-shirted AARP people. There was this *Shining* vibe of a big opulent room with no one in it. Or maybe the Titanic.

I went over to join the AARP peeps cuz the other ghosts scattered around the room kinda scared me. They had the two tables right in front of where Weld would speak, and I grabbed a seat just a few feet in front of his mic. Turns out only about 3 of them stayed at the table, so this huge banquet table right in front of the speaker was largely empty except for me and my monkey. I mean, my notebook.

C-SPAN was the only camera covering it. It was a beyond-long-shot challenge to trump's nomination, not only because of his in-party disciples, but also because he got about 10 states to cancel their primaries altogether. The Dead-friendly Weld was a two-term Massachusetts governor in the '90s — a Republican governing a Democratic state — and more recently he was Gary Johnson's running mate for the Libertarian ticket in 2016 who got more third party votes than anyone since Ross Perot's Reform Party in 1996.

Another kinda voodoo scary storyline was — I'm always going to Democratic events, surrounded by like-thinking Democrats, and here I was talking to the red-shirted AARP folks who seemed just like the AARP people at all the other rallies — and like some *Twilight Zone* episode or that excellent recent movie *Get Out* by Jordan Peele — I started to realize the people around me weren't who I thought they were. As I vanished into my solitary note-writing world and became invisible to the banquet tables of political talking locals, I started to overhear conversations slamming the poor, and about "the immigrant problem," and all the parasites living off these people's tax dollars.

One guy said to another, "You know, when I heard that George Bernard Shaw quote — 'A government which robs Peter to pay Paul can always depend on the support of Paul.' — that really summed it up."

These were sure not conversations you'd hear at any of the other rallies I attended. I suddenly realized I was the lone blue-shirt deep in the red zone. The 30 people had grown to 50 . . . and I swear I saw muskets and pitchforks in the back. Straw hats and beards. Backwoods militia members and leather-clad bikers. This sure wasn't a bed-in for peace.

After playing Grand Funk Railroad's *We're An American Band* — a song about rock stars banging groupies — the socially awkward perpetual candidate took the microphone and started in on his rambling talk about deficits and "privatizing everything."

Usually political candidates, especially veterans of the profession, are extremely comfortable in front of a crowd — and no disrespect, but Weld was physically awkward the whole time — never knowing what to do with his non-mic-holding hand, putting it in his pocket, taking it out, letting it just hang at his side. And I don't want to be mean, but he had snot dripping down from his nose the whole time.

I was right there in front of him. Caught everything, as it were. And in the continual *Twilight Zone* of this whole trip, for long stretches of time, he was staring right at me in front of him — giving his talk directly to me. I had my reporter's notebook out, and maybe he thought I was some wig-big, but either way it was freaky — and ol' Mr. Awkward was makin' *me* feel awkward.

He mentioned that Mitt Romney was the only
Republican in the Senate who voted that afternoon to
impeach the president, and that there needed to be more
within the party who stood up. And around this time
I noticed he hadn't said a single thing that had gotten
applause in the room. I mean, usually candidates have
worked up some guaranteed applause lines they drop in
early and often to their speeches. Y'know, get the room
involved. Toss 'em some red meat. Or a veggie burrito.
Whatever it takes to get some engagement. It wasn't

until nearly the end of the hour that anyone applauded anything — and it was for some guy in the audience who was addressing another guy in the audience who commented about the social problems he faces being a Republican in the trump era. And the second guy says, "Well, the best thing you can do is vote for Bill Weld," and *finally* a round of applause broke out — and it wasn't even Weld who said it!

And in the continuing sureality, somebody asked him about his position on gun laws, and he rambled away about how hunting rifles were okay, but assault style weapons were not and they were "highly illegal." (!) Huh? He thinks assault weapons are not for sale just about everywhere in America? It was bizarre.

And for my Prankster friends — when he was extolling the virtues of Big Pharma even while lamenting their profiteering, he actually cited the old DuPont ad slogan that became an inside joke for psychedelic rangers worldwide — and sounded so funny coming from the lips of a stiff 74-year-old Republican in a suit —

"Better living through chemistry."

I was glad I wore my tie-dye shirt.

~ = ~ = ~ = ~ = ~ * ~ = ~ = ~ = ~ = ~

The next day — Thursday, February 6th — was **The Great Mayor Pete Adventure**.

It was his first appearance in the state since he won the most delegates at the slow-reporting Iowa caucuses, and it was held at a small American Legion Hall in Merrimack — a 20 minute drive — my furthest Road Trip to date.

I got there an hour before the 2:30 start time, and had to park in a snowy field a half-mile away. The little Legion parking lot was already full of press & staff with license plates from Illinois, Indiana, Ohio, Maine, Massachusetts,

New York, Virginia, Maryland . . . it was like a freakin' Dead show!

Pete had been live on *The View* that morning, and was flying in from NYC as the new surprise frontrunner coming out of the first state voicing an opinion.

I was right near the front of the line talking to fellow undecided voters, including one with the unusual name Enid, like my late great Mom, and both the public and the press check-in lines were growing rapidly outside the modest Legion building. When this was booked for Pete to connect with his fellow veterans it was clearly not done with him being a newly minted frontrunner in mind. The crowd was soon to become a national story itself, with not only hundreds of New Hampshire voters not getting in, but scads of late-arriving national press as well.

When I walked in with the initial batch, the two rows of seats in back of the "stage" (really, just part of the floor with a microphone on a stool) were open, so I plopped myself down right in the front, and promptly had my non-veteran-looking ass moved to the second row.

I counted a total of 75 folding chairs in the little Legion Hall, and by the time they stopped letting people in, there were maybe 100 standing around the perimeter. I could see Howard Fineman from the *Huffington Post*, Dana Bash from CNN, and David Weigel from *The Washington Post,* who would interview me at length later — all managed to make it in early.

With the great and astute Dana Bash from CNN

It was a cool crowd waiting for the arriving star — with more electricity in the room than anything in New Hampshire so far. Next to me was some character who flew in from Seattle the night before just to ride the buzz of the small town rallies. Next to him was a lifelong Deadhead who saw his first show in 1976. Across from me was a young beauty pageant contestant actually wearing a tiara. And playing over the PA was the best collection of tunes heard so far On The Trail — Bowie rocking *Rebel Rebel*, Aretha singing "Freedom" over and over as she implored us to *Think*, George Michael coming right out with *Freedom*, and The Who's old song for the new insurgents, *Won't Be Fooled Again*.

Pete finally took "the stage" an hour after it was supposed to start and it was really clear this was intended as a veteran-to-veteran moment. He made the point about American citizens, like troops in the field, trusting one another and working together — something that the Divider-in-Chief has made a point of destroying. "When we got in a vehicle to go on a mission, the people in the vehicle could not care less if I was a Democrat or a Republican, or if I was going home to a girlfriend or a boyfriend, or what country my father immigrated from. They wanted to know if I was prepared to do my job, to keep them safe, and vice versa. And we learned to trust one another even though we came from radically different backgrounds, geographically, racially or politically. And yet we formed that trust. And that is a touchstone that we need today."

And he talked about composure, something else genetically missing from the current president's DNA. This youngest candidate is in so many ways the most mature, the most respectful of others, the least flappable, and the best at improv verbal sentence construction that these writer's ears have heard in this campaign.

After his talk connecting his philosophy and life experience to his time in the military, and the advantage of having a Commander-in-Chief who had actually served, he took a bunch of questions from the audience.

Two things every candidate does after every question asked of them is say — "Thank you, [person's name]." And "That's a great question."

He rocked inquiries about child abuse ("We've got to be proactive and not reactive"), healthcare ("Obamacare was a big leap forward, but there's a lot of gaps we've got to fill in"), and lessons learned in Kabul (that societies aren't free if they don't have basic services, the importance of a sense of humor to lift each other up, and that being in charge is not about being exulted but to do right by the people who call you "sir").

Author in second row corner, tiara in foreground

I learned in advance that Pete wasn't much for the post-show hang. And with him now being the frontrunner, and in this tiny packed room, I knew there was pretty much no chance of getting any time with him or a picture or anything. But what the hell?

The moment he put the mic back down on the stool, I slipped out from the second row and crossed the "stage" and was standing next to him within a handful of seconds. He was autographing a sign for one of the people who asked a question, and as soon as his pen lifted off the placard and he was starting to turn in the other direction, I put my arm around his shoulder and said, "Pete, can I get a picture," and he *super* friendly said, *"Sure!"* But, dig — he was already surrounded by staffers who were circling him like football blockers to get him out of there. There was one right in front of us, I handed her the camera and she got the cramped close-up, then as soon as she handed it back, I felt an arm on my shoulder unsubtly tugging me the hell away.

I went back the 10 feet to my seat, checked that the shot came out, looked at my coat and was wondering whether I should put it on or hang s'more, when suddenly Mayor Pete was whisked past me out of the building — about 30 seconds after this picture was snapped, and maybe a minute and change after his speech ended.

But I was six-for-six getting a pic with every candidate!

After it was over, I lingered with some of the press peeps while fellow veteran John Fogerty's band played *Up Around The Bend*. Weigel from the *Post* and Joey Garrison from *USA Today* interviewed me at length, and CNN's Dana Bash was super friendly, and there was really a feeling that something was in the air with this Buttigieg guy. Was he going to be the unknown who emerged from the pack as the challenge to Biden & Sanders? If Obama prompted the (erroneous) term "post-racial America" were we now in a "post-homophobic America"? Was this the new face of what

a military veteran presidential candidate looked like after
John McCain?

Whatever was happening, it was electric.

When I finally left the Legion Hall, which really felt
like the old community clubs that were built all around
Winnipeg after WWII and that I grew up in, there was
the exulted feeling of finally stepping outside after a
great concert. Everyone was still jazzed at what they'd
experienced and strangers were stopping strangers just to
shake their hand.

There were a couple of friendly looking bohos I'd
seen inside, Wolfgang and Erik, and we started talkin', and
turned out they're from the biggest newspaper in Sweden.
I don't know what it is, but I've really connected with every
Scandinavian I've ever met, and became good friends with a
few of them, including my Swedish Kerouac brother Johan
Soderlund ever since we first met in Amsterdam when I
was inducting Jack into the Counterculture Hall of Fame
there in 1999 and Johan's Levi's Jeans were sponsoring
it; and more recently the Danish Danger Duo I met in San
Francisco during the Dead's Fare Thee Well shows and
recently did the Woodstock 50th with.

So me and the Swedes start jammin', talkin' hockey
and good beer, and they asked if they could interview me,
and what the hell, it was a beautiful sunny afternoon, and
we've all had a helluva day already, so I start flowing in
typical animated Brian fashion, feeling quite loose cuz I'm
not talkin' to the frickin' *Washington Post*, and, knowing
these homies know hockey, I riffed something about
Buttigieg being like the Gretzky of politics — how it's his

first season in the big leagues and he's taking it by storm.

We all got along like the bunch of northern country socialists we are, and made vague plans for beers later, but they had to head off to some other rally, and in that moment I was glad that I wasn't a working journalist with a daily deadline so I could just let all this New Hampshire magic soak in like the warm winter sun.

Imagine my surprise the next morning when I heard from ol' brother Johan in Sweden — "I just read you in the biggest newspaper in the country! It had the name 'Brian Hassett' and I thought, 'Hey, I know somebody by that name.' Then you started talking about hockey and I knew it was you. But get this — you're the quote in the headline! It says, 'After Iowa, interest soars for the 'Gretzky of politics'.'"

With the Swedish brothers — Wolfgang & Erik

~ = ~ = ~ = ~ = ~ * ~ = ~ = ~ = ~ = ~

Friday February 7th was the big nationally televised Democratic debate from Manchester. I tried every angle to get tickets, but even longtime plugged-in politicos told me they were shut out. Made me feel a smidge better.

The obvious thing was to go to the DoubleTree Hotel in Manchester.

Manchester's the main city in New Hampshire and only has one major hotel downtown. It used to be a very cool Radisson, but Hilton took it over in 2018 and frankly it's nowhere near as happening as it was in 2004 when there was a massive bar with an overlooking restaurant and it was a helluva scene. Now it's all different, but I'll get into that shortly.

There's a little hidden sidestreet right next to the DoubleTree that nobody seems to know about — the perfectly named Pleasant Street. I parked on it in 2004, and my very last memory of *that* whole New Hampshire campaign Adventure was at the end of election night calling out as I drove away to that funny British reporter / character Richard Quest who was outside taking a solo smoke break. I howled, "Hey man! I love your stuff!" And I could see his huge white teeth smiling back as he waved to my fleeing rent-a-car. In fact, not only was I back on the same street, but the exact same spot was the only one open on the block the first three times I went there! Don't tell me this town ain't got no heart.

As I walked into the lobby to head to the bar, I noticed a long line going in the other direction. "What's this?"

"It's a live taping of the Chris Hayes show. It's the debate-watch, then you have to stay to be in the studio audience until 1."

"Do they serve beer?"

Awkward pause. "I don't think so."

So I went and checked the lobby bar — and it was so small I had to ask if it was the only one. The old Radisson had this *giant* bar lined with TVs with all the different news networks on them, plus a big open restaurant space. All of that was gone and replaced by this small airport lounge type joint in the lobby with a meager two TVs behind the bar ... showing *sports* in the middle of the primary!

This wasn't right.

So I went back over to the Chris Hayes line, and found out everybody had to be registered in advance to be in the studio audience, but I went and talked to the organizers and pitched the idea of filling in for somebody who didn't show up, and they let me stand on the side until the line went through the metal detectors and into the hall — and sure as heck they let me in!

Come for a bar hang — end up in a live TV show taping. That sounds about right. I pulled out my wallet and cashed in a couple Karma Coupons.

I had no idea what to expect, but they had a free fancy coffee station and were bringing out nonstop boxes of pizza so it seemed to be off to a good start. Apparently in the complete architectural overhaul of the hotel, they built a massive open exhibition space about an acre in size attached to the hotel that NBC had rented and turned into their "New Hampshire Election Headquarters," broadcasting almost all their MSNBC shows from different temporary studios built throughout it.

Going in, they'd given New Hampshire residents wristbands, and had them all sit in the middle section in front of the Chris Hayes set, so for the post-debate live show he could walk among them to get local undecided voters' reactions to the debate. (Amy won.)

The two-hour ABC debate was shown on a cube of giant 10'-x-20' hi-def screens in the center of the massive room, while the *All In* production crew did different camera blockings and chair markings for the various segments that were all gonna go down live as soon as the debate ended. Hanging around the perimeter were a bunch of politicos who would end up taking an on-air chair later — Michael Moore, Howard Fineman, Jonathan Alter, Lawrence O'Donnell, Joy Reid, David Corn and others.

The debate itself was the last of the civil exchanges before the gloves came off in Nevada and South Carolina in the coming weeks. It was also the last one with ol' Andrew Yang, and the last without Michael Bloomberg. Newly crowned co-frontrunner Bernie Sanders finally started to take some direct challenges on a debate stage, including on his history of voting against the Brady Bill and other gun legislation, and about what trump was gonna do with Bernie's self-attached label of "socialist." Like the lifelong politician he is and his base pretends he's not, he deflected and pivoted with the best of them.

His co-winner out of Iowa, Pete Buttigieg, the young "debate team captain" as I call him, and the one who can compose complex sentences on the fly better than anyone on the stage, also took lots of incoming, including from Amy Klobuchar about how he said the impeachment hearings were exhausting and how he'd rather turn the channel and "watch cartoons instead" — an unfortunate comment from someone who looks not far removed from cartoon watching age.

After his disappointing fourth-place finish in Iowa, Biden picked up his game and was more forceful and articulate than he'd ever been before. "We should pin a medal on Colonel Vindman not Rush Limbaugh," he said with fire in his eyes, speaking to both the moment and the room, and to great applause. To my eyes, leaders are very clear as soon as they walk in a room. It's a specific strain of DNA that says, "Look at me — I'm in charge." General Schwarzkopf had it. Obama had it. Ken Kesey had it. But Biden is more of a Charlie Watts. Great guy to have on the backbeat, but he doesn't seem to be a frontman who can galvanize a stadium.

My first-choice candidate Liz has just never caught on and didn't win many converts in this debate. Particularly Liz, but really all these candidates, do better in the hour-long town halls that CNN and others occasionally host. Although she'd distinguish herself by coming out swinging in the debates that followed, her attempt at being "the unity candidate" didn't seem to be uniting voters behind her.

I don't know what Tom Steyer was doing on the stage. I understand his ad buys juiced his polling numbers in a couple states allowing him to qualify, but over the last year talking politics with thousands of people I've never come across a single Steyer supporter.

And poor ol' Andrew Yang. It felt like it watching, but got confirmed afterwards — both Bernie and Biden had the mic for roughly 20 minutes each, and Andrew Yang spoke for 8. He's a nice, smart, funny, altruistic, forward-thinking guy — but that and a dollar will get him on the subway.

Which all brings us to Amy Klobuchar, who seemed to be the consensus pick for winner of the debate. She would be rewarded a few days later by a strong third-place finish in New Hampshire and become a poster child for how debates can change momentum. The first thing I noticed — I know it's absurdly superficial, but — her hair looked great! I even mentioned it to the woman sitting next to me, about how it oval-arced around her face like Jennifer Aniston on *Friends,* and the woman about Amy's age next to me heartily agreed.

She had a funny line about how "59 is the new 38" to Mayor Pete, and managed to get in that she had been endorsed by the three biggest newspapers in New Hampshire, to go along with the *New York Times'* dual endorsement of both her and Warren. And the escalating poetry of her closing statement about empathy brought down the house — the combination of all of which spiked her up into the top tier of candidates.

As soon as the debate wrapped, the EMT-like production team leapt into action. The woman director patrolled the perimeter of the giant studio with a headset directing everyone. Her second-in-command physically directed camera movements with his long arms as a visual to her audio directives, as well as clapping and cueing the audience of around 200 when needed. Chris was center stage reading the intros and outros from the teleprompter but otherwise improvising. This is his game and his life. He could riff this stuff till tomorrow and not run out of ideas.

At the 2016 Republican National Convention in Cleveland 2016
Photo by Jeremy Hogan

In the first segment, he wandered out into the New Hampshire wristband-wearing part of studio audience. I saw a seat chart on somebody's clipboard with certain aisle seats highlighted — I guess people they'd assessed were articulate and camera-friendly. "Who do you think won the debate and why?" was the go-to question — and "Amy" seemed to be the come-back answer.

They did remote interviews with both Amy and Liz that looked like every other cross-country satellite interview — except the two rooms were only two miles apart in tiny Manchester.

The first post-debate panel was the first-line all-stars to open the show — Chris Matthews, Joy Reid, Lawrence O'Donnell, and Alicia Menendez for the Latino perspective. And then there was another one with David Corn and a couple others it's driving me nuts that I can't remember their names. And then Michael Moore came out for a fun one-on-one with Chris to close the show.

To be completely confessional I didn't take notes on what they were saying because 1) — It wouldn't look proper as a studio audience member to be sitting there taking notes like a reporter. They told us "no photo taking during the taping" — that we were part of the show. This isn't a rally in a gymnasium — we're on-camera extras in a live-broadcast movie. I can respect that. And 2) — I figured the whole show (like the debate itself) would be posted to YouTube or the NBC site or something, so this would be one part of The Epic Adventure I could relive later and not have to be committing to memory as it happened. But I was wrong. The one gig I thought would be preserved in hi-def in perpetuity doesn't even have notes on paper to show for itself.

After the live show, the audience mostly left, but of course I hung and jammed with the band. Ol' Michael Moore was hangin' around and we started talking about growing up in the Midwest and how that's so different from the coasts. And about Canadian healthcare and that Bernie was so right to be saying we can do it 50 miles from his house. And I told him with a laugh how I loved that scene in his *Sicko* movie going to the teller's booth at the hospital in England — but how they were actually paying him money. He's such a great storyteller. And he's on our side. And that's a good thing.

And then there was the whole post-debate hang in the airport lounge bar in the DoubleTree lobby. *This* was the jam. It ain't the old Radisson big-bar scene — but it's sumpthin.

It was packed and noisy and buzzing like the big family reunion it was of journalists and politicos from all over the country gathered in a tiny New Hampshire town in an even tinier New Hampshire bar with a presidential nomination on the line.

There was diminutive Delaware Senator Chris Coons encircled by a friendly gaggle of press and operatives I didn't know, but everybody was smiling and super upbeat even though his man Joe didn't get one of the "three tickets out of Iowa."

And there was DNC Chair Tom Perez, seemingly the man of the hour judging by the crowd around him. I'd loved to have talked to him about the expedited primary schedule and the upcoming convention in Milwaukee and how they plan to handle the militant Bernie supporters, but he was surrounded by a pack of wild journalists and functionaries cueing up ad hoc around him, and it didn't seem worth the battle to try to get a word in edgewise.

Elsewhere in the party were any number of other interesting people I recognized — Ari Melber, Lawrence O'Donnell & Joy Reid from MSNBC; Jonathan Martin from *The New York Times*; Sam Stein from *The Daily Beast*; Ed O'Keefe from CBS; Lisa Desjardins from the *PBS NewsHour;* David Corn from *Mother Jones;* authors Michael Izikoff and Jonathan Alter; and Biden spokeswoman Symone Sanders was locked into position on one of the dozen barstools. I schmoozed around talkin' to a bunch of them and others, but then ol' Amy Klobuchar joined the party! How great! — the only candidate in downtown Manchester to actually come out post-debate and talk to a non-controlled public gathering.

And before long I fell into the best conversation of the week.

Lawrence O'Donnell and Amy Klobuchar

I saw Lawrence O'Donnell and Amy start talking, and since I'd spoken to both of them before, I left them alone to have a few minutes together. Then after a bit, I went over, and what the hell, joined them! As I walked up she broke into an ear-to-ear smile and pointed at me — "Manitoba!" Couldn't believe she remembered!

What a happy, fun person she is. I told her how her hair looked great, and immediately she gushed a genuine, "Thank you for saying that." So I riffed furthur — "It looks like the Jennifer Aniston cut from *Friends*. And the woman in the audience I mentioned this to agreed!" "Oh, thanks!" she said, beaming even more. My mother always taught me to complement people. Say the nice things. It's an easy way to make people feel better. A nickel toss-off complement

318

from you can be worth a million dollars to the person who receives it.

And suddenly Lawrence O'Donnell, Amy Klobuchar and I were a trio talkin' the campaign, and it felt like jammin' with old friends. We riffed Romney ... Schiff ... McConnell ... how she wants Bloomberg in the debates ... and Lawrence said he wants her to "give it" in the next one like she did in this one ... and I told her to keep stressing that she wins rural districts.

Eventually Lynn Sweet from the *Chicago Sun-Times* joined us, and then David Corn from *Mother Jones* came up behind and said, "I wanna get in on this!"

Suddenly I had the taller-than-I-expected Lawrence O'Donnell on my left, the fairly petit Amy Klobuchar right in front of me, the even more petit Lynn Sweet and bespectacled David Corn on my right in this classic quintet riffing a fabulous freewheeling conversation about the impeachment hearings that just wrapped up, and every time Amy would share some insider detail, she'd preface it with, "This is off the record," because she was talking to three known journalists. It was so interesting to experience how they talk to each other. She and they knew the rules. And we were in a bar. And everyone was enjoying an adult beverage, but could converse with one another unencumbered. This was off the record.

And Lynn Sweet had some great stories about being in the Senate press gallery during the impeachment, and observed how different presidential candidates interacted with their colleagues. She mentioned a column she wrote earlier in the week where she played with the idea of — what if the Senate were a high school lunchroom? and sketched out which cliques different presidential candidates would be in, saying of Amy — "Klobuchar, of Minnesota, would be the kid welcomed at any table. She could fit in with the jocks, nerds, popular students, brainy kids, and the student newspaper clique."

Amy's face lit up right away with her big natural smile, and she said her staff read that to her over the phone. It was so nice to be standing next to a writer while the subject of her prose responded that she had read it (or heard it) and loved it. Knowing you got it right in the eyes of one of your subjects is one of the invisible gusts in the sails that keeps any writer's ship in the race across the unchartered unwritten seas.

Amy riffed about the trouble in a crowded field of getting on news talk shows cuz there's so many candidates. Shows themselves, and networks writ large, don't want to show bias, and so they sort of have to wait till everyone has cycled through before bringing someone back. But with time of the essence now, a regular avenue of message impartation was bottlenecked.

I so much wanted to have a picture taken of the five of us in this long colloquy, but I knew asking someone to take it would break the magic of the moment.

At some point in all this madness, I snuck into debate broadcaster ABC's adjacent after-party, cuz that's whatcha do, but it really wasn't much of a party, except for the mile-long tables of classy food. The great warrior reporter Martha Raddatz was there, but mostly it seemed to be staffers coppin' a free buzz. I started talking to a couple young fire-blazing babes who seemed to be enjoying themselves, and had just been in the audience for their first presidential debate. "We were right up front, but we were sitting right behind George (Stephanopoulos) and David (Muir) so we couldn't really see the candidates, but we were right there near all their families, and it was so cool during the ad breaks, they'd all talk to each other. Warren's husband Bruce was really friendly. And Klobuchar's ... what was his name — John."

"And Andrew Yang's wife . . . Evelyn, right?" the other one chimed in.

"You guys should host a candidate's spouse roundtable," which as soon as I blurted it out somewhat blew my cover as not working for ABC.

"What are you doing with the election?" one of them asked, and I told them about the book I was writing that you're now reading, and that seemed to be enough to buy another round of blue-eyed sparkles.

I asked what they were doing. "We're interns at the news bureau in Washington, so whatever needs doing."

"Oh — that's cool! That's basically how I got into the music business. You get in — get to know people — prove how good you are. (pause) Make yourself *invaluable*," I advised them. "And it's all about personal connections. Every person you're working with is your potential employer. Hey — lemme ask ya — what about sexism and the Me Too thing. Do you experience anything like that there?"

"Not at all," one said and the other nodded.

"That was my experience at MTV. I was there at the Times Square headquarters for six years, and people were hooking up, but it was a very equality-based place."

"Yeah, ABC is, too," the talkative one said. "At least in Washington. I've never been to the New York office."

And we riffed on how cool Manchester is, "Yeah people

are really nice here," the big city Washingtonians observed.

Then I suddenly remembered there was a whole bar full of cool reporters and senior politicos, and as appealing as the visuals were, I had giants to meet.

"Okay — enjoy the rest of the campaign. May the best woman win!"

"*Yeah, baby!*" the non-talker suddenly chimed with gusto.

Back in the center ring — there was ol' Joy Reid who I remembered from the Cleveland Repugnant Convention. We never really talked then, but I saw her enough to know she was fun and cool. She's a very socially comfortable person, and I bet when she's off for a weekend with just close friends, that is one helluva fun time.

She has a two-hour political show on MSNBC every weekend morning called *A.M. Joy,* but sometimes they give her one-off evening slots and call them *P.M. Joy,* and I told her how much I liked those, and she said with a big smiling twinkle, "Yeah, they're cool."

She's a real people person, and I told her how great she was in that funky coffeeshop they were broadcasting from in Iowa working the room talking to random voters. "That's so much fun," she confessed. "Who wants to talk to all these political experts," she said with a laugh and dismissive hand wave. "Lemme talk to real voters any day."

"Hey — I know there's no African-Americans on the stage, but the two women are kicking ass," I said.

"Women kick ass," she bounced back in her very enthusiastic kick-ass way, and all with a smile and I-mean-it eyes. I love this woman!

Over in the corner I noticed ol' Ari Melber in a chair deep back in an enclave, and figured he was hanging off the beaten trail for a reason. But I was keepin' my eye on that mofo. There's nobody in the history of political journalism who quotes rock and rap lyrics with the frequency and ease he does.

He finally got up to go to the bathroom or sumpthin, and I was BOOM! right there!

"Hey man, I dig your stuff."

"Oh, thanks."

"Are you a Deadhead?" I asked, since he quotes them frequently.

"Yeah. I first saw them with Jerry in '94," he said with a big proud smile.

He was wearing a plaid Neil Young or Kerouac-type workingman's shirt — the least dressed-up guy in the joint.

I just told you Joy Reid was prolly a weekend warrior under the right circumstances — but I request permission to revise and extend my remarks.

Ari Melber is the guy I wanna go to a concert with! Including the pre- and post-show hangs.

I was getting to like these politicos. Every one of them's got the lights on, and all the ones I met were curious and open and you could tell they were learning all the time. As much of a buzz as it was for me to get a few minutes insight into these mass-media thought leaders, I got the feeling they were gleaning at least as much from me as I them. Maybe more. They're all like writers in that way. *Everything* is information. Everything is a story. Every detail is important. Every person a character. Every person has a story. Maybe that's why I connect with these guys. We're all reporters with a slightly different medium. We don't have the same audience size, but we're all practicing the same art. And it made communication easy.

I told Ari how his Robert Hunter quotes reverberate through Deadlandia, which he beamed to hear. "It's so great the way you . . . *weave* them in," I said dramatically with a whoosh of my weaving hand like a Dead show dance.

"Oh God!" I suddenly remembered. "That Chris Matthews / Three Dog Night moment the other day!" and I bent over in pain with laughter. He laughed a crack, but not too hard cuz he didn't wanna rub it in. But it was priceless. It was during one of those wide oval desk panel discussions after some big event, I don't know what they were talking about, but Matthews said something, and Ari responded with, "Well, as Three Dog Night said, 'Two can be as bad as one.'" To which Matthews responded obliviously — "Well, I'm not hip enough to quote Three Dog Night." (!)

And BOOM! A month later he was gone.

"Are you having a good time in New Hampshire?" I asked.

"Yeah — it's great to get out of New York and meet people . . . like yourself," he said with a huge smile and hand gesture. "What are you doing here?" he asked, practicing his inquisitive nature.

I started to tell him about this Adventure Book, and about eight seconds into it, he goes, "*Fear & Loathing On The Campaign Trail!*" and smiled wide enough to let me know we're both in on the same joke. I bet ol' Alice D. and he have met.

We riffed on about poetry and politics, and songwriters capturing our moment — and I mentioned Dylan and Neil ... and he mentioned Jay-Z and Jeezy ... and suddenly I felt like somebody who thought Three Dog Night was cool.

Then I remembered he prolly had to go to the bathroom or something so we did the ol' photo and huggin' "see ya brother" routine. And that was the melting with Melber in Manchester moment.

~ = ~ = ~ = ~ = ~ * ~ = ~ = ~ = ~ = ~

One guy I didn't have a freakin' clue about coming in was **Andrew Yang**. Ever since my friend Brad hipped me to the non-politician with zero name recognition I'd been paying a close eye to this upbeat cat with the offbeat ideas. In his first answer in his first national debate he got a laugh and caught my attention saying, "The opposite of Donald Trump is an Asian guy who likes math." And then he dropped his break-out proposal of promising every American $1,000 a month as some kind of "freedom dividend" much to the jaw-dropped surprise and some snickers from all the other candidates on stage. This guy was taking the "free ponies for everyone!" idea to the moon! He called it a "Freedom Dividend" based on all the financial success the country had, like Alaska's payment to residents coming from their massive oil revenues. Yang's a successful tech entrepreneur who's bringing some fresh ideas to a staid political conversation. And this, combined with his youthful positive facile demeanor brought in waves of young voters who became known as the Yang Gang.

I got to his rally at the Nashua Community College where I'd also seen both Amy and Liz, and in diametric contrast to Warren's lack of any buttons or stickers, ol' Yanger was giving away MATH hats *and* t-shirts and all the buttons and stickers you could carry. He had begun using "Math" as the buzzword for his campaign, which he then cleverly/comically started to say stood for Make America Think Harder. His placards they give away for people to hold in the crowd said "Humanity First" which is a pretty spot-on mantra I've never heard used on a campaign before — and by 2020 it's pretty hard to come up with new poetry no one's phrased before.

The gym was packed — about 100 people behind the stage, 100 chairs filled on the floor, 200 sitting on the floor or standing around the perimeter, and another 50 hanging over a balcony walkway above. There were the red-shirted AARP crew in the front row as always, but there were more young people — or is that Yang people? — than any other rally I'd been to.

His paid staff all had cool little "MATH" buttons on their lapel to distinguish them from others for the local production hosts at each venue. It was pretty slick. No other campaign had such a thing. I wonder how many other good ideas this guy's got?

But, interestingly, for a cool guy who appeals to the young and has a cutting-edge vibe to everything he does, there was no pre-rally music (cutting edge or otherwise) like every other candidate had.

When he finally hit the stage, it was immediately obvious he and Liz Warren were the only two in this race with a dynamic high-energy stage presence. Both grabbed the handheld mic and prowled back & forth like stalking cats; both waved their arms conducting their words as they spoke; both enjoyed being in front of people and engaging with them in real time, and making them laugh. Natural performers. And there were only two in the field of ten in New Hampshire in 2020.

The guy is funny, empathetic and a self-made multi-millionaire — things that rarely all come in the same package. And he'd make a great math teacher. He *is* a great math teacher — the kind of guy who can make numbers the most interesting subject in the world! He told us how, because of the small population of New Hampshire versus the large population of California, each New Hampshire voter is worth 1,000 Californians. (!)

Or he could be a great history teacher when he talked about "the fourth industrial revolution" — the first being the birth of machines & factories; the second the advent of electricity, and the production of steel and automobiles; and the third being computers. And now the fourth is Artificial Intelligence, robotics, self-driving cars, 3D printing and the like — which we're just entering now, and how America is woefully unprepared for the changes in automation ahead.

He has lots of great lines — "I talk to the forerunners in the technology world, and I have this one friend, I'll call him 'Elon' ... " huge laugh . . . but it's true that he's interwoven into the furthest frontiers of technology — and that somebody with this insight is able to share it with a wider audience than would ever otherwise hear what's happening and where we're going is certainly one of the historic pluses and legacies of his campaign. He's definitely got a Big Picture vision. It would be a real long-shot for him to win the primary, but he's a straight-shooter with a fresh perspective on where we're at as a civilization, and way closer to how to tackle the problems than any other candidate in either party.

Bernie talks about a theoretical socialist "revolution" he'd like to start — but Yang is on the front line of a revolution that's already happening. Pete and Tulsi may be in their 30s, but Yang at 45 has the freshest perspective on our global landscape. He has a platform of *now*. And we ignore him at our peril.

8 for 8! — hanging with candidates and getting a shot for posterity!
:-)
I'm wearing one of his MATH hats here, but I tilted it upwards cuz I figured it was either my face or his word.

~ = ~ = ~ = ~ = ~ * ~ = ~ = ~ = ~ = ~

Saturday night (Feb. 8th) was **the big all-candidates McIntyre-Shaheen 100 Club Dinner in the 10,000-seat hockey & concert arena** in downtown Manchester.

This annual Democratic fundraiser has been held every year since 1959 when it was initiated to help neighboring Massachusetts Senator John F. Kennedy with his presidential bid. Over the years, every Democratic President, Vice President and major candidate has spoken at it, but it's usually held in a fancy ballroom, as per normal fundraisers. This year, with all the candidates running — 10 by the time of the dinner — they did what they did only once before, in 2016, and held it in the arena!

The donors at their $1000-a-plate dinner were sitting at round white linen tables covering the whole arena floor — including fellow Canadian-American actor Michael J. Fox right in front of me — while the entire lower bowl of arena seats had been bought section-by-section by different campaigns. Liz had four; Pete three; Bernie, Amy & Deval two; Biden one; and Yang had a couple up in the upper deck; with Tulsi, Bennet & Steyer scattered in pockets here and there. You got the sense that Deval, being from neighboring Massachusetts, knew to get in on this early (and get his two big center-ice sections), and ol' Yanger didn't know its importance until too late and ended up in the rafters.

When I first walked in, *Come Together* by The Beatles was blaring over the PA, and that was really the theme of the night.

And this is another good time to mention the camaraderie of Democratic voters. If a person only saw us on Facebook or Twitter, you'd think we all hated each other. But when there was a whole arena full of fans of ten different teams, I never heard a single cross word spoken during five hours of us hanging together.

So, of course I went on a full exploration of every person and place I could find before the program started. Every candidate had multiple tables & booths set up around the concourse.

You know how when you go to anywhere from a food court in a mall to a Shakedown Street in a parking lot, there are some places that have a line and crowd around them, and others with sadly forlorn workers behind a table of wares with no customers even stopping to look? Well, that was kinda the case here.

Pete, Bernie, Liz, Amy, Yang and Deval (of all people) had large buzzing crowds around their tables with free buttons and pamphlets and sometimes petitions or a candidate's book for sale, with vibrant excited conversations going on; and then you'd move on a few feet, and there would be these sad tables with three or four volunteers and nobody stopping, and you felt so bad for them — poor ol' Tulsi . . . ol' fourth-place Biden . . . Tom Who? Steyer . . . and the guy no one even knew was running, Michael Bennet. The volunteers behind their tables were as committed to their candidate as anybody else was to theirs, but thousands of Democrats just streamed past by the hour, with nary a nibble.

And it was funny how the volunteers kinda reflected their candidates. Pete's were largely gay, and I also mean that in the happy sense. There was a helluva party going on at each of his two or three booths spread around the giant oval concourse. They had a photo booth at one where you could get a picture with a life-size cutout, and people were striking all sorts of funny poses. And at another they were giving out Pete 2020 beer koozies of all things! Liz's volunteers were mostly female and all looked like law school students. Yang's looked like an undergrad keg party. Biden's was a bunch of older polo shirt-wearing straight-streets. And Bernie's crowd was as unruly as his hair in a wind storm.

Being the guy I am, I wanted to make the lonely tables feel better, so I'd stop and engage them, and hope to prompt somebody else to stop too. They just looked so forlorn and abandoned with *no one* talking to them. I found out about a Michael Bennet rally in Manchester on Monday, so I had the tip to catch one of the last ones I hadn't yet. When I stopped at the Tulsi table, I picked up a button and was told they're a dollar each! Kinda wish I'd bought one now, but at the time it seemed so off-putting that these promotional materials to advertise a candidate had to paid for when everybody else was giving them away for free.

But the coolest score of all was at a Biden table. Seeing as there was no crowd in front blocking my view, I spotted some "Joe Biden for President" buttons I hadn't seen anywhere else. I started talking to the polo shirt, and it turns out, get this, the state Chair for his *1988* campaign still had boxes of them from that aborted run . . . *32 years ago!!* I had just been time-traveling back to 1988 while writing about it for this book — and now I was holding in my hand a rare artifact of a campaign that never even made it to Iowa!

Heading back into the arena, the large stage was in-the-round, covering what would be center ice, and I had an aisle seat near the red line. Just before it started, I noticed four seats open in the front freakin' row! So Boom! down I go.

The idea of the evening was that each candidate would speak for ten minutes. It was the proverbial political "elevator pitch." Other than single-candidate die-hards, everybody in the arena had probably attended rallies by multiple candidates — but certainly no one had seen all ten. And this was the night we all got to do that.

Another thing that was cool about the Deval Patrick campaign, when I was checking in and they gave me the Deval placard, I asked what I was supposed to do with it and what I was expected to do in general, and the woman said, "Wave it when he comes on and cheer for him — at least louder than you cheer for the others." And that last part was so key. This wasn't a "You must hate everyone

else" campaign. I really appreciated that. As Democrats —
the other candidates are not the enemy. And when you get
offline and get in the middle of 10,000 of us all rooting for
different candidates, *We Are Family*, as the Sister Sledge
song they played before it started said.

Oh and speaking of good tunes — as the warm-
up music, they played a whole buncha upbeat songs
thematically linked to our mission — *You Ain't Seen
Nothing Yet* by Canada's own BTO!; *We Are The Champions*
by Queen; *Happy* by Pharrell; *Simply The Best* – Tina
Turner; *Go Your Own Way* – Fleetwood Mac; *Move On
Up* – Curtis Mayfield; *Higher Love* – Steve Winwood; *Love
Wins* – Carrie Underwood; *Land of Hope and Dreams* –
Springsteen; *The Bullpen* – Dessa; *(Your Love Keeps Lifting
Me) Higher & Higher* – Jackie Wilson; and *O-o-h Child* by
Nina Simone were a few I remember.

The two New Hampshire Democratic Senators
Jeanne Shaheen and Maggie Hassan spoke first, then Iowa
delegate-winner **Mayor Pete** came out as the leadoff
candidate to a prolonged ovation and chants by his yellow-
shirted supporters of Boot-Edge-Edge (as their signs spelled
it). He wisely compared the town he was mayor of to the
one we were standing in — and that small towns are more
the heart of America than anywhere else.

Amy was next, and she wisely turned and said, "Hi,
Bernie people!" to their section with a big smile, after they'd
occasionally booed Pete. That was also, sadly, the section
that when one of the candidates would say "We've all got
to pull together to beat trump," and everyone in the arena
would stand and cheer, the Bernie section would be visibly
sitting including on their hands. "What unites us is bigger
than what divides us," Amy stressed. "This election is an

economic check on this president. It's a patriotism check. A decency check," she said, reminding us of the indecent face of our country right now.

Joe Biden came running out the runway to the stage to show his youth and energy, I guess. His speech began disturbingly stilted with him having to read off a script on the podium, and I was thinking the same thing as at his earlier rally — *"Oh no!* This guy only has to do ten minutes and he's been on the trail ten months . . . *and he needs to read it?!"* But then a kind of amazing thing happened — he suddenly just walked away from the podium and started wandering around the big stage talking directly to the Bernie section, then the Liz section, about poverty asking "How this could be happening in our country?" Then wove into violence against women — both the subject and the Act he wrote. And he really became possessed and suddenly had the whole arena enwrapped. He transitioned into trump mocking the disabled and how the man didn't have a shred of decency in him. And like a great musician he just kept building and building in intensity. What started out as a doddering old man reading a script morphed into a fireball that had the whole arena captivated — and looking back on it now, it seems like a microcosm of the stumbling start of his campaign that suddenly exploded into something no one saw coming. Section by section people started rising out of their seats as he built and built — "We have to **stand up** against bigotry, hatred, the abuse of power. We've got to stand up America! And we've got to do it now! *Now!"* and he had a standing ovation by the end of it.

Then **Yang The Younger** came bouncing out — seizing the rock star arena moment and prowling the stage from end to end, smooth as Chinese silk, with a Bill Nye The

Science Guy skill at making the complex fun. He had the place in the palm of his performance hand — from Berners to Warren warriors. And I respected that he was the only guy who talked about small town newspapers closing. "It's very hard to have a democracy function when people don't know what's going on in their community." I hope this ethical thinker is going to be in our national discourse for a long time.

Tom Steyer came out to Pete's signature *Up Around The Bend* — "There's a place up ahead that I'm going, as fast as my feet can fly." This was the only time I ever caught him in person because he left New Hampshire the next day, and the campaign entirely two states later. He hit every key issue on the minds of Democrats — minimum wage, healthcare, education, the environment — but in the inexplicableness of politics, he just never caught on with voters. He was ahead of the curve on impeaching trump, but ended up in a traffic jam of more appealing candidates.

Warren came out to an ovation that wouldn't stop even as she tried to start her speech. She told the story of her reading a letter by Coretta Scott King on the Senate floor that was stopped by the Repugnant majority, and how Moscow McConnell's line attempting to silence her, "Nevertheless, she persisted," became a rallying cry for feminists and resistance movements worldwide. "Fighting back is an act of patriotism. We fought back against a king to build this country. We fought back against the scourge of slavery to protect this union. We fought back against a great depression to rebuild our economy, and we fought back against fascism to protect our democracy. That's who we are," said this fighter. "This is our time. This is our moment to choose hope over fear. This is our moment to dream big, fight hard, and *win!*" For an Okie from Bostonee she's sure got a lot of Baptist preacher in her! And to the strains of Aretha Franklin's *Respect* she literally danced off the stage.

To which **Bernie Sanders** responded — I'll see your Aretha, and raise you one John Lennon — playing his *Power to The People* as he walked to the podium. And speaking of podiums, only he and Joe used one — and they ended up being the last two standing in this fight, so maybe podiums are the key. One of the things I love about Bernie, and that I hope his most fervent supporters embrace as much as they do everything else he says is — "I know that there are differences of opinion in the room. I *detect* that. (laughter) But what I want to say, is that despite the differences of opinion and the candidates that we are supporting, and I know that I speak for every candidate, is that no matter who wins the Democratic nomination we are going to come together to defeat the most dangerous president in the history of this country." And yes, even the Bernie supporters in the house cheered this. I just wish this sentiment of his and his in-person supporters were reflected more by those who stay home and type their intransigence onto social media. And he very validly pointed out that, "Four years ago when I was here in New Hampshire, many of the ideas that we talked about like raising the minimum wage to a living wage of 15 bucks an hour were considered radical. They're not radical today. Seven states have passed a $15 an hour minimum wage." (thunderous applause) "Now is the time for us to come together, to end the divisiveness, the racism, the lying, the homophobia, the xenophobia, the religious bigotry of the trump administration." The guy's not wrong. And I was happy to hear his boppin' joyous dancing outro — *Takin' It*

To The Streets by the Doobie Brothers — which I had just danced to at their show live with a bunch of Pranksters at the Woodstock 50th last summer.

Then it was the friendly ol' **Deval Patrick**, the dude who invited me to the party — and a guy most people didn't even know was in the race! He told a great story that summed up his approach to governance and life — about when he was Governor and supporting refugees fleeing violence, he went to a store and was confronted by an angry man who shouted at him that he was wrong. But in that same store, six other people came up and whispered that they supported his decision. And in that moment he realized — "We have learned to shout our anger and to whisper our kindness, and it's completely upside down. We need to learn again to shout kindness, to shout compassion, to shout justice. *That* is who we are." "Shout Kindness" should be his campaign slogan.

Next up was the Senator from Colorado, **Michael Bennet** — another guy just about nobody knew was running. And the sad part was, by now the lower bowl seats for the big-name candidates were starting to empty after hours of candidates talking, so very few heard him speak about the importance of winning purple states to retake the Senate. We better have a longer collective attention span if we wanna win this November.

Last up was **Tulsi Gabbard**, in her signature white pantsuit, who had the good sense to open with, "I want to thank the entire crew who made this evening possible, especially because they had the wisdom to save the best for last." She actually got a pretty good response for a half-empty house, particularly from the remaining Warren and Buttigieg supporters. The "Aloha" peace warrior

338

was stressing her experience more than her vision, which seemed an odd tact for a 38-year-old, but it got her a solid 3% of the vote 3 days later.

I sure as hell never saw ten presidential candidates speak in person on the same night in the same place before, and probably never will again. As goofy and dysfunctional as us Dems are — as Will Rogers put it, "I am not a member of any organized political party. I'm a Democrat." — the spectrum of voices & visions blended into a harmonious choir proactively addressing climate change, improving healthcare and public schools, creating economic fairness, relieving poverty, taxing giant profit-reaping corporations responsibly, protecting women's rights, being kinder to one another, uniting together, and being involved.

And that is why I'm a Democrat.

~ = ~ = ~ = ~ = ~ * ~ = ~ = ~ = ~ = ~ = ~

Sunday was sort of an "off" day. The only two candidates I hadn't caught — Tom Steyer and Michael Bennet — were not appearing anywhere near me. In fact, Steyer wasn't appearing *anywhere* — today *or* tomorrow. He left the state entirely! And on top of that, attempting to confirm what didn't make sense, I discovered he didn't even have a functioning website! He *had* one, but it wasn't maintained, and there was no place to check for appearances.

With Bennet and Bernie scheduled for Monday, my Kerouac buddy Steve gave me a personal tour of all the Jack spots in Nashua, including the family plot in the local cemetery where his mother, father, brother and daughter are all buried, and is the very site where not one, not two, but three of his novels climax. (!) (*The Town & The City*, *Visions of Gerard*, and *Vanity of Duluoz*)

That night was the Academy Awards. Heading to New Hampshire, I had visions of watching it with a roomful of politicos, but couldn't find a single damn person planning to catch it! And the people at the campaigns thought I was crazy even suggesting it two days before Get Out The Vote election day!

It was broadcast on ABC, and I kicked myself realizing that when I snuck into their party Friday night, that's when I needed to hustle up a network watch party! So I was home alone when Brad Pitt won Best Supporting Actor and said, "They told me I only have 45 seconds up here, which is 45 seconds more than the Senate gave John Bolton this week. I'm hoping maybe Quentin does a movie about it, and in the end the adults do the right thing."

I was really rooting for their collaboration *Once Upon a Time in Hollywood*, but it turned out more of a *Parasite* night — which pissed off donald trump, so at least that was good.

~ = ~ = ~ = ~ = ~ * ~ = ~ = ~ = ~ = ~

On the very last day of the New Hampshire primary, I went to the very last presidential campaign rally ever held by **Michael Bennet**.

It was at Franklin Pierce University in a converted old 1800s mill building on the banks of the Merrimack River in Manchester — up in a student lounge conference room on the third floor. This was sure not a gymnasium-packing act I was catching! In fact — I rode up in the elevator with the candidate and his family! Wanted to take a picture but it was just too intimately closely weird.

We all walked out of the lift and into the room together as a woman was at the microphone vamping because we were all a smidge late. "Oh, and here's the star of our show now . . . " she said to the 50 or so people seated. He walked straight to the mic, and I straight to a second row aisle seat.

This was the end of small-room campaigning in 2020. After tomorrow, everything would move to Las Vegas, then South Carolina, then Super Tuesday, and the days of rallies in rooms with 50 people would be long over.

But here we were — the presidential candidate from Colorado in his pullover sweater and blue jeans having a conversation with a handful of voters. This was so "small town" — we could've been in Woody Creek! And I was wearing my Tilley hat in Hunter's honor.

Bennet's three daughters were standing at the back of maybe ten rows of chairs. And even though we were on a college campus, it was almost all voters older than me who probably have their radios tuned to NPR at home and have never missed voting once in their lives. We were mere hours away from ballots being cast, and these people were out listening to a candidate who was polling at 1% in the state. My kinda people.

Bennet's a really funny guy with a quirky offbeat view and dry delivery so you don't see the lines comin'. I think his whole campaign was really just a cover to launch his stand-up career.

I was so happy to hear him call Colorado legend Gary Hart a friend and mentor, and that Gary and Bennet's dad were friends, and he and Gary have been since before he ever ran for office.

He talked about being respectful of others, and the importance of coming from a swing state — that Colorado is 1/3 Democrats, 1/3 Republicans, and 1/3 independents, like New Hampshire — and how that teaches you to look at all sides and reach across the aisle and how this is so sorely lacking in our politics today.

Somebody asked about marijuana legalization in Colorado and he said not only is it working there but that he co-sponsored a bill to legalize it federally and expunge all prior convictions — adding that Mexico should legalize it and how that would stop so much violence and gang warfare down there. And he described the buses that fill up and leave from old folks' homes to go to the pot dispensaries. It's sure a new world for the old nowadays.

When it was over, it was such a casual small scene we were able to have a nice talk. I told him the story of Ken Kesey saying in Colorado at the Kerouac Conference in Boulder in 1982 that the first state to legalize marijuana would have a big jump on the rest of the country. "Smart guy. Good for him. I'm sorry that he's not still here," which heartened me both that he knew that, and would say that.

And we got to talk about Gary Hart a little bit, and he loved the story I told you in the opening chapter about one of his rallies changing my life. "Yes, Gary changed a lot of young people's lives with that campaign. And New Hampshire was the state that changed *his* life back in '84. I hope it's as lucky for this Colorado Senator," he said with a twinkle.

After we snapped the picture together — making me 9-for-9 with candidates at rallies — myself and a young millennial woman were both packing up our stuff at the same time. "Cool coat," I said of the full-length old-west leather duster she was putting on.

"It was my uncle's."

"It's still in great shape."

344

And we started talking and it turned out she was Alexandra Petri from the *Washington Post* and she asked to turn our yak into an interview which turned into a long discussion about the Dems prospects in November. Only Iowa had voted at this point and we had no idea who the Dem nominee was going to be, but I pointed out the two big other factors as she scribbled notes furiously. "First, there's the whole Bloomberg thing. Even if we Democrats screw up — and we sometimes do — he's going to be running a whole parallel campaign on his own. And he's really good at it. He didn't just throw money at those 24 House candidates in 2018, he hooked them up with strategists and ad makers and came up with entire strategies that the rookies never even thought of. If Bloomberg was involved in 2016, he would have seen the problems in Michigan and Wisconsin and moved to fix them. I don't think we're going to make the same kinds of electoral college mistakes in this year — but it's gonna be great to have this guy — who won us the House back for godsakes — running a cousin campaign.

"And the other thing is The Lincoln Project — y'know, Rick Wilson, Steve Schmidt, George Conway, all those guys — that's going to be a whole other battalion on the battlefield. And they're as dedicated to beating trump as we are, but they've got the inside scoop of how the Republican Party works. So they're gonna be waging their own war," and I started using the table beside us as a battlefield map drawing out the troops placements of the Allied Forces — "And Bloomberg's gonna be waging his, and then there's the whole Democratic machine coming up the middle."

She heard me mentioning Kesey and Kerouac to the senator, so we veered off in that direction for a bit, which she was as interested in as the campaign. She said the Beats were a literary movement she wanted to learn more about, so I told her she came to the right place, and off we riffed.

I later checked out her column in the Opinions section of the *Post*, and although she didn't write one on me, I discovered she's a really funny political satirist! If you like your politics with a twist, she's pretty twisted!

And as we walked out of the old mill building, the late afternoon sun was just beginning to set on the 2020 New Hampshire primary — and there was only one rally Adventure left.

~ = ~ = ~ = ~ = ~ * ~ = ~ = ~ = ~ = ~

And then there was **Bernie**.

He'd never appeared in Nashua, Manchester, Merrimack or anywhere else I was able to catch him — and now I was gonna have to drive an hour out to the coast to the University of New Hampshire campus in Durham.

In a two-hour window, I went from 50 old folks in a conference room . . . to 7,000 screaming college kids with rock bands and movie stars in a hockey arena. Democracy takes many forms in America.

From the time I drove up in the dark to swirling flashlights pointing me to overflow parking lots, this felt like every arena rock concert I've ever been to.

There was a half-mile-long line of people, so I went to look for my imaginary friend holding a place for me at the front, and there was a guy in a wheelchair who made me flash on my old pal (and Kerouac's) Henri Cru, and we got talking primary politics. Through the glass doors I could see they were checking bags like they do at arena concerts, and by the time we'd inched to the door, I just pointed to my new friend like I was his "plus one" and walked through with a sidebag full of cold Heinekens.

I entered this primary as a Liz Warren supporter, and also came in with fond feelings for ol' Obama VP Joe Biden, and figured I might like Andrew Yang — but walking into this Bernie event, I had the oddest feeling that **I was coming home**.

The big stage was set up in front of the players' benches on one side of the ice rink floor, with the circling white hockey boards — and there was another slapshot of "home." I got a great aisle seat on the side and watched these thousands of kids create their own form of participatory democracy. Spontaneous cheers would rise up and roll around the arena like a wave for no reason except wanting to scream joy for The Berning Man and the moment. They even started doing The Wave around the arena bowl with all of us standing up and waving our arms as it rolled past.

Since this was shaping up as such the perfect setting to climax the primary, I hooked up with my old Prankster pal Alice D. who added a whole extra layer of color to the proceedings.

Thusly enhanced, I left my coat on the seat with my new best-friend neighbors and went to meet the wild cats filling the Wildcats' arena. I learned that this UNH campus has about 15,000 students, and that Bernie's appeared here twice before (but never in the arena), and that the student body was split roughly 50/50 for trump/not trump — just like the state itself had voted by a difference of only 0.4% for Clinton in 2016. Of the Democratic-leaning students, I was told about half were Very Bernie, and half were very Not Bernie.

I met a bunch of Berners at the big Dem dinner on Friday night, but this was the first time this cycle (see, also, 2016, page 179) I was in a building full of them. I talked to both official t-shirt-wearing volunteers and regular students and every one of them was as nice as could be. Polite, engaged, informed, friendly . . . in such stark contrast to the Bros & Brats typing into Facebook every day. That was the overwhelming takeaway from this experience — the night-&-day difference between these happy love-filled positive people and the destroy-others / conspiracy-theory crap you see online.

Bernie's 2020 campaign slogan — "Not me, us" — was written in lights all around the arena, which seemed to me to be him attempting to get away from the messianic cult of personality that had arisen around his campaign. I guess we'll learn in the summer and fall of 2020 whether his furthest out supporters embraced this signature line of his campaign or not.

And just like the rock concert vibe this whole night was, they had an opening band! **Sunflower Bean**, a psychedelic punk quartet from New York City, with a lead singer, Julia Cumming, who had invited Alexandria Ocasio-Cortez to speak at her *first ever* public forum as she was beginning her campaign in the Democratic primary for the seat in the Bronx she would eventually win. The band ripped a letter-perfect *My Generation* by The Who, including the funky John Entwistle bass breaks and a Keith Moon flurry to climax, so they won me over.

Bernie supporter **Nina Turner** came out in a flowing floor-length black-&-white leopard-skin-patterned dress, and prowled the stage like a stalking wolf, reminding me of her nearly namesake Tina Turner, using a repeated "Hello somebody!" call-&-response cue to the audience to cheer. I'll tell ya, this woman makes Angela Davis look like a stay-at-home mom.

With the packed arena and fervently cheering fans, I thought — "Boy, if only people under 30 could vote, Bernie Sanders would win in a landslide!"

Sex In The City star and New York Democratic gubernatorial primary challenger **Cynthia Nixon** came out, and when she mentioned voting for Hillary four years ago and people started booing at the mention of her name, Cynthia put up her hand in an emphatic stop sign and said, "Oh no. Oh no. We're not going to do that here," and actually got cheers as she began listing Hillary's qualities that made her vote for her. She went on to say why she flipped in four years — because of Bernie advancing the discussion on Medicare for all, free college for all, a $15 national minimum wage, the Green New Deal — and did it all with an actress's dramatics. She was something of a fixture in the New York City theater world of the 1980s and I saw her do Shakespeare In The Park and both on Broadway and Off, so I appreciated seeing the continuum of her on a stage again in our common passion play of democracy.

And speaking of dramatic! Good Lord! **Cornel West** came out next! This guy reminds me of the Beat poet Amiri Baraka. Or maybe Dick Gregory. Or Don King. Or Bobby Seale. Or all four.

Obviously he and Bernie both went to the same Arm Flailing School of Dramatics, but Cornel is definitely from the Baptist preacher side of the family. He rhymes, he testifies, he drops scripture, and drops names like John Coltrane, Stevie Wonder, Martin Luther King Jr., Cesar Chavez and Harvey Milk into his passionate animated sermon on love and democracy that had the audience screaming with a fervor even rock concerts don't produce. These kids were sure getting their money's worth tonight!

And speaking of rock stars! **Alexandria Ocasio-Cortez** — the Beyoncé of Congress — came out to a building-shaking scream-deafening ovation. Between Julia Cumming & Cynthia Nixon from Manhattan, Bernie from Brooklyn, and AOC from the Bronx there was definitely a whole lotta New York in da house. I heard a few people say that whether it was Bernie or Biden or whomever got the nomination, they were only a placeholder till AOC came of age. And I'll tell you — watching her on a campaign stage — I can't think of any candidate ever who comes close to her combination of articulation, delivery and buoyant energy. She's a blend of Cornel's Baptist preacher with Bernie's political philosophy. She has an Obama-like mouthful of beaming white teeth when she smiles, and an Andrew Yang-like ability to explain big ideas in a way you can follow and understand. I'm not saying that I agree with every position or action she takes, or that she could actually win Ohio or Florida, but this woman is a political superstar. I don't know how her storyline will play out, whether she can broaden her appeal beyond her deep blue base, but boy, she's got all the tools — and they're all brand new. As Kerouac and Cassady talked about in *On The Road* — she has got "IT."

At one point she mentioned that she'd been in Washington for a year, and I blurted out in disbelief to the civics student beside me — "Wait — she's only been there a year?!" And his eyes bugged open in confirmation. "Yep." It seems like she's already an institution — How could it only be a year?!

After her incredible rousing "Forward! Forward! Forward!" climax, once again John Lennon's voice singing *Power To The People* came blasting over the PA — and the old white-haired messiah appeared!

I love how he opened with — "People are sick of a president who is a pathological liar, who is running a corrupt administration, who is a bully, and a vindictive person, who is a racist, a sexist, a xenophobe, a homophobe, and a religious bigot. (pause) And those are his nice qualities. Americans understand that that is not the kind of human being who should be in the White House."

And one thing was clear — Bernie's health seems great! He was in command of the room, full of energy and in strong voice. As we've all aged beyond "don't trust anyone over 30" I've learned with each passing decade that age numbers that once seemed unfathomably old are now attached to people like my energetic 80-year-old stage partner George Walker, or the irrepressible 89-year-old

David Amram who I perform with every year at Lowell Celebrates Kerouac. We've all learned in recent years — if you keep your mind and body active there's more life to this life than we thought before.

As Bernie the rock star kept conducting the room like a long-armed maestro with set crescendos to get cheers and other cues to get boos, and I saw these kids fist-pumping from the mosh pit to the rafters, I wondered if this could translate to an audience older than college students?

But it was easy to see, at least for this old dude, why he's so popular. "Are you ready for a radical idea? My administration will believe in *science*." . . . "Two years ago, trump and his friends gave a trillion dollar tax break to the 1% and large profitable corporations. If Congress can give tax breaks to billionaires, we can cancel all student debt in America." . . . "500,000 people a year go bankrupt because of medically-related debt while the healthcare industry last year made $100 billion in profit."

So much of what Bernie says makes such level-headed reasonable sense — it's so tragic there's this fringe of vocal supporters who're exactly the opposite. I've been reading the same intractable judgmental viciousness on social media in Bernie's name since 2016. With the plainly inclusive anti-messiah "NOT ME, US" flashing all around the arena, and the "we're all in this together" theme of his entire speech, and the love-bunny John Lennon blessing his entrance to the stage, how have so many of his supporters ended up being extremist hate-mongers like no other campaign's? Bernie could have been curled up with John & Yoko in their bed-ins for peace — but some of his supporters sound like they just got out of a trump rally. All the people I was sitting surrounded by were funny and smart and polite

. . . and as soon as I opened Facebook when I got home it was a firehose of hate from them directed at every other candidate and institution of governance. **How does the guy preaching the communal sharing gospel of Woodstock end up creating an army of Hells Angels at Altamont?** It's such a shame — and disrespectful disservice to both the man and the message.

And in the Something I Never Thought I'd See Dept.: — Bernie Sanders playing Bill Graham introducing the rock band The Strokes! — yet more New York City in the house! And they even opened with hometown heroes the Talking Heads' *Burning Down The House!* The arena floor was closed off hours earlier, but security stepped away when the rock 'n' roll started, and a stream of students flew past me down the stairs.

Here I was at a rock concert — a *political* rock concert — in 2020 . . . the very connection I made with the Gary Hart rally in 1984. I first understood what politics were by seeing a young rock star of a politician playing to a crowd from a concert stage on a street in Greenwich Village. And now here it was in a packed arena all these decades and pages later . . . with a light show, and video screens, and dry ice, and a costumed band sounding like early Alice Cooper, and a mosh pit, and a thousand kids pogo dancing to post-punk with political placards waving.

"Will the circle be unbroken, by and by Lord, by and by."

"Come senators, congressmen, please heed the call . . . there's a battle outside and it's raging."

"Kids want a savior, don't need a fake, I want to be elected."

And the band invited the audience up on stage for the climactic number, blending the performers and the fans, the one voice with the many, the pedestal with the populace, the stars with the groundlings. This was Bernie's message of inclusion manifesting in action in the masses. You say you want a revolution, you better get on stage right away.

Power to the people, right on.

~ = ~ = ~ = ~ = ~ * ~ = ~ = ~ = ~ = ~

Then the most extraordinary thing happened when it was over. As the thousands of kids streamed out of the arena, right next to it was a big outdoor skating pond, and in the joy of the frozen midnight moment in New Hampshire, students began climbing over the fence and figure skating on it without skates.

Here were the children of the euphoric night, inspired by a politician to dance the light fandango, waving blue Bernie signs as their batons — running and sliding, cheering and laughing, pirouetting in moonlight, and celebrating their first brush with democracy.

Bernie's rock star rally had flashed me back to Gary Hart in '84 — but this was taking me all the way back to my childhood in Winnipeg and going for skates in the early darkness of winter nights on a pond full of happy people in a tranquil town reveling in the simple pleasures of frozen water.

Snowbanks surrounded the ice, everyone's breath was visible in the misty night, cheeks were turning rosy, and strangers were hugging strangers in the land where they

let the children hug. Democracy had played out for the last
week in New Hampshire, and now voters were out playing
in the last hours before tomorrow's voting.

I'm the guy who spots a cool assemblage of friends
and wrangles everyone together to get a group photo, but I
didn't know anyone here, and everyone was spread out all
over the ice.
Then the next amazing thing happened.

You know those sprawling group photos taken at
center ice when an NHL team wins the Stanley Cup?
And you know who Wayne Gretzky is? Did you know he
invented those?
It was when he won his last Cup with the Oilers
in 1988 at a game in their Edmonton home town —
their fourth in five years. After the players had skated
euphorically around the rink hoisting the Cup above their
adrenaline heads, Captain Gretzky grabbed it back and
suddenly started waving the players to center ice to take
a group shot with the authentic sweat and victory joy still
fresh on all their faces. First it was just the core players,
but more and more trainers & coaches & managers and all
the people who made the team work came running from the
sidelines sliding into the group.
Well, that very scene played out on the frozen pond
with this team celebrating the Sanders Cup on home ice.
First, about a dozen friends gathered for a group shot,
and I ran over in the role of photographer to capture their
collective joy, including because there wasn't a single
member of press present. I was it.
And as I snapped their hooting faces, more people
saw what was happening and came shushing across the ice
and sliding into them like a crazy cartoon of calamity. I had

to keep backing up to get their ever-expanding team in the frame, and more student photographers with phones joined my press pool. All that was missing was a big silver Cup in the middle.

From first catching Deval Patrick in a small dark basement room in a library, the New Hampshire primary built to a massive open-air love-in of screaming laughing joy. This was democracy in action in real time in America. From old folks gathering in a gym on a Tuesday afternoon to hear Joe Biden to thousands of college kids filling an arena and spontaneously creating their own escapades of Ice Capades, participation in the political process is healthy and thriving. It's not any one group or one voice, but a collective of choirs singing songs of joy and progress, of innocence and experience — and forever Going Furthur.

~ = ~ = ~ = ~ = ~ * ~ = ~ = ~ = ~ = ~

New Hampshire Primary Election Night
Tuesday, February 11th, 2020

For some reason I was under the mistaken notion that the campaigns were all going to be throwing private "victory parties" for their staffs and volunteers. But thanks to the handy-dandy New Hampshire NPR "candidate tracker" website I found out they were all holding events open to the public!

I caught every candidate twice (except Tom Steyer) — once solo, and once at the big dinner. And now tonight every candidate was throwing a party — and once again it was New Orleans Jazz Fest time — you gotta pick a stage out of a whole lot of cool choices.

My bright idea was — since ol' Yanger was giving away shirts and hats and everything else at some random rally — imagine the party he was gonna throw on election night?! I looked up the locations of a few candidates — Liz was having hers at some Health & Sports Club that didn't sound very fun, and Bernie was going to be in a big box university field house, but Yang's was in some fancy joint where you'd throw a nice wedding reception.

I put all three Manchester addresses into my GPS and started driving not knowing where I was going. Turned out, **Liz's** was on the south end of town which I'd get to first, so I figured I'd check that out on the way to Yang's royal spread. Even though polls didn't close until

8:00, by 7:00 this massive sports complex parking lot was overflowing and it seemed like a big victory party was indeed at hand.

Inside this huge high-ceilinged industrial warehouse-type building there were two massive areas roped off and filled with press, and they had a well-catered feast of pulled pork, Swedish meatballs, fresh veggies and homemade cookies! Plus there was a bar selling beer & wine so people could be in an extra good mood, and everything looked set for a party. Except it had the buzz of some Kiwanis dinner my parents would drag me to as a teenager when I knew there was better stuff going on everywhere else.

Over in the corner they had one TV, muted, on CNN, and for some reason they were reporting results before the polls closed — and Liz was getting about 8%! "Oh no! This is a disaster!"

I took one more look around this roomful of my parent's friends and got the hell out of there!

Yang's wedding reception was eight minutes away. After seeing the spread that Liz's broke campaign laid out, I walked in expecting a royal feast, an open bar and free iPads — but was greeted with a tray of celery sticks.

New Year's Eve at The Ritz this was not! But Yanger's supporters are young and fun, and everybody was hitting the cash bar with vigor. There were only three news cameras set up — as opposed to the wall of them two-deep at Liz's — so I kinda had a feeling I was not in the center of the universe.

Within minutes of the 8:00 poll closings, Andrew and his wife Evelyn came out and the 150 or so Yang Gangers in the fancy reception room went bananas. I was standing maybe ten feet directly in front of him and noticed that the happy warrior candidate didn't seem to have his normal buoyant visage, but I figured he was just tired after three rallies a day for months.

He gave a standard election night speech, thanking all the voters and volunteers, and rattled through the key bullet points of his stump speech, then said, "You know that I'm the Math guy, and it is clear tonight from the numbers that we are not going to win this race," which I obliviously thought was referring to the New Hampshire race. Then he dropped the bomb right in front of me — "And so tonight I am announcing that I am suspending my campaign for president."

What?! Never been in the room for one of those before! Boom!

Then whaddya do?

Me — I jumped in the car and bolted over to **Bernie Sanders**.

Another eight minutes later I pulled up to the field house intersection to find spinning police car lights and roads blocked off. The cop told me I gotta go to some satellite parking lot way down some road. I turned, saw an office building that was obviously closed for the day, took the chance, grabbed the last spot, and begin the mile long walk to wherever it was people were streaming to.

A few others were coming the other way towards us and I was concerned he'd already spoken — or why would they be leaving? Turned out, when the cluster of us finally got to the building, there was a line four people wide going all the way along the end of the field house . . . then all the way through the long parking lot . . . then all the way back out of the parking lot . . . then up the long ramp to the road . . . then continuing along the street!!

Unless this "field house" is way the hell bigger than I think it is — most of these people are never getting in! It was time for Adventureman to pull a magic trick.

I went to the front doors to get the lay of the land. They were letting press, staff and volunteers in, with no set time for the rest of us, and they didn't cotton too well to me hanging around. So I started working the line, lookin'

for familiar faces from eight days On The Road, and right near the front bumped into somebody I'd been looking for since I first arrived in his native New England — my old pal from the Repugnant Convention in Cleveland — the mighty **Vermin Supreme**!

Vermin has been treating every presidential election since the '80s as performance art. He actually gets on the ballot in some places — and this year he was trying to win the Libertarian nomination, "And I think I might get it," he tells me. He wears this custom-made two-foot-high black rubber boot on his head, and he's *always* performing.

He's a bit like Wavy Gravy, who also ran a playful parody campaign — Nobody for President — from '76 thru '84 when I actually tried to book him for a rally at NYU, but it never happened. He had all sorts of great campaign slogans — "Nobody's perfect!" and "Who's going to look out for you? Nobody!" and "Who keeps all his campaign promises? Nobody!" and "Nobody should have too much power!" which was all in the grand Abbie / Prankster / Dadaist spirit.

And in keeping with this great American tradition of comedic presidential candidates from Gracie Allen to the Yippies running Pigasus to Pat Paulsen to Deez Nuts in 2016, Vermin runs on platforms promising zombie preparedness, free ponies for everyone, and time travel research.

As he worked "the room" I played Ed McMahon to his Johnny until they opened the doors. I could see in advance that people weren't just streaming in, so I assumed that meant they were checking bags, and I quickly took off my coat, put my brewski-filled sidebag over my shoulder, put my coat back on, and as we went in I played the old lost-in-the-crowd / center-line routine with uniforms checking on both sides I slipped up a hole in the middle and once again got in with a bagful of cold ones!

I went straight into the field house rally room and — "Oh-oh!" It was basically just a basketball court in a high school gym, with a ten-row bleacher running along one wall that was reserved for staff & press, a giant roped off stage at one end, an enormous two-tiered riser the width of the room at the back overflowing with cameras and reporters, and the other side wall was all sectioned off with working press tables. There was barely a basketball court open. I shook my head picturing that line outside that was already stretching down the far road an hour ago. "90% of those people are never gonna get in!" And the other crazy thing was, they closed off the doors very shortly after I hit the hardwood. The court was not crowded at all — maybe a couple hundred people. The fire marshals were on hand, and they didn't want it to be unsafely mobbed — and boy it sure wasn't.

I immediately found my Swedish reporter brothers and we shared a blazing international buzz. And there on the packed camera risers were Ed O'Keefe from CBS, Ryan Nobles from CNN, and MSNBC's Sanders Road Warrior Shaquille Brewster all at the front. *This* was clearly the center of the universe.

I don't know what happened to Vermin, but he never made it in the room. Maybe they didn't like his hat.

After some roundabout hellos, I went to the center of the floor, about five people back from the stage-front rope-line, and got an excellent spot with all short people between me and Bernie's podium.

And it was a party! I talked to a huge krewe of various Europeans from some university over there who were all in the same Poli-Sci program, and I learned all about how the multi-party system mostly works in the Netherlands, and how Angela Merkel is who she is cuz she grew up in the austere conditions of East Germany. It's so great that all these different universities are getting their students to on-the-ground events in democracy and not just babbling in a classroom. And this same experience is open to every American every day of every election — and we don't have to pay tuition or fly across an ocean to do it.

In the background they were playing the soundtrack to our lives: Simon & Garfunkel's brilliant Kerouacian *America* — that actually had the room singing along! And the also-Jack-triggered *On The Road Again* by Willie Nelson. And Tracy Chapman's *Talkin' 'Bout A Revolution*. And they even played two Canadians back-to-back — Rush's *Closer To The Heart*, and Neil Young's *Rockin' In The Free World!*

Then a writer from the B.U. (Boston University) newspaper started interviewing me about Yang dropping out, and how Michael Bennet also had, and about how the field was gonna keep shrinking. And we riffed about how Tulsi came across so much better in person than TV. And about how Amy did so well here and deserved to be coming in third. And how Mayor Pete was the undeniable rising star, coming in one point behind Bernie!

Cornel West and Nina Turner came out shaking hands and talking up the crowd without getting on the stage. They had one big TV screen up in the corner so we could see (but not hear) other candidates giving their speeches. When 2nd place Pete finally came on he was the only guy to get booed. Then before he'd even finished, we heard over the PA — "Ladies and gentlemen — please welcome — *the next President of the United States!! — Bernie Sanders!!*"

And the floor shook and the meters pinned as he came out with his wife and kids and grandkids in a very family affair that reminded me of that *Music From Big Pink* Band album sleeve photo — except with waving blue and white placards framing it.

He was positively giddy and couldn't stop smiling ear-to-ear as the audience couldn't stop cheering. He thanked his volunteers, like you do, and expressed his appreciation for the other candidates, which was nice, and added once again — "What I can tell you with absolute certainty, and I know I speak for every one of the Democratic candidates, is that no matter who wins — we certainly hope it's going to be us — we are going to unite together," and the room cheered, and I prayed for those words to be carved into Moses's tablets.

Then he went into a greatest hits list of things he wants to do — "Healthcare is a 'uman right, not a privilege. The wealthy and powerful will start paying their fair share of taxes. We will make public colleges and universities tuition-free, and cancel all student debt. Unlike donald trump, we know climate change is very real, and an existential crisis for our planet. We are going to end a racist and broken criminal justice system. We are going to pass comprehensive immigration reform. Our gun safety policies will be determined by the American people not the NRA. And under our administration it will be women not the government who control their lives."

All great stuff — that I sure hope his supporters will stick around to help make happen if he doesn't win the nomination.

He only spoke for about 10 minutes, but it was the climatic winning-moment finale of a wondrous week-long ground game by ten candidates all working their tails off to win Democrats' votes.

New Hampshire is the first primary in the nation and the last of small town retail politics. Tomorrow the campaigns move to Las Vegas for the Nevada caucuses in what will likely be the last year caucuses are ever held. But Nevada is basically a two-city neon-light state, and the days

of 25 rallies in little libraries and legion halls ended tonight.

He did a quick rope line handshake pass while Neil Young's *Rockin' In The Free World* blasted a reprise and this fellow Winnipeger cracked a fresh beer in both their honour.

~ = ~ = ~ = ~ = ~ * ~ = ~ = ~ = ~ = ~

Bernie would go on to win Nevada giving him an unbeatable 3-&-0 start. In the history of public voting primaries in America (which began in 1972) no candidate has ever won the first three contests and didn't win the nomination. But he then lost 20 of the following 25 states in the biggest primary turnaround in the history of either party.

Bernie never pivoted after his 3-&-0 Nevada win into a front-runner general election candidate reaching out to a wider constituency than his core. He had a week to become President and presidential — but he never seized the moment — deciding instead to defend Fidel Castro.

After a passionate, personal and emphatic endorsement for back-of-the-field Biden by South Carolina's senior political titan James Clyburn in something that will probably forever be known as "a Clyburn endorsement," everything changed. Biden won S.C. in a 30-point landslide, and Bernie didn't carry a single county — a rare unanimous primary verdict that would soon repeat itself in Michigan, Mississippi, Florida, Wisconsin, Ohio, Oregon, and 101 of 102 counties in Illinois.

Three candidates dropped out within 24 hours of South Carolina (Steyer, Pete & Amy), and two more right after Super Tuesday three days later (Bloomberg & Liz), leaving it a two-person race between Biden & Bernie (with Tulsi Gabbard lingering for another couple weeks).

Bernie would go on to lose eight of the nine states in the two Tuesdays following the Super one for a combined wipe-out loss of over 220 delegates that would determine the Democratic nomination.

Then a global pandemic hit and the whole country including the primary shut down.

In early April, the Republican-led Wisconsin legislature, backed by Republican-appointed judges, tried to kill off some Democrats by insisting they vote in-person during the most contagious and deadly viral disease in a hundred years. Who knows how many got sick or died, but the unconscionably immoral maneuver backfired on a national level when it prompted Bernie Sanders to finally drop out of the primary, allowing Democrats to begin consolidating around Joe Biden in early April rather than late June.

Here's to hoping voters on the left have 2020 hindsight and don't repeat what happened in 2016.

May the four winds blow us safely home.

New Hampshire Primary 2020 Playlist

Songs I noted at different rallies. Would make a great mix tape.
All intentionally thematically chosen with a purpose by the campaigns.

Deval Patrick:
No music at his library appearance

Joe Biden:
Pre-rally:
Aretha Franklin *Respect*
Paul Simon *You Can Call Me Al*
The Beatles *Come Together*
Post-rally:
Bruce Springsteen *We Take Care of Our Own*
Stevie Wonder *Don't You Worry 'Bout A Thing*

Tulsi Gabbard:
No music at her library appearance

Amy Klobuchar:

Pre-rally:

Bob Dylan *The Times They Are A-Changin'*, *Lay Lady Lay*
& others

Post-rally:

Prince *Raspberry Beret* & others

Elizabeth Warren:

Pre-rally:

The Big Chill soundtrack

Diana Ross

Neil Diamond

Bill Weld:

Pre talk:

Grand Funk Railroad *We're An American Band*

Pete Buttigieg:

Pre-rally:

David Bowie *Rebel Rebel*

Aretha Franklin *Think*

The Who *Won't Get Fooled Again*

George Michael *Freedom*

Post-rally:

Creedence Clearwater Revival *Up Around The Bend*

Yang:

Pre-rally:

No music (!)

Post-rally:

Billy Preston *Nothing From Nothing*

Democratic dinner:

Before the 10 candidates spoke:

The Beatles *Come Together*

Sister Sledge *We Are Family*

Bachman-Turner Overdrive *You Ain't Seen Nothing Yet*

Queen *We Are The Champions*

Pharrell *Happy*

Tina Turner, *Simply The Best*

Fleetwood Mac *Go Your Own Way*

Curtis Mayfield *Move On Up*

Steve Winwood *Higher Love*

Carrie Underwood *Love Wins*

Bruce Springsteen *Land of Hope and Dreams*

Dessa *The Bullpen*

Doobie Brothers *Takin' It To The Streets*

Jackie Wilson *(Your Love Keeps Lifting Me) Higher & Higher*

Nina Simone *O-O-H Child*

Creedence Clearwater Revival *Up Around The Bend*

Bennet:

No music at his conference room appearance

Bernie election-eve rally:

Martha & The Vandellas *Dancing In The Street*
The Who *My Generation* played by Sunflower Bean
John Lennon *Power To The People*

Bernie election night victory rally:

Simon & Garfunkel *America*
Rush *Closer To The Heart*
Neil Young *Rockin' In The Free World*
Tracy Chapman Talkin' *"Bout A Revolution*
Willie Nelson *On The Road Again*
Marvin Gaye *I Heard It Thru the Grapevine*

and now . . . here's . . .

The

DESSERT

Menu

A Cup of Joe

by

Lance Simmens

This book, as you just experienced, is all firsthand Adventure Tales. Since the Democrats settled on a nominee just as this was going to print, and I don't have too many firsthand Joe Biden stories, my friend and author and lifelong political practitioner, Lance Simmens, offered to jump in with a firsthand view of Joe in action in Washington.

Growing up in Philadelphia I was familiar with Joe Biden since he was first elected to the Senate in neighboring Delaware in 1972. Born and raised in Scranton, Joe would fondly be praised by many in the political hierarchy of the Keystone State as the "third Senator from Pennsylvania." But it was not until 1981 that I would have a chance to watch him up close on a regular basis.

After having served in the Carter Administration and having watched our bid for a second term in 1980 enveloped in the firestorm that would become known as the Reagan Revolution I secured a staff position on the U.S. Senate Budget Committee working for Tennessee Senator Jim Sasser from 1981-87. Biden was a member of the committee and sat several seats down the dais from my boss. There were Senate heavyweights on our side of the aisle — Moynihan from New York, Hart from Colorado, Hollings from South Carolina, Chiles from Florida, Metzenbaum from Ohio — but none quite like the ebullient Senator from Delaware. While he was a serious student of the legislative process he possessed a cavalier attitude that exuded both confidence and competence, but oh that full-toothed grin which would break out in a flash, even in heated debate. You just couldn't help but like the guy.

If you have ever seen a Senate hearing you'll notice the phalanx of Senate staffers sitting dutifully behind their Senators, occasionally supplying them with reference notes on the issues being discussed or leaning over whispering in their ears, which often ends up being repeated in the form of a question to whomever was testifying. Well, that was me for six years of a professional career in public service which would ultimately span nearly four decades. It is a heady experience to hear your advice transmitted directly into the Congressional record of proceedings, whether it's a floor statement, written remarks either in support of or dissent of legislation, or direct questioning. My story is written from that perspective.

One day in the early 1980s, during a break in the Senate hearings on Reagan's supply-side economic proposals, several Senators and staff were gathered in the Committee cloak room discussing a strategic line of questioning. I was chatting with my boss while Senator Biden was busily engaged in conversation with several other Senate members when he called my boss from across the room to come join them. I stood back and Biden motioned to "bring the boy from Tennessee with you." I looked at my boss and we both grinned at the idea of me gaining an immediate Southern heritage and we approached the gaggle assembled across the room.

When we got there my boss smiled and told Biden that I was not from Tennessee, but was from up near his neck of the woods, Philadelphia. Biden smiled with that infectious ear to ear grin of his and looked at me and blurted out, "Get the fuck outta here!" I told him, "No shit." That exchange established a connection that would last decades. Biden immediately engaged me in discussion, "How did a boy from Philly end up working for a Senator from Tennessee?" I told him I had worked in the Carter Administration and after our loss the Senator had offered me a position he had on the Budget Committee.

In quintessential Joe Biden fashion he next asked me, "What Parrish?" Smiling, I told him St. Cecilia's in Northeast Philly. "Were you an altar boy?"

"I most assuredly was," I responded, and immediately launched into a recitation of Latin phrases that any altar boy in the early 1960s would have had ingrained in their brains for life. "Dominus vobiscum, Et cum spiritu tuo, Corpus Christi, in nomine Padris et Filii et Spiritus Sancti, Amen." In unison, there we were reciting Latin phrases from the mass that eventually were changed in the mid-to-late-'60s by the Second Vatican Council.

I must admit that there was considerable consternation on the faces of the assembled Senators as their conversation was temporarily hijacked by this unexpected interruption, with a staff person no less. But that was Joe Biden, charging ahead on every topic with unbound enthusiasm. You got the impression that he was really enjoying himself, because he was.

If you want to get a true picture of the man and his unquenchable thirst for human interaction and genuine interest in the plight and story of others, here it is. He possesses an empathy that is sorely missing in the contemporary political dialogue in the way he interacts with total strangers, with little regard for their position in life, or whether they are constituents or potential voters in an election somewhere in the distant future. He is the consummate old-school politician, a lost art in the politics of the era of social media.

From that point forward, for years, Biden would continue his predilection of turning around during Committee hearings to not only his staffer but to all of us and ask whether what the cabinet official or economic expert, or whomever was testifying that day, was talking "bullshit?"

On more occasions than I can remember he would shoot a look with that grin of his towards me and ask "What's the altar boy from Philly think about this?" Typically I would in a low hushed voice say,

"Its pure bullshit." He would teasingly look back and ask, "Should I say that?" "Of course," I would tease back, surely sending shivers up the spine of his staffer, a venerable former elected official from Delaware, Dick Andrews, who mentored me when I first came to the Budget Committee and to whom I am gratefully indebted.

One day it would be OMB Director Stockman, another Defense Secretary Weinberger or Secretary of State Shultz or Federal Reserve Chairman Greenspan, or any one of a number of economic heavyweights discussing an unproven economic theory called supply-side economics buttressed by an unproven economic metric called the Laffer curve. Biden would seek counsel from those of us who were dedicated to the proposition that government and public service were serious and worthwhile concepts and that despite the political rhetoric of the 1980 presidential campaign "government was the solution not the problem." He brought levity to a situation that at its core was as serious as it gets. And that is Joe Biden.

Flash forward twenty years or so. I was working for the Governor of Pennsylvania, Ed Rendell, in Harrisburg, the state Capitol, and he asked that I represent him at a large labor convention in neighboring Hershey where Senator Biden was giving the keynote address in the run up to the 2008 presidential election. Dutifully I attended and waited afterwards to give the Senator the Governor's regards after he finished the backslapping and advice-gathering that is required following a major speech.

As I approached him and stuck out my hand, starting in with, "Senator, I don't expect you to remember me but many years ago I worked for Senator Sasser on the Budget Committee and ..." he immediately cut me off and in an exuberant voice with eyes sparkling he hit me in the shoulder and blurted out "the altar boy from Philly."

Not wanting to let the moment slip without a retort, I looked at him and said, "Get the fuck outta here, you remember that?" We both laughed and proceeded to share a couple of minutes of Budget days in the 1980s. That's Joe Biden.

The importance of this is to validate a couple of things that I believe have relevance and importance during these political times when interpersonal skills are so sorely lacking: first, nobody in Washington doesn't like Joe Biden; second, he is a consummate old-school politician, backslapping and jovial, but truly concerned with the person he is talking to and the issues being discussed; third, he wears his heart on his sleeve, battered by numerous personal tragedies that might have destroyed a weaker soul he is driven by the need to make a difference; fourth, he is the embodiment of the type of leader our founding fathers envisioned when they constructed a foundation for government that is dependent upon civility, compromise, commitment, and competence; and lastly, he carries a reservoir of experience with respect to how representative democracy works.

In early March of 2020, I was standing in the rope line at a Biden speech in Los Angeles and as he got to me and shook my hand and our eyes met he stopped and pointed his finger at me and repeated three times "I know you, I know you, I know you." When I told him I used to work for Jim Sasser, he pulled me into his body and said "The altar boy from Philly!" Truly astonishing. But the look on his face when he realized our connection was priceless.

It is that kind of political instinct that is needed to pull this country back together now. Hell, I can barely remember what I did a couple of weeks ago and here he is, former Vice-President of the United States, and nearly forty years after our encounter that day in the Senate Budget Committee he still remembers me. This is one of the key reasons that people who know him genuinely like him — he makes you feel important, not because it is advantageous to do so, but because he actually cares.

After the last four years of self-promotion, incessant chest-beating, indescribably narcissistic behavior, temper tantrums, petty name calling, policy-making by Twitter, an absence of even a scintilla of empathy and persistent prevarication that has shrunk the standing of the nation among allies and adversaries alike, a return to professionalism is long overdue and desperately needed.

I am confident that I am not alone in my reflections upon the value of a true public servant reclaiming the moral legitimacy of the nation in the upcoming presidential election. This is just one story among many, but it is an indelible sign of hope that brighter days are in the offing. I will follow Joe Biden to the ends of the Earth. He offers the best chance to recapture the soul of a nation that is drifting through treacherous seas. That is my story and I am sticking to it.

Lance Simmens 2020 — Malibu, California

No Regrets

A Celebration of Abbie Hoffman's Life

June 17, 1989

The Palladium, 14th Street, NYC

An account written immediately following the event —

The New York memorial for Abbie Hoffman, the card-carrying Groucho Marxist, brought to the fore many leaders of social and artistic change to discuss the progress and setbacks in the ongoing struggle for freedom and fairness.

The afternoon gathering attracted a capacity crowd to hear the likes of Norman Mailer, Allen Ginsberg, Wavy Gravy and Paul Krassner recite alternatingly rousing and tearful accounts of their life and times with a fallen comrade.

The issue of how he died was set in proper context early on by one of many video and audio taped eulogies. The novelist William Styron (*Sophie's Choice*, etc.) discussed the horrors of living as a manic-depressive in such haunting terms his voice hushed the bustling crowd of 4,000 summer afternoon New Yorkers into a stunned stillness. Afflicted himself, Styron described the incurable disease as "worse than any physical pain," and told how we

The Abbie Hoffman Foundation Presents

No Regrets

A Celebration Of Abbie Hoffman's Life

Written By	Paul McIsaac
	Ed Sanders ‛
Conceived And Developed By	Johanna Lawrenson
	Paul McIsaac
	Ed Sanders
Directed By	Paul McIsaac
Metaphysical Consultant	Wavy Gravey
Executive Producer	Abigail McGrath
President Of The Abbie Hoffman Activist Foundation	Johanna Lawrenson

Speakers * Phyllis Hoffman—her sister

Jack Hoffman	Danny Schechter ✶	Fred Duke
‛ Andrew Hoffman	Jeff Nightbyrd	Ramsey Clark
‛ Ilya Hoffman	Brad Fox ⁄	Jonathan Silvers
. america Hoffman	William Kunstler	Christine Kelly
Marty Kenner	Bobby Seale	Allen Ginsberg
Marshall Efron	Lee Weiner	Norman Mailer
Jerome Washington	Daniel Ellsberg	Ralph McGehee
Anita Hoffman wife	Paul Krassner	Amiri Baraka
Bob Fass •	Jerry Lefcourt	Christopher Hitchens
Walli Leff ‛	Steve Ben Israel	Victor Navasky
Marty Carey ⁄	Johanna Lawrenson	Sonia Santchez
Ed Sanders	Rick Spencer	** scheduled to appear,*
Tuli Kupferberg	Lisa Fithian	*subject to change*

often misunderstand its victims as cowards or quitters. "He was a martyr only to a malignant disease," he said.

Held at New York's Palladium theater (after similar services in L.A. and his hometown of Worcester Mass.), other taped eulogies included Whoopi Goldberg, who credited Abbie as "a mentor who taught us who we could be," Ed Asner, Barbara Walters and many other contemporaries.

Citing the advances in segregation, environmental law, housing, and voting rights since the 1960s, Hoffman himself reminded us via video tape, "Change was made because people gave a damn. This isn't the Peloponnesian War we're talking about here. These things happened while most of you were alive."

Musical tributes abounded but were best epitomized by David Amram who scored an obscure movie written and narrated by Jack Kerouac called *Pull My Daisy*, the title song jointly composed by Amram, Kerouac, Allen Ginsberg & Neal Cassady. Amram's incredible rendition brought a prolonged standing ovation after he composed verse after verse of spontaneous be-bop poetry about Abbie and the collective spirit of all pranksters living and dead, including the much quoted Hoffman motto: "Act on your imagination."

Also performing throughout the afternoon were The Fugs doing the ironic *Protect and Survive* and a new song about Abbie in Beijing; John Hammond; Buster Poindexter (David Johansen); The Washington Squares; Peter Yarrow; and a chilling version of *I Shall Be Released* by Monica Behan, a friend of Abbie's.

Allen Ginsberg, appearing to be one of the more rehearsed and focused speakers of the day, recited a recent poem which brilliantly captured news stories which happened up to two days prior.

But it was Abbie's P.T. Barnum of the street's poignant sense of humor and ability to turn a bad situation to the good that was the prominent theme of the day.

Gerry Lefcourt, a lawyer who made a pact with Abbie on St. Mark's Place back in 1961 — "You do the protests and I'll keep you out of jail," — defended him during the famous trial over the revolutionary's desire to wear a U.S. flag as a shirt, something the federal government took exception to in 1968.

On the morning of his arraignment, Hoffman arrived at the courthouse wearing the very shirt his government objected to. On the front steps, with the cameras rolling, the police ordered its removal, only to expose a huge Vietnamese flag hand-painted on his back.

Asked by the judge at the end of the hearing if he had anything more to say, evoking Nathan Hale, Abbie replied, "I only regret that I have but one shirt to give for my country."

After his acquittal, when grilled by the press, he said, "You're gonna have to cut off a lot of hair to stop *this* revolution."

Different guests read from the many books Hoffman wrote over the years. The excerpts revealed, despite the simple narrative autobiography, an astounding succinctness, clarity, and perception into our psyche during this age of cataclysmic change. Among other things, he illuminated the suppression & disenchantment we feel today by putting it in terms of the innocent but honest questioning of childhood.

Hoffman's three children appeared on stage and gathered around a microphone, obviously unrehearsed. Although some speakers had been, they were not choked up, but rather stood together, smiled, and told us, "Abbie's over in China right now helping the students. Let's send him a postcard." As they left the stage, america, the youngest, shouted with raised fist, "We'll see you in the streets."

Paul Krassner, another of the many who seem to have been in touch with Abbie since his most recent underground disappearance, reported back that he's currently working on his next book — *Resurrection For The Hell of It.*

When Jerry Rubin took the stage during the chronological, oral biography program, he became the only person other than Richard Nixon to get booed all day. Ignoring his detractors, he retold touching stories of Abbie in such a reverential manner one wondered how he'd wandered so far astray. Their college debate tours of a year ago were described by Abbie's life-mate Johanna Lawrenson with, "*God* he hated those."

The Palladium, long a cathedral for Gotham's counterculture, was an ironic setting for a memorial to the cofounder of the Yippies. Now a temple of yuppie overindulgence with its Disneyland bombardment of video screens, flashing lights and mirrors, it seems a long cry from its heyday as a movie house in the 1950s and '60s, and concert hall filling the Fillmore's void in the 1970s. Once the sight of all-night Grateful Dead shows, it's more recently been home to Jerry Rubin's weakly Wall Street "Networking" parties.

Some of the other eulogists who spoke included

Sydney Schanberg (the Pulitzer-Prize-winning journalist immortalized in *The Killing Fields*), Jacques Levy (the Broadway director and Dylan collaborator), Amiri Baraka (the Beat poet originally known as LeRoi Jones), Daniel Ellsberg (who first liberated and then cowrote *The Pentagon Papers*), fellow Chicago 8 defendants Bobby Seale and Lee Weiner, his brother Jack Hoffman, and his partner of the last 15 years, Johanna Lawrenson.

The most poignant moment of the afternoon, however, occurred not on the stage but out in the lobby — much to the delight of Abbie's Cheshire spirit grinning over the gathered assembly. It was protest in its truest and most dramatic sense:

A group from the Tompkins Square Park Association who are working to expose violent actions being taken against East Villagers during gentrification had a table with information that for some reason the event's organizers had taken exception to. With Palladium bouncer heavies on the scene, the eclectic group was being asked to pedal *their* protest elsewhere. This was Abbie's day.

What organizers forgot, a handful of the attendees milling about seemed to remember.

The group with the table didn't want to leave. Security wrestlers grew in number. Walkie-talkies squawked. People's heads cocked. A few feeble tablers argued their case. Voices grew louder. The walkie-talkies signaled more troops. Shouting. A crowd gathered. One man walked to the table and asked what the information was about and took a flyer. The crowd moved a little closer. The white-uniformed oafs looking like staff from *One Flew Over The Cuckoo's Nest* lifted up the table and began to carry it outside, whereupon the now nestled crowd reached out and began leaning on the table. The wrestlers continued their bulldog march. Someone started chanting, "Let them stay, let them stay . . . " The entire crowd chorused in, not meekly mouthing the words like a national anthem, but vehemently reciting and seeming to grow in number. More walkie-talkies squawked. Suddenly a decision was made to allow them to stay. The people overturned security brutality! And when was the last time you saw that happen?

Back on stage, Wavy Gravy was in typical fine form, seeming most at home whooping a crowd from the stage for a good cause. He had the audience don distributed paper bags and engage in an exercise of hyperventilating through the bags *en masse* while simultaneously making the sound of a kazoo with every breath. He provoked the loudest response of the wake — and generated the most money, too! by encouraging everyone "to give away a few pictures of dead presidents you may be carrying around with you."

The Abbie Hoffman Activist Foundation, the beneficiary of all the door and donated monies, is a posthumously formed clearing house for information and assistance in opposing anything you think is wrong. A sort of civil disobedience center.

Henry David Thoreau may have been the most appropriate of the many free-thinking Americans to whom Hoffman was compared. His words of 140 years ago echoed through the church of Abbie's memory: "I think it is not desirable to cultivate a respect for the law, so much as for the 'right.' I think it's not too soon for honest men to rebel and revolutionize."

If you are within reading distance of this and there is an environmental or social injustice occurring in your community, you can gain assistance in challenging it from: The Abbie Hoffman Activist Foundation — which — editor's update — a quick search online reveals it's still operating as of 2020! Yay us!

Many people who met Hoffman as Barry Freed when he was living underground in the late seventies spoke of the unifying effect he had on the small border community on the St. Lawrence River, which was then under siege by an army dredging project. The small town residents were getting military slide shows and Reagan rah-rah in community club settings that danced around questions of the environmental impact reports. It wasn't until a new resident arrived and stood up before the uniforms, hollering in a Boston accent, "Aaaaaa the U.S. army ain't won a war since 1945, we ain't scared of you," that the citizens began to feel they had a chance. No less than a dozen of these people traveled all the way down to the city to pay tribute to the man "Abbie Hoffman" had nothing to do with.

Norman Mailer, sort of the Abbie Hoffman of authors, delivered the final toast — which riveted the crowd despite the five-hour proceedings. Looking a little like Yoda, Mailer held court from a stool at the podium, news cameras floating around him. Having written the preface to Hoffman's book, *Soon To Be A Major Motion Picture*, he read from it calling him, "One of the smartest, bravest, finniest, most spontaneous people I've ever met." Of the sixties he said: "I learned that Abbie live it. I observed it." Perhaps the reigning godfather of American letters, Mailer's presence made an important statement about the reach of Hoffman's influence and respect.

DESSERT

One was left with a sense of renewed opposition, that the struggles we face in overcoming life's daily impediments are actually trivial and surmountable: that it is the larger challenges of how to drink safe water with the current EPA that are tougher to overcome. Which only makes what this man did for almost 30 years all the more remarkable. 'Twas truly a Wake worthy of Finnegan.

And although James Joyce was unable to attend, in his absence, wrote the evocation: "He's tiff but he's steady. 'Twas he was the decent gaylabouring youth. Sharpen his pillowstone, and tap up his beer!"

Narrators	Music
Paul McIsaac	Monica Behan
Caryl Ratner	Razor's Edge
Gustin Reichbach	Jackson Browne
	David Amram
Readers	Peter Yarrow
Marty Garbus	John Hammond
Rip Torn	The Fugs
Jacques Levy	Buster Poindexter
Al Giordano	Washington Squares
Sam Leff	Dennis Pearne
Bob Fass	
Sydney Schanberg	

PROGRAM

THE BROOKLYN PHILHARMONIC ORCHESTRA

Introduction... ....Caroline Stoessinger

Trumpet Fanfare...Traditional
Ben Peck, herald trumpet

The Ringing of the Bells for Freedom

Sinfonietta.. Janacek Allegretto
Zubin Mehta, conductor

The Ringing of the Cathedral Bells

Greeting...................................The Right Reverand Richard F. Grein, Bishop of New York

Remarks..Milos Forman

Agnus Dei...Bizet
Placido Domingo, tenor   Zubin Mehta, conductor

Reading..Paul Newman

"Bridge Over Troubled Water"...Paul Simon

Reading..Ellen Burstyn

Final Chorus from "The Abduction from the Seraglio"..Mozart
Cathedral Singers   Tom Hulce, conductor

Reading..Maximilian Schell

Performance...Roberta Flack

Performance...Dizzie Gillespie

Reading..Ron Silver

Serenade from "Don Giovanni"..Mozart
Ferruccio Furlanetto, bass   Marcello Panni, conductor

La ci darem la mano...Mozart
Dawn Upshaw, soprano
Ferruccio Furlanetto, bass   Marcello Panni, conductor

New York City Salutes The World's First Avant-Garde President

written February 1990

"Imagine there's no countries."

We've witnessed the oppressive dictatorships of communist Europe vote themselves out of power. The impossible became possible. "War is over if you want it." Utopian romantic visions do come true.

Now, one man has stepped out from the darkness of a prison cell and into the spotlight of conscientious global change.

This could be the story of Nelson Mandela who never surrendered a single ideal even if it meant he could not live with his family or friends or be a part of the world he was born into. He chose to stay in a cinder block prison if the only life offered him was of oppression and degradation.

This could be the story of Mikhail Gorbachev who opposed the most powerful, autocratic and dangerous government on earth to affect a more equitable life for the people of his homeland.

But this is the story of Václav Havel.

Havel is a Czechoslovakian playwright who just became president of the nation at the center of Europe.

Imagine this: You're growing up. You're in your twenties, your energy is boundless, your dreams infinite.

393

You write; you play an instrument; you plan to make movies with your friends. Then some war starts outside your country somewhere. Who cares? But then your country is taken over and the government — *the world* — you had ceases to exist. *Your* country. And the people who take it over say you can't play your instrument any longer, and those movies? Forget it.

But let's say, you say, "No way." And you go on writing and playing and dreaming in the immensity of it. Then one day, while you're sitting at home reading a subversive magazine and practicing your instrument, your door suddenly gets kicked open and uniformed police officers storm your house.

You're arrested and taken away for reading and writing things that are not acceptable. You're actually thrown in jail and nobody even *mentions* the idea of a trial. And you're only offered freedom when the occupying government decided to rotate the incarcerated pests.

Then you get out, but instead of giving in, you write a play — only this time it's even *more* passionate about the integrity and importance of personal choice. And one night while friends are performing it behind pulled shades, the doors are again broken down and now all your friends are going to the same jail you just left, and it starts all over again, only ten times worse.

These are the real stories and conditions of a First World nation in our lifetime.

First you are one of many, and then one of only a few, who are willing to stand up against what you know is wrong.

You are imprisoned, you hurt, and part of you

dies. But maybe it's only the bad part. Maybe, just maybe, through it all, through all the horror around you, through all the lies your peers regurgitate, through all the prison terms and burned manuscripts of your tortured philosophy, what if, just maybe, maybe you never give in. What if the crimes around you only make you angrier and stronger and more determined to oppose a lie no matter how small or large?

What if there is a peaceful revolution, a groundswell you never thought possible, and suddenly the occupying government leaves as abruptly as it arrived?

Then, what if the newly freed people decide to elect *you*, the lowly lonely playwright, to be the first president of their reborn land?

Right?!

It's the stuff of fiction. *Science* fiction. But it just happened. The story is true. An artist, a writer, and a philosopher has just been elected the leader of the nation at the heart of Europe.

*

In something that may have been called *Mr. Smith Goes To Washington II*, President Havel recently visited our nation's capital to spread understanding and gather whatever advice he could. Havel addressed the Congress, breaking three D.C. laws at once: He wrote his own speech, he told the truth, and he flashed the peace sign in the face of his standing ovation.

Then *playwright* Havel flew to New York City for the first time since the failed 1968 uprisings in his homeland that grounded the very last of their freedoms.

On his first night in The Apple this world leader went bar-hopping! He cruised the streets of Greenwich Village with childhood friend, the film director Miloš Forman, stopping in at The Bitter End, then continuing down Bleecker Street to CBGB. Could you imagine Thatcher or either of our two recent puppets, a) walking anywhere, b) going to CBGB, or c) doing either without first consulting their press secretary?

The following night, in a hastily prepared gathering, the world artistic community paid tribute to the playwright at the Cathedral of St. John The Divine in Manhattan, in a program broadcast via satellite to Czechoslovakia and taped for a PBS special.

An amazing array of people jammed the largest cathedral in North America to cheer loudly for this kindred spirit who had hit the big time. Every inch of the marble floor was covered by emigrated Czechoslovakians, PBS documentarians, writers, political junkies, Beats, Deadheads, clergy and councilmen. Sitting near me I spotted beneath the six-story columns activist actors like Sigourney Weaver and Willem Dafoe, rock stars Frank Zappa and the Grateful Dead's Mickey Hart, and paparazzi favorites like Ric Ocasek & his Czech-born babe Paulina, Richard Gere & Cindy Crawford, and so many others I can't even remember them all.

From the marble pulpit, Miloš Forman began a stunning evening of tributes to a petit man who toppled a communist government without a single bullet being fired.

A reverential Paul Newman stressed our personal responsibility to strive for internal credibility, then introduced Plácido Domingo, who led into Paul Simon singing *Bridge Over Troubled Water* directly to the man who just crossed it.

Ellen Burstyn read from a letter that Havel wrote to his wife from prison: "Hope is a dimension of the spirit. It is not outside us, but within us. When you lose it, you must seek it again within yourself: not in people around you, not in objects, nor even in events."

Then *Amadeus* actor Tom Hulce conducted the Brooklyn Philharmonic playing Mozart's final chorus from *The Abduction from the Seraglio*. This was followed by Roberta Flack singing: "Can you imagine all the people sharing all the world ... " playing Lennon's dream to the man who overthrew Lenin's.

Austrian actor Maximilian Schell said, "Tonight I am trembling — trembling for Václav Havel, because maybe we'll read in the newspapers tomorrow that that brave man in the Kremlin is out of power. And what will happen then?"

Soviet emigre Mikhail Baryshnikov introduced slave descendent Dizzy Gillespie who blew his wild Beat horn 15 feet from Havel's head.

In perhaps the most inspiring speech of the evening, actor Ron Silver told us bluntly, "Václav Havel has shown the world that art matters. He has reminded us that artists speak to people in ways that politicians cannot." Regarding Havel's persecution he said, "People and politicians censor art because they're afraid of what it means. In America we pride ourselves on our freedom of expression. But we must not grow complacent, because we too, sir, have censors that would like to control what artists say and do. We too have ideologues who want to impose their narrow view on us."

Treat Williams talked about making *Hair* with Miloš Forman, about how that story was the individual's struggle

for freedom of expression, and look how complacent some
have become. A beaming Arthur Miller welcomed his fellow
PEN member to the global literary political community
and you could just picture Biff confronting Willy at the end
of *Death of a Salesman*, demanding they have an honest
relationship.

James Taylor performed, then Nobel laureate Saul
Bellow pointed out how in Czechoslovakia, writers have
to fight to print whatever few words they can, while in the
West we have complete freedom of the press but no one's
reading.

Then Gregory Peck, who if he were British would
be knighted by now, read eloquently from Havel's *Long
Distance Interrogation*, about how being a responsible
citizen of the world is larger than one's own life. Barbara
Walters segued into Romanian author Elie Wiesel who
introduced Harry Belafonte who said, "We're forever in your
harmony."

Which all led up to Joseph Papp, the show's
organizer and New York theater producer. He created
and has continued the free Shakespeare productions every
summer in Central Park, which last year, for instance,
featured Gregory Hines, Jeff Goldblum and Michelle Pfeiffer
in a hilarious *Twelfth Night*. He is the guy who brought
Robert De Niro back to Off-Broadway to do a 26-year-old
Puerto Rican kid's first play. And when Havel was in jail
and his plays were banned in his homeland, Papp staged
them here so the words could breathe life.

This night the producer reminded us that poets
are the unacknowledged legislators of our world, then
introduced the man we were all there to support.

The stocky, determined Havel ascended the sculpted

pulpit to a standing ovation. He bowed and bowed with hunched shoulders and twinkling impish grin. The assembled priests and politicians, reporters and musicians, Soviets and Americans all clapped with raised hands and whistles echoing through the largest cathedral on the continent as others broke down in tears.

He didn't talk long. Writers can be a pretty shy bunch. And he could hardly speak English, of course. Imagine how you would sound suddenly being honored in Czechoslovakia.

He seemed like just a man, everyman. He was nervous, almost embarrassed with his role in the spotlight. He hasn't learned how to inspect the troops yet or how to hold his spoon at lunch. He seemed like someone who's living in a *Twilight Zone* fantasy of suddenly becoming a president. I mean, in his country there wasn't even the position of president to dream about growing up and being!

Then the bishop came out and presented Havel with a plaque — but he didn't know how to receive it, or how to hold it. And his suit didn't fit right. And he is the President of Czechoslovakia.

An American Tribute to Václav Havel
And A Celebration of Democracy in Czechoslovakia

at the Cathedral of St. John the Divine on February 22, 1990 at 7:00 pm.

Great Americans

Not Born in America

It's funny when some Americans talk about who is American and who isn't.

It made me think of some commonly-perceived "Great Americans" who weren't born here, like ...

Christopher Columbus (Italian) ("discovered" America, and for whom cities & holidays, and circles & squares are named after)

William Penn (English) (founder of Pennsylvania and champion of religious acceptance)

Thomas Paine (English) (author of *Common Freakin' Sense*, 1776)

Alexander Hamilton (British West Indian) (Founding Father and co-author of *The Federalist Papers*)

General **Lafayette** (French) (huge hero in the American Revolution under George Washington)

Charles Darwin (English) (scientist, naturalist, founder of evolution theory)

Albert Einstein (German) (relatively important physicist)

Alexander Graham Bell (Scottish) (scientist, living in Canada when he invented the telephone)

Adam Smith (Scottish) (a founding father of modern economics)

John Kenneth Galbraith (Canadian) (economist, Presidential advisor, ambassador, author)

Andrew Carnegie (Scottish) (patriarch of the industrialist and philanthropist family)

Meyer Guggenheim (Swiss) (patriarch of the other industrialist and philanthropist family)

Joseph Pulitzer (Hungarian) (publisher who bequeathed the journalism awards)

James Smithson (English) (scientist who bequeathed the Smithsonian Institution)

John Roebling (German) (designed The Brooklyn Bridge and many others)

John McIntosh (Canadian) (farmer who invented the original McIntosh apple)

Levi Strauss (German) (inventor of blue jeans)

C.F. Martin (German) (founder of the company making the best acoustic guitars in the world)

the **Gimbels** brothers (German) (founders of the department store chain)

the **Warner Brothers** (Jack was Canadian; Harry, Sam & Albert were Polish [temporarily Russian])

Marshall McLuhan (Canadian) (philosopher, author, teacher)

Stephen Hawking (English) (physicist, author, teacher)

Madeline Albright (Czech) (Secretary of State)

Isaac Asimov (Russian) (author)

I.M. Pei (Chinese) (architect of the Rock n Roll Hall of Fame and many other masterpieces)

Joe Shuster (Canadian) (creator of Superman)

George Soros (Hungarian) (financier and philanthropist)

Bill Graham (German) (producer/promoter and essentially the inventor of rock concerts)

Peter Jennings (Canadian) (journalist, ABC news anchor, and practicing Deadhead)

Morley Safer (Canadian) (journalist, *60 Minutes* reporter)

Mort Sahl (Canadian) (political satirist, comic pioneer)

Jerzy Kosinski (Polish) (author)

~ = ~ = ~ = ~ = ~ * ~ = ~ = ~ = ~ = ~

Not to mention . . .

Bob Hope (English) (comedian)

Charlie Chaplin (English) (actor and director)

Stan Laurel (English) (comedic partner to Oliver Hardy)

Harry Houdini (Hungarian) (magician, escape artist)

Alfred Hitchcock (English) (film director)

Walter Huston (Canadian) (actor and father of John)

Mary Pickford (Canadian) (actress, and co-founder of United Artists)

Norman Jewison (Canadian) (director, *In The Heat of The Night, Jesus Christ Superstar*, etc.)

Miloš Forman (Czech) (director, *Cuckoo's Nest, Hair, Amadeus, Ragtime*, etc.)

Roman Polanski (French-born, Polish raised) (director, *Rosemary's Baby, Chinatown*, etc.)

Robert Frank (Swiss) (photographer, filmmaker)

Arnold Schwarzenegger (Austrian) (former Governor of Caleefornia)

John Lennon (English – famously applied for U.S. naturalization)

Bob Marley (Jamaican) (musical philosopher)

Neil Young (Canadian) (musician, green car investor)

Joni Mitchell (Canadian) (songstress)

Yo-Yo Ma (French) (cellist)

Itzhak Perlman (Israeli) (violinist)

Leonard & Phil Chess (Polish) (founders of Chess Records)

and **Martin Short, Jim Carrey, Seth Rogen, Mike Meyers, Michael J. Fox, Dan Aykroyd, Phil Hartman, Howie Mandel, Catherine O'Hara, Samantha Bee, Lorne Michaels, David Steinberg, Norm Macdonald, Tommy Chong, John Candy, Rich Little** . . .

every damn one of them Canadian ;-)

En-Cora-gement —
Give The Kids The Vote

By

Dale "Gubba" Topham

Here's a beautiful inspiring story about proactively engaging young people in democracy. And I mean young people under 18!

It's a story about generosity and generations, empowerment and inclusion, doing the right thing, and putting your good where it will do the most (as Ken Kesey used to advise).

It's told by a fellow Canadian Prankster Brother who's technically named Dale Topham, but is known in preferred circles as "Gubba" — which this New Yorker expanded to "Gubba Gubba Hey!" to refrain a certain hometown punk band.

As Brutha Gubba tells it . . .

In the most recent Canadian election [2019], I let my 11-year-old granddaughter, Cora, choose how I would cast my ballot.

Rene, Cora & Gubba
in the Okanagan Valley in British Columbia

It started because I was in an unusual muddle about whom to vote for. I generally vote Liberal in Canadian elections. In 1963, my first time voting, I supported Lester B. Pearson, then became a full-fledged member of Trudeau-mania (for Justin's father Pierre). Since then I don't believe I ever cast a federal vote for anyone but a Liberal, right up to supporting Justin Trudeau his first time out in 2015.

But Justin disappointed me in spades. Once he was elected he changed 180 degrees from opposing to supporting the Trans Mountain Pipeline [bringing dirty tar sands oil across the Rocky Mountains to the Pacific Ocean]. And then he used political pressure to intercede in a case against a Quebec-based construction company.

It was clear to me that for the first time in my life, I would not be voting Liberal.

To muddy the waters further, our Liberal candidate, Terry Beech, was far and away the best choice of those running in my riding! He's a hard working young man who's on the right side of all the issues I care about, but all he could do was promise to apply whatever pressure he could when those issues were discussed.

When the election was called, the Conservative candidate was Heather Leung. About a week into the campaign, some film surfaced of her making extreme anti-gay remarks from a Christian religious right point of view. They were so bad that she was kicked out of the party immediately.

To make this tricky choice even harder, the NDP Candidate, Svend Robinson, was once our long-standing Member of Parliament. He was also the first Canadian MP to declare himself openly gay, but had left politics about ten years ago when he was convicted of stealing an expensive ring from an auction house. Now he was back looking for my support. From a philosophical point of view, I would tend to support the NDP over the Conservatives, but a jewelry thief? I think not!

Among all these flawed choices, there was a young woman representing the Green Party. She looked like the best candidate to me, but the Greens got less than 2,000 votes in our very populous riding last election. To me, this looked like throwing away my vote.

So there I was.

In other news — once a week I would pick up my granddaughter Cora after school and take her to her climbing class, about a 20 minute drive. All the street-side political signs turned our conversation to the election. I told her about my dilemma with Trudeau, and she told me they were having a mock election at her school, and that they were going to be learning about the issues and about what the parties were representing. I told her that if she could figure out who to vote for she should tell me! And we both laughed.

Over the next few weeks we talked about what she was learning. She told me if the election were held today, she would vote Green, and said it was mainly because of their position on environmental issues and climate change. I said her reasoning was very sound and that I thought young people would probably make better choices than their parents.

And that's when the lightbulb came on!

I told her then and there that I would give her my vote in the real election, and that if she ever changed her mind from Green (she never did) just to let me know and I would vote for whomever she said.

I told my wife Rene what I had promised Cora and that I would be voting Green. Every time we discussed it, Rene would say something like, "You know Terry Beech (the Liberal) is the best candidate in our riding," which I would counter with, "... but I just can't support Trudeau!" Obviously she was still

408

going to vote Liberal, as we always do.

On election day, as we left the polling station, she asked me, "Did you vote Green?" I said "Yeah." And she said ... "So did I." Boy, was Gubba happy! And I couldn't wait to tell Cora!

For the record, our Liberal candidate won, the jewelry thief came second, and the ousted religious zealot came third. Our Green candidate came fourth with over 4,000 votes — but more than double what she got last time.

My granddaughter is so proud & pleased that she was involved. She's always been very adult and we treat her that way. And now she's voting before her time and feeling the power of having her voice heard and counted. Of everything we've happily given her over the years, we all three agree this was maybe the best present ever.

~ = ~ = ~ = ~ * ~ = ~ = ~ = ~

Giving the gift of the vote.

We're always reminded that "people died" so we could have the right to vote. Well, now you can give it to somebody who doesn't have the right — and nobody has to die!

It's such a mind-flippingly beautiful twisteroo Prankster concept — giving the power to the purity of smart young people who see the world with unpolluted eyes to suss the good guys from the bad, the good ideas from the baloney. Adults listening to pundits or their pub pals sure haven't been installing the most evolved visionaries ... or even functionaries. So how 'bout if we go ahead and let some fresh voices in the choir.

Vote swapping is already something gaining popularity in both the U.S. and Canada the last couple elections — how about giving the gift of political engagement to someone younger who will get in the habit of using it including long after the gift-giver is gone.

And now — about that wife swapping ... I mean, vote swapping . . .

Gubba reading Kerouac to Cassady
during Lowell Celebrates Kerouac, Oct. 8, 2018

Vote Swapping
& Third Parties

And in a related story . . .

Vote trading or vote swapping was big in Canada in the 2015 federal election, and also employed in the Democratic primary and the general election in 2016.

In America, it usually manifests between Democratic and Green voters. Let's say you live in a close tossup state like Florida and you really want to vote Green. You know the Green candidate has no chance of winning, but you want to support their positions and add your vote to their national total so maybe they get on the next Presidential debate stage and on more ballots or at least more respect & stature next cycle. Using an app or website, you can find a voter in a safe blue state who will cast your Green vote there if you will cast a vote for the Democratic candidate in your swing state. This is totally legal — anybody can vote for whomever they want to for whatever reason they want.

What it does is reduce the impact of fracturing of the vote on the left.

It flourished in Canada in 2015 largely because of the soulless science-denying profiteers of the Conservative Stephen Harper government. Canadians were so repulsed by his Repugnant ways, that voters from coast-to-coast made promises to other Canadians they'd never met to vote for whichever non-Conservative Party's candidate was the strongest in any given riding. If you wanted to vote Liberal where you lived, but that candidate/party was in a distant third place, you could vote NDP in your riding, and have someone who wanted to vote NDP instead vote Liberal some place else where that candidate had the best chance. It was the ultimate in collaborative strategic voting.

This kind of vote swapping got known in Canada as ABC voting.

Anything But Conservative.

Maybe we should call it AIR voting in America.

Anyone Instead of Republicans.

The websites and apps for this seem to change for each election cycle, but an internet search should find one for you whenever you need it.

Obviously a person should vote their conscience, but there's also logistics and political reality at play.

In 2016, I assume the people in Michigan, Wisconsin and Pennsylvania who voted Green did so because they were voting their conscience. However, they were in close battleground states, and the number of votes that went to the Green Party in each of those states was more than the small difference donald trump won by. Their well-intentioned Green votes ended up putting a science-denying environmental monster in power. They thought they were doing something good (voting their conscience) but their vote did more damage to the Green cause and our green world than has ever been done by any president in history.

You don't need me to tell you to vote whichever way you want — but I highly suggest you know the political landscape of your district or state before going third party.

A Word about Third Parties

Every election I hear some Americans grouse that they wish they had more choices. I'd like to know which country in the world they think multiple parties works. In Canada, it's a frickin' disaster — and is exactly why vote swapping had to be invented by grassroots voters in the first place. What happens in The Great White is — the two parties on the left split the left vote, and the conservatives win even though it's a liberal country.

Plus — there *are* third parties in America.

There's the Greens (which gives people on the left an alternative), and the Libertarians (for voters on the "less government" right), then a whole bunch of smaller ones that get on ballots in different states. But as much as you may hear people bitch about how they want a third party — there already *are* major third parties on both sides of the spectrum. Plus far-right voters have the Constitution Party, and far left voters have the Party for Socialism and Liberation, or rebels in the middle can go for Ross Perot's still-existing Reform Party.

But here's the thing — even in the historically disastrous election of 2016 when we had the candidate with the highest disapproval rating in the history of polling (trump) running against the candidate with the second highest disapproval rating in history (Hillary) and both the Green's Jill Stein and the Libertarian's Gary Johnson got lots of media coverage, and the egalitarian social media allowed regular people to become their own "news channels" sharing whatever they wanted — even with all of that — the best possible political landscape ever for third parties — *all the Libertarian & Green & all other third party votes* <u>*combined*</u> didn't even add up to 5% of the total vote. With the two most disliked major party candidates in all of history — and the full-on explosion of social media and blogs and texting and selfies and podcasts accessible to all — with *everything* going in third parties' favor — all their votes plus all the write-ins added up together couldn't even reach 5% of the vote.

With the grousing you hear about "we need more choices" or "we have to get rid of the two party system" — when voters had the most favorable landscape in 2016 to make that choice — less than 5% of voters actually wanted to do it.

So, next time somebody bitches about wanting a third party, tell them about Canada, and remind them that they've already got at least two functioning third parties — which don't help —and News Flash — nobody actually cares. Well, maybe 5% of people who actually vote.

In 2020, if you're in a safely blue or landslide red state — please do a one-second internet search for "vote swapping app or website," and register. You will probably be able to cast your vote in a swing state where it will be needed.

And if you live in a swing state — I'm looking at you Florida – Pennsylvania – New Hampshire – North Carolina – Ohio – Michigan – Wisconsin – Minnesota – Nevada – Arizona – Georgia — and

are thinking of voting Green, by all damn means register on one of these sites and you'll easily find a Dem somewhere around the country who will cast your Green for you if you'll add one to the blue column where you are.

We have to do everything we can to prevent the freakish occurrence with the freak in 2016.

When Conflict Television Was Born

or . . .

"I'll sock you in your goddamn face."

Best of Enemies

Film Review

1968 —

The year so much changed . . .

Martin and Bobby . . .

North Vietnam's Tet Offensive galvanizing Americans' opposition to the war . . .

The Prague Spring and Soviet invasion of Czechoslovakia . . .

President Johnson announces he won't run for re-election . . .

The Beatles carve open their Apple Core . . .

The Electric Kool-Aid Acid Test is a bestseller . . .

2001: A Space Odyssey packs theaters . . .

Hair opens on Broadway . . .

Rowan & Martin's Laugh-In debuts on TV . . .

Madison Square Garden opens on 33rd Street, and the Fillmore East on Second Avenue . . .

* And that was all before the political conventions hit! *

And boy – did they hit!

Although the three television networks were broadcasting in color, almost no one had color sets at home — it was still an absurd luxury — B&Ws continued to outsell color TVs until 1972.

And of those three networks, late start-up ABC was so far behind the others, as someone joked in *Best of Enemies*, "They would've been fourth, but there were only three."

To try to do something different than the rote "gavel-to-gavel convention coverage" of Huntley & Brinkley on NBC and Walter Cronkite on CBS, the new kids came up with the smart low-budget idea of putting talkative spokesmen for the right and left in chairs next to each other and let them go at it for each of the two weeks covering the Republican and Democratic conventions.

This decision was to become as transformative in its field as Dylan plugging in at Newport a few summers earlier. But sadly, just as that gutsy maneuver led to some godawful electric music, this initially admirable idea similarly led to a lowbrow *Crossfire* hurricane of right-left hate-speech that's dominated American political coverage for decades.

This now-famous tete-et-tete between two reigning intellectuals on either side of the ideological spectrum has taken on a sort of Lincoln-Douglas mythological status. But just as reading a transcript of those 1858 debates reveals — they were often far from civil or high-minded. In fact this more recent Great American Debate Legend was bitter, petty, vicious, uncomfortable, conniving, mean-spirited — and absolutely riveting live television.

ABC's ratings spiked through the roof — even as the roof of their cheaply-built "studio" at the convention hall in Chicago literally collapsed on their heads. But network television, much like Hollywood, is nothing if not a rip-off-and-replicate industry. And thus the no-budget *Point/ Counterpoint* style of belligerent blowhards yelling over each other was born.

And this documentary — made by the same team as the magnificent recent Academy Award-winning *20 Feet From Stardom* — time-travels you back to the summer of 1968, but with 21st century perspective from the likes of Christopher Hitchens, Frank Rich, Dick Cavett, Andrew Sullivan and loads of erudite others. And it's really fast-paced — running through the whole set-up, the ten "debates" and the aftermath in less than 90 minutes.

The entire movie is smart filmmaking — opening with dramatic old aerial footage of the Italian coastline that looks like unused B-roll footage from *To Catch A Thief* taking us to where pondering Gore Vidal lived and paced for decades — and ending with a machine-gun-collage of clips of shows that were born out of this television summer of '68 — from Jon Stewart telling the *Crossfire* hosts, "You're doing theater when you should be doing debate." They use the clang of a boxing bell to start each round of "debate," and a perfect piano and cello-based soundtrack by Jonathan Kirkscey that sounds a lot like Philip Glass at times. In fact, there's a real harmony here with Glass's work on another great documentary, *The Source* (1999) by Chuck Workman, about how the Beat writers changed history.

And speaking of the Beats ... who are these guys and why do they keep following me?

Not seven minutes into the film do we get Buckley walking and pontificating next to a four-foot-high photo of Allen Ginsberg! — wearing the "Pot is Fun" sandwich board, no less! Which then goes into a slow "Ken Burns pan" up the photo until it's resting on Allen's face (!) as Buckley's voiceover spews his dopey Ayn Rand-ian gobbledegook, "As long as liberalism suggested that it could bring happiness to the individual, then people tended to look to government agencies for those narcotic substitutes in a search for happiness and contentment which they ought to have found in their religion, in their institutions, and their culture themselves."

And of course on the streets outside the Chicago convention hall where Buckley and Vidal were debating, Ginsberg was leading the crowds with chanting and other non-violent protests, alongside Jean Genet, Ed Sanders, Terry Southern, and William Burroughs who was there covering it for *Esquire*.

And then Allen shows up again when he was a guest on Buckley's *Firing Line!* And of course any casual Jack Kerouac fan knows of the author's legendary appearance on that same show — which was — get this — taped the very first day Buckley returned to the studio following the conventions! Immediately after this historic Chicago smackdown that would define Buckley's television career (much to his chagrin), Kerouac was in the Vidal seat taking the flamethrower's heat — and as he told his agent Sterling Lord afterwards, "Buckley kept kicking my shoes and telling me to shush." (And the Ginsberg episode was taped just three weeks after this!)

And there's not just Beat cultural references.

This particularly inclusive & colorful doc also features *Rowan & Martin's Laugh-In*, Muhammad Ali, *Sunset Blvd.*, Aretha Franklin, *The Flying Nun*, Norman Mailer, *The Best Man*, Woody Allen, *Playboy After Dark*, Henry Gibson, *Ben Hur*, Paul Newman, *Saturday Night Live,* with John Lithgow and Kelsey Grammer voicing the authors' respective left / right writings . . . and on and on appropriately appropriating mass culture into this political news philosophical debate story because it really was the beginning of the blending of the two.

Prior to this, television news was formal, staid and nonpartisan. Yes, there was a time when journalists reported news objectively. But this was televised New Journalism — just as was being invented in the literary form at the same time by Tom Wolfe, Hunter Thompson, Norman Mailer and others.

ABC's slogan for their unexpected hit broadcast was "Unconventional convention coverage" — and this documentary captures every part of it — from the executives' initial decisions to the carpenters rebuilding the studio roof that collapsed just before showtime. It sneaks inside the minds of both the two prize fighters in the ring, as well as those in the rings of repercussions rippling out from the splash in still waters these two giants made.

Aaron Sorkin (of *West Wing, The Newsroom* and *The American President* fame) has signed on to write a feature-length dramatization a la *Frost/Nixon,* and every network has pledged to give you the same on-the-verge-of-violence "debates" for the next year of the 2016 Presidential campaign.

Make sure you see this movie soon or I'm going to sock you in your goddamn face.

Tim Russert

May 7th, 1950 – June 13th, 2008

Written the day and evening it happened.

Tim Russert just died.

I'm in shock. I just got home and will have MSNBC on all night. I was at the hospital with my Mom when my cell phone went off five times. I couldn't answer it but knew something happened.

For non politicos, this is on the level of losing John Lennon. The best of the best is now gone.

He was so far beyond the rest. There was him . . . and everybody else.

Obama just called him: "The standard-bearer for good journalism. But also a great person."

Barbara Walters just said, "This is a huge loss to *America*." And she's right.

He set the standard, and every journalist in the business was his student.

Time magazine just listed him this year as one of the 100 Most Influential People In *The World*.

The mayor of his hometown Buffalo just put all flags on government property at half-mast.

Election Day this November should be dedicated to him.

He became the nation's go-to voice during the disputed 2000 election.

The white board he used on air where he wrote "Florida Florida Florida" is now in the Smithsonian Museum's permanent collection.

TV Guide recently ranked that as one of the Top 100 Moments in all of Television History.

MSNBC did not run a single ad starting from when the news first broke (around 3PM) until 8:30 at night.

Journalists are sitting on air stunned, red-eyed and choked-up — Al Hunt, Mike Barnicle, Keith Olbermann, Campbell Brown, NBC CEO Jack Welch . . . barely making it through their tributes. 73-year-old Welch: "This has affected me like only a few days in my life."

Crew members are working on set with tears in their eyes.

In the spontaneous hours of coverage we heard from every giant in journalism and politics.

Olbermann — "If he wasn't the story, he'd be the one here guiding us through tonight."

"He was a player-coach to other journalists — one of the players, but also the coach of the team. And we lost our quarterback today."

"He was always the smartest guy in the room," said more than one person tonight.

"If Tim said something, you could take it to the bank."

Eugene Robinson of the *Washington Post*: "He understood politics so much better than everyone else. His encyclopedic knowledge, and his work ethic made him so outstanding. He's such an institution and presence in Washington." People aren't even talking about him in the past tense yet.

Mike Barnicle named his son Timothy — and Tim was at his Christening.

Chris Matthews talked about how everyone in the room would say, "Russert is here," if he showed up anywhere. His presence meant more than anyone else's. But he was not a cocktail party guy.

Meet The Press has been on the air for 61 years — since Nov. 6th, 1947 – the longest continuously-running show on television, period. And Tim was its host for the last 17½ years! — the longest serving host ever.

He was the guy (because of his credibility and clout) who changed it from a half-hour to an hour show. And then the other Sunday morning shows followed.

"History is about stories – and he understood that, and could bring them out of others."

He reinvigorated *all* the Sunday morning news shows – forcing all the other networks to up their game.

He didn't want *MTP* to be an argumentative program. He knew exactly what he wanted to do with that show, he transformed it, and it transcended journalism.

There was no easing into interviews with him — no letting the guest get comfortable with their own bullshit — from the very opening question he would deliver a knock-out punch to the center of their face — in the form of a question. If this was baseball, he would be the first batter up in the first inning, and slam the first pitch right out of the ballpark.

And he had video and newspaper quotes already cued up of answers the guest had given differently than Tim knew in advance they were likely going to respond on his show. He would challenge — live on the air — the most powerful people in the world with their own words and force them to reconcile them . . . all with the cameras rolling and the nation watching.

He was the guy who popped the David Duke bubble. When Duke got the chance to appear on *Meet The Press*, it was Russert's questions that ended his political rise.

As Chris Matthews remembered it — "That David Duke takedown! Tim didn't say Duke was a racist — he forced Duke show it himself."

Ben Bradlee (Executive Editor of the *Washington Post* for 25 years) — "When the Saturday news release of your next morning's guests becomes a must-know in Washington, you know you've arrived."

Frank Rich (*New York Times*): "He changed Sunday Morning. *Meet The Press* was the biggest meeting of newsmakers. There isn't another single entity in news that had that position. Yet he wore himself lightly. He took on the most powerful people in America — but he was never a gotcha wiseguy."

The statements that he got from senior officials on *MTP* are part of the historical record — from Cheney and others during the lead up to the Iraq War, to every historical event of our time. He was creating a record for history week after week.

He changed not only *MTP*, but every other serious news show on television. He set the bar. As Matthews put it, "He was the gold standard."

An elder and legend in his own right, Bob Schieffer, Tim's competitor from *Face The Nation*, confessed, "He made me better."

NBC news anchor & reporter David Gregory – "There's a giant crater left here in the news world."

NBC Nightly News anchor Brian Williams — "This is a staggering, overpowering loss."

This hockey fan remembers him just a couple months ago holding up the Washington Capitals jersey on *Meet The Press* after they made the playoffs for the first time in years.

I've got so many *MTP*s on tape, man — going back 20 years. They were *that* important — I had to record them.

Tim's hour-long "Tim Russert" show on MSNBC on the weekend is also gone. He just had Jim Webb on last weekend – and I've got the tape of it.

He was the guy who called the 2008 Democratic primary for Barack Obama.

It was the night of the North Carolina / Indiana primaries on May 6th when he said, "We now know who the Democratic nominee is." It was when Russert said it — and *that* definitively — that even the Clinton campaign knew it was over. It was like a judge rendering a verdict from the bench. Other people may have tried to declare it over, but when Tim said it, it meant everything to both campaigns, and every journalist in the world.

David Gregory shared, "when the word got to the Hillary campaign headquarters that Russert had called the race over, the air went out of the room. He had that gravitas. And no one else had it."

His first big Washington job was being Chief of Staff to New York Senator Daniel Patrick Moynihan, and they became personally very close. What smarter person could he have been around?!

He knew Moynihan's voice so well, he would actually impersonate him and field calls on his behalf.

He steered the Senator's ship through his first re-election and on to being one of the most respected giants of the Senate.

Moynihan said to street-smart Russert about the Ivy League hotshots in the Senator's office — "What they know, you can learn. What you know, they can never learn."

He was known as the brightest aide when he served

on Capital Hill. He knew where everything was and how to get anything done.

He unintentionally intimidated his colleagues because he was so smart.

Tim loved the game of politics.

He had a passion and child-like enthusiasm with a genius's intellect.

"When talking about politics, his face would light up like a kid on Christmas morning. And he listened to people's answers."

"He jumped through the phone with enthusiasm."

He often joked, "I have a face for radio."

"Hair spray never touched his Irish locks."

"He was clinical. He diagnosed people."

He was the guy who brought Chuck Todd into NBC and expanded his role.

As Chris Matthews put it: "He was 'us' as a country. He was a role model for me. He was the hardest worker I ever saw. The preparation. There is no one who beat him. He constantly reminded us to look for the truth. It's a competitive business, but he shared with everybody."

He had such undeniable leadership qualities . . . plus a solid family base.

His father Big Russ had just gone into an assisted-living facility in Buffalo, but he felt "blessed" to still have his father here.

His only child, son Luke, is also really into politics, and just graduated college with a major in history.

He had such a joy for family and children. And this Sunday is Father's Day.

He was so grateful for the life he was living. He was very spiritual.

And he was a devoted friend to all who knew him.

His doctor, Michael Newman, said he had asymptomatic coronary artery disease. He did his best with exercise and improving his lifestyle. On April 29th he had a stress test. "He was on the treadmill this morning, as he was most days." But he was burning it on both ends.

"These heart attacks occur without warning — there's no way to detect them. There was a rupture of cholesterol build up." He had an enlarged heart. They did the autopsy and found the break in the artery.

He was in the studio recording voiceovers for this Sunday's *Meet The Press* when he collapsed.

Within seconds everyone knew he was in trouble.

An intern who knew CPR began doing it.

They needed a defibrillator.

Even in a witnessed cardiac arrest, survival is only about 5%.

He had taped his weekend "Tim Russert" show in the morning, There's one last episode!! Political reporter John Harwood was the guest. And apparently Kelly O'Donnell was on a different segment.

Lindsay Graham was scheduled to be on *MTP* this Sunday.

He and Tom Brokaw were both big Chuck Berry fans! They had a bet who was going to lose the most weight – and the winner would get a platinum Chuck Berry album!

He was also a huge Springsteen fan – he even booked him at his college long before he was famous. At a recent Springsteen show he was described as more into it than anyone around him.

He said to my jaw-dropped amazement one week on *Meet The Press* that he actually went to Woodstock in 1969! . . . "wearing a Buffalo Bills jersey with a case of beer."

Mario Cuomo, who was a mentor to Tim, said, "We've lost him when we needed him the most."

I met him on election night in 2004 and we shared a leprechaun Prankster's wink and smile. "Can you pass the Russert test?"

I can't believe he's not here anymore.

"Go get 'em!" was how he signed-off letters to good colleagues.

Now he's gone got 'em.

As Bob Dylan ended his tribute to Jerry Garcia —
"There's no way to convey the loss. It just digs down really
deep."

Rest In Peace and

Fly In Spirit,

Mighty Warrior Brother

40 YEARS IN PRINT

A CHRONOLOGY OF THE PUBLISHED
REAL-LIFE ADVENTURE TALES

1980 – April – John Anderson in San Diego – *Blissfully Ravaged in Democracy* – 1980–1984 chapter – pp: 2-3

1980 – June – First Grateful Dead show – *The Hitchhiker's Guide to Jack Kerouac* – ch. 14; pp: 156–159

1980 – October – Carter–Reagan Presidential debate – *Blissfully Ravaged in Democracy* – 1980–1984 chapter – pp: 4-6

1982 – June–August – Kerouac Super-Summit in Boulder & Kesey farm visit – *The Hitchhiker's Guide to Jack Kerouac*

1984 – March – Gary Hart rally – *Blissfully Ravaged in Democracy* – 1980–1984 chapter – pp: 6-8

1987 – April – Engagement on rooftop – *Blissfully Ravaged in Democracy* – 1988 chapter – pp. 9-10

1988 – June–November — "Political Parties" – *Blissfully Ravaged in Democracy* – 1988 chapter

1992 – March — The Tsongas campaign – *Blissfully Ravaged in Democracy* – 1992 two chapters

1993 – January — Clinton's Inauguration – *Blissfully Ravaged in Democracy* – 1992 chapter

1994 – May — The NYU Beat Conference – *Blissfully Ravaged in Democracy* – 1996 chapter, pp: 48-50

1994 – May — First bonding with Carolyn Cassady – *The Hitchhiker's Guide to Jack Kerouac* – ch. 21; pp: 227-228

1994 – August — Woodstock 25th Anniversary Concert – *Holy Cats! Dream Catching at Woodstock*

1995–1996 — Life as a Temp in Manhattan – *The Temp Survival Guide*

1996 – April–November — The Clinton re-election – *Blissfully Ravaged in Democracy* – 1996 chapter

1999 – Beat shows in NYC – "Be The Invincible Spirit You Are" – *How The Beats Begat The Pranksters* – ch. 14

2000 – November–December – the Gore–Bush election – *Blissfully Ravaged in Democracy* – 2000 chapter

2001 – April – *On The Road* 50th anniversary of Jack Kerouac writing it – shows in New York and L.A. – *On The Road with Cassadys* – ch. 1 & 2

2001 – May — *On The Road* scroll auction – *On The Road with Cassadys* – ch. 3

2001 – July — *Big Sur* reading in Northport – *On The Road with Cassadys* – ch. 4

2004 – February — Al Franken, Howard Dean & the New Hampshire primary – *Blissfully Ravaged in Democracy* – 2004 section

2004 – November — Election night in New York – *Blissfully Ravaged in Democracy* – 2004 section

2008 – February–October — The 2008 primary – *Blissfully Ravaged in Democracy* – 2008 section

2008 – November — Election Night in NYC – *Blissfully Ravaged in Democracy* – 2008 section

2009 – January — Obama's Inauguration – *Blissfully Ravaged in Democracy* – Inauguration Adventures section

2012 – June — Living with Carolyn Cassady in England – *On The Road with Cassadys* – ch. 9

2012 – June–August — Haiku for Carolyn – *On The Road with Cassadys* – ch. 10

2012 – August — *On The Road* film premiere in London – *How The Beats Begat The Pranksters* – ch. 6

2012 – September — *On The Road* film premiere in Toronto – *How The Beats Begat The Pranksters* – ch. 7

2012 – November — John Cassady / Walter Salles *Road* trips in Bloomington, Columbus & Cleveland – *On The Road with Cassadys* – ch. 5

2012 – December — *On The Road* film premiere in New York – *How The Beats Begat The Pranksters* – ch. 8

2014 – August – "Woodstock with The Pranksters" – *How The Beats Begat The Pranksters* – ch. 9

2015 – May – "Pranksters in Wonderland" – *How The Beats Begat The Pranksters* – ch. 10

2015 – June – Meeting Phil Lesh – *How The Beats Begat The Pranksters* – ch. 4

2015 – June – The Beat Shindig at The Beat Museum in San Francisco – *How The Beats Begat The Pranksters* – ch. 3

2016 – May – Bernie Sanders in Bloomington – *Blissfully Ravaged in Democracy* – 2016 section

2016 – July – Republican Convention in Cleveland – *Blissfully Ravaged in Democracy* – 2016 Republican Convention section

2016 – October – Lowell Celebrates Kerouac – *How The Beats Begat The Pranksters* – ch. 2

2016 – November – Election Night in New York – *Blissfully Ravaged in Democracy* – 2016 section

2017 – May – Reconnected with original Merry Prankster George Walker & started doing shows together – *How The Beats Begat The Pranksters* – ch. 11

2018 – Published *On The Road with Cassadys* and did a buncha shows

2019 – Published *Holy Cats! Dream-Catching at Woodstock '94* and created *Blissfully Ravaged in Democracy* and did a buncha shows

2020 – February – New Hampshire Democratic primary – *Blissfully Ravaged in Democracy* – 2020 section

Books

The Temp Survival Guide — published December 1, 1996

The Hitchhiker's Guide to Jack Kerouac — The Adventure of the Boulder '82 On The Road Conference – Finding Kerouac, Kesey and The Grateful Dead Alive & Rockin' in the Rockies – published April 13, 2015

How The Beats Begat The Pranksters & Other Adventure Tales — published September 26, 2017

On The Road with Cassadys & Furthur Visions — **completing The Beat Trilogy** – published September 5, 2018

Holy Cats! Dream-Catching at Woodstock – published May 6, 2019

Blissfully Ravaged in Democracy — **completing The Five Books in Five Years Mission** – published April 27, 2020

Acknowledgements

In the I-Couldn't-Have-Done-It-Without-You Department:

David S. Wills for the Michelangelian layout and craftwork over five books in five years;

Marci Zabell — for the word-saving proofread and feedback, and for being the cool English teacher on stage & off (I mean "and");

My Beat Detective Agency fellow cofounder, The Beat Museum's Jerry Cimino, for the vivid Introduction and multi-discipline proactivity;

and his Museum cohort Brandon Loberg for always being left and visually justified;

Lance Simmens for sharing his firsthand Joe Biden stories in a pinch;

Dale "Gubba" Topham for creating the beautiful "Give Your Kids The Vote" program;

Kenneth Morris for the 2020 intro and Cleveland 2016 housing and being the eveready cameraman and poli-Beat brother of eternity;

443

Reverend Steve Edington for New Hampshire 2020 and for being so central to the best Jack party in the world — Lowell Celebrates Kerouac every October;

Allan Robinson for housing both ways on so many Road trips, for music back when it was needed, and for his invaluable website tips;

the late great Beat & poli brother John Grady for hosting and housing in New Hampshire 2004, and prompting me to writer *The Franken Fracas*;

Mitch Potter for the housing assistance during Obama's inauguration, and for 10,000 hours of political discussions spanning four decades;

Rob Salmon for the housing and fun in New York during Obama's election in 2008;

Aaron Howard for housing and support in New York during the 2016 election disaster;

the entire crew of Democrats Abroad in Toronto — especially Karin Lippert and Julie O'Neal Buchanan — for creating such a fun, inviting & engaging culture of proactivity for expats;

Cynthia Johnston for the loving & perfect New Hampshire chapter title;

and Barnaby Marshall for hosting my website — BrianHassett.com — where some of these stories first found life.

For the architectural inspiration — Sam Shepard's *Rolling Thunder Logbook* — how a chapter/story could be one paragraph or ten pages or one poem or one dialogue. That book changed my life as much as *On The Road*. Jack exploded sentences, but Sam exploded structure. I couldn't have done this book without him showing me it was possible. And thanks to Walter Raubicheck for gifting me his own copy of it back in the magical days of New York in the '80s;

For the vocal inspiration — Hunter Thompson's *Fear & Loathing on the Campaign Trail '72* for first making political reading fun, and is up there with *OTR* and Sam in the Books That Changed My Life;

For his storytelling, playfulness, attention to detail, and big picture perspective— Quentin Tarantino;

For the early engagement inspiration — Abbie Hoffman;

For the incredible lightness of being and lightening our burdens — Stephen Colbert, Jimmy Kimmel, Seth Meyers, Jon Stewart, Trevor Noah, Andy Borowitz, *SNL*, John Oliver, Bill Maher, Larry David, Seth MacFarlane for *Family Guy* and so many other heroes of laughter.

Some books read or reread while writing this: *Janis* by my friend Holly George-Warren; *The White Album* by Joan Didion; *1984* by George Orwell; *Brave New World* by Aldous Huxley; *Why We're Polarized* by Ezra Klein; *Game Change* by John Heilemann & Mark Halperin; *Lies and the Lying Liars Who Tell Them* by Al Franken; *Molly Ivins Can't Say That Can She?* by Molly Ivins; *'Scuse Me While I Whip This Out* by Kinky Friedman; *The Big Picture* by A. Whitney Brown; *Dave Barry Hits Below the Belt* by Dave Barry; *Stupid White Men* by Michael Moore; *Banana Republicans* by Sheldon Rampton & John Stauber; and *Bushworld* by Maureen Dowd.

Photo Credits

<u>1988</u>:

Jesse Jackson '88 button — author

<u>1992</u>:

"We the People want Tsongas" button — author

<u>1996</u>:

author at citizenship swearing-in ceremony — girlfriend

"Role Hemp" sticker — author

author in polling booth voting for the first time!! — girlfriend

<u>2008</u>:

Obama Pow! button — author

Barack For Jazz button — author

Grateful Dead Steal Your Barack button — author

Beer Connoisseurs for Obama button — author

Obama HOPE poster button — author

"Rose of Hope" — voting booth lever — Alex Nantes

author with black coat open with buttons — Alex Nantes

author in Obama t-shirt after Phil Lesh show — Alex Nantes

<u>Inauguration Adventures</u>:

intro — author arms outstretched Obama inaug — unknown

16th — author at "re-entered space" Blue Bomber car — Mitch Potter

17th — author and Garth Brooks — unknown

20th — author outdoors pointing to podium — unknown

20th — camera boom crane and helicopter — author

20th — author & Nadette sitting under Capitol dome — unknown

20th — Andrea Mitchell on flatbed — author

20th — approaching Presidential limousine — author

20th — author at Capitol dome, arms upwards — unknown

Road to Woodstock Michael Lang book cover — author

<u>2012</u>:

author peace sign Dems Abroad debate party — Brian Humniski

Photo Credits

2016 — Hillary Clinton Election Night:
Inside Javits Center — "H" — author
author seated with flag and buttons — unknown
author's predictions sheet — author
Chuck Schumer — author
author standing peace sign — unknown

2020:
Vote Blue No Matter Who button — author
author & Deval Patrick — unknown
author in Biden audience — unknown
author & Biden — Biden staffer
author & Tulsi Gabbard — unknown
author & Amy Klobuchar — Klobuchar staffer
author & others in front row at Liz Warren — unknown
author & Liz Warren — Warren staffer
Bill Weld with notebook on table — author
author and Bill Weld — unknown
author and Dana Bash — unknown
author and Mayor Pete Buttigieg — staffer
Mayor Pete wide shot with author in corner — unknown
author and Swedish reporters — unknown
author at NBC Decision Desk — unknown
author and Chris Hayes in 2016 — Jeremy Hogan
author and Michael Moore — unknown
Lawrence O'Donnell and Amy Klobuchar — author
author and Joy Reid — unknown
author and Ari Melber — unknown
author and Andrew Yang — unknown
author in arena dinner front row — unknown
author at Kerouac grave — Stephen Edington
author and Michael Bennet — unknown
author with peace signs at Bernie rally — unknown

Photo Credits

Bernie supporters group shot outdoors on ice — author
author and Vermin Supreme — unknown
author with Bernie over shoulder — unknown

<u>Dessert</u>:

Joe Biden promo shot — unknown
Lance Simmens author shot — Lance Simmens
Abbie Hoffman Memorial program — author
Abbie Hoffman Memorial program page 2 — author
Vaclav Havel program listing — author
Vaclav Havel program cover — author
Alexander Hamilton dollar bill — unknown
Rene, Cora & Gubba — by the waitress
Gubba & Cassady at Kerouac's grave — author
Gore Vidal & Paul Newman — film promo
Buckley pointing finger — film promo
author at *Best of Enemies* film poster — unknown
Tim Russert on *Meet The Press* set — NBC promo
Tim Russert waving goodbye — NBC promo
author at Adventure Travel Office — unknown
book collage — author

(Total: 115 — with 5 cover/interior repeats = 110 different)

The front cover arms-outstretched photo was taken by one of a trio of middle-aged women who'd come up to sit in the front after the Obama Inauguration and soak it in. They were all obviously very proactive Adventurewomen, and you could tell good friends by the rapid-fire way they talked to each other. But what was really memorable was — one was a feisty petite Mexican, one was a large dark-skinned African, and one was a skinny white woman who coulda been my mom on a serious coffee buzz.

I relished listening to them like music for several minutes — in awe of their different timbres and speech patterns, and the way they interwove like a jazz trio who'd been playing together for decades. They were each _so_ different — yet they spoke together like they'd been sisters from birth. I can still see them vividly in my mind. Wish we'd exchanged numbers and become friends. But it was just one more great magic moment memory from that historic love-filled day with Barack.

When I was envisioning the back cover, I knew I wanted to do a trademark Brian-collage scattered on an American flag backdrop — but not a digi flag, or even a modern one that I have many of made out of synthetic crap. Then I remembered an old flag I used to have . . . went digging through the boxes of antiquity until I found the ragged Old Glory — even older than I remembered — a pre-1960 48-starer!

To lay out the collage I used actual-size paper replicas of the buttons & photos the size you see them on the cover, moving them around into the right assemblage.

I thought at first we could never just have diagonal stripes as the spine . . . until the lightbulb went on that that might actually look really cool!

And that's also the old flag's stars and stripe on the front cover.

So dig thusly — that's an original 1950s or older flag scored in NYC that Kerouac & Cassady coulda drove past flapping in the bright-colored optimism of the endless post-war American road.

Index

(The coolest cast of characters in any political book *ever.*)

Index

Index

Index

Index

Index

The Hitchhiker's Guide to Jack Kerouac

"You did a fine job of bringing this back, far finer than my own memory, and I thought I had a decent one."
Dennis McNally
Kerouac & Grateful Dead scholar & author

"This book is a youthful memoir with all the never-to-be-recaptured frantic zest of a young man. Everything is wonderful in the Hassett world, even bad luck. Every cloud he sees has a silver lining. This attitude takes him far. It's the sheer unbridled enthusiasm that pours from Hassett that is so engaging."
Kevin Ring
Beat Scene Magazine

"Both Kerouac and Hassett worked incredibly hard to seek out truth and beauty in this world. And then sit down to tell us what they found. Read the *Hitchhiker's Guide* for the history. But don't miss the larger lessons within."
Kurt Landefeld
author of *Jack's Memoirs: Off The Road*

See many more in front pages of book.

How The Beats Begat The Pranksters

"Brian Hassett has made it his life's work to present to all of us the insights of the Beats and the Pranksters, and all the history, all the important things that came out of that, which have been perpetuated by the incredible vision, the incredible energy, of this man who is now one of our prime spokesmen, and we are so fortunate for that."

George Walker
original Merry Prankster and practicing Neal Cassady

"This is an excellent new addition to the collective cultural canon from the people's Prankster Brian Hassett, Beat evangelist and voice of the living Dead. Our rocking roisterer and bebop brother has done it again!"

Simon Warner
author of *Text Drugs & Rock & Roll* and *Kerouac On Record*

""Brian Hassett doesn't just write ABOUT the Pranksters! He IS one! This book is great insider stuff about Ken Kesey and the Pranksters, about Jack Kerouac and the Beats, and especially about the late, great Neal Cassady, who did more than "bridge the gap" between those two points in the Bohemian universe — he closed it!"

Lee Quarnstrom
author, journalist & original Merry Prankster

On The Road With Cassadys

"Brian Hassett has perfected the art of getting backstage and into the presence of the main characters, the musicians, writers, actors & directors. He gets there by knowledge, intuition, a feel for a situation, and a very big smile. He's always in the middle of things and his passion gets him into situations that might daunt others. Once there, he is invariably embraced, his sense of camaraderie, spirit of fun, his knowledge of the people he has just been embraced by, gets him the nod. This makes for unusual stories, insider ones where you think he'll never manage to infiltrate. It's all a testament to the author's perseverance and personal fascination with it all. And it is all so much fun to read."

Beat Scene
(out of England, the last print Beat magazine going)

"This is the third book in the highly acclaimed and entertaining Beat Trilogy. Everyone should check out all three of these. There are very few people in the world who know as much about the Beats and the Pranksters as Brian, and we should know because we meet everybody at The Beat Museum."

Jerry Cimino
(founder, owner, curator of The Beat Museum)